THE
BOOK OF
NUMBERED
LISTS

THE BOOK OF NUMBERED LISTS

The Unique Numerical Reference Guide to Just About Everything You Can Count

Gwen Foss

A Perigee Book

New York

A Perigee Book
Published by The Berkley Publishing Group
A member of Penguin Putnam Inc.
200 Madison Avenue
New York, NY 10016

Copyright © 1998 by JSA Publications
Book design by Jennifer Ann Daddio
Cover design by Julie Duquet
Interior illustrations by Gwen Foss

First edition: August 1998

Published simultaneously in Canada.

The Penguin Putnam Inc. World Wide Web site address is
http://www.penguinputnam.com

Library of Congress Cataloging-in-Publication Data

Foss, Gwen.
    The book of numbered lists : the unique numerical
reference guide to just about everything you can count /
Gwen Foss. — 1st ed.
    p.   cm.
    "A Perigee book."
    Includes bibliographical references and index.
    ISBN 0-399-52421-5
    1. Curiosities and wonders.   I. Title.
AG243.F69   1998
031.02—dc21   97-35041
                                             CIP

Printed in the United States of America

10 9 8 7 6 5 4 3 2 1

CONTENTS

ACKNOWLEDGMENTS

While this volume has been a labor of love for me, several people have taken time to provide information I was unable to find on my own. There were often occasions I had only the title of a numbered list and was unable to find the names of the items themselves. The following individuals gave me invaluable service by completing some of the more difficult entries: Yvonne Wyborny, Rebecca Swartz, Marilyn Smith, Linda Rindt-Frantz, Barbara Rice, Suzanne Paul, Nancy Ohl, Robert F. Johnson, Carole Hund, Carol Hansen, Peter H. Foss, Millie Foss, Ron Elkin, Earth Poet, Sherry Deeg, Steve Asman and Jane Alstrom.

The following people supported and encouraged me through the many hours I labored on this project: Skip Rosenthal, Kathleen Jacobs, Steven L. Held, John Foss, Darren Ezzo, Norma Cole, Robin Bowns, and Deanne Bednar; my agent, Joseph S. Ajlouny; and editors at Putnam/Perigee: John Duff, Bill Harris, and Martha Ramsey. My heartfelt thanks to you all.

THE
BOOK OF
NUMBERED
LISTS

Introduction and How to Use This Book

Among many kinds of reference books available, none takes a concentrated look at the numbered lists that underlie religion, philosophy, science, and popular culture. We encounter these nuggets of knowledge every day, without realizing what makes them special or noteworthy. Yet when one hears terms like "Third Reich" or "Fourth Estate," the serious researcher or casual reader know not where to find out what the first two Reichs were or what the other three Estates are. How often have you been called on to name the Three Musketeers or, more popularly, Snow White's seven dwarfs, and been unable to find a source for the answers? This book was formulated to be the singular source for this type of numbered information. As such, it fills a sizable reference gap.

How does one define a numbered list? Quite simply, it is a finite group of items with a specific numerical title, such as the Three Magi or the Five Great Lakes, in which each element on the list has a specific name. For example, the Twelve Months of the Year is a numbered list, but the Thirty-one Days of March is not, because each day of March isn't separately named. Similarly, the Five Great Lakes clearly fits the definition, but an "eighteen-wheeler" does not.

Top Ten lists and similar enumerations are not numbered lists because their content is not comprehensive. For example, lists such as Ten Reasons to Purchase Life Insurance, the Seven Warning Signs of Cancer, or the Five Longest Rivers of the World represent only an opinion, a set of priorities, or selected bits of information about a specific topic. A true numbered list includes an entire collection, not just an interesting or logical assortment.

Numbered lists, by their very conciseness, attain a degree of relevance matched only by their perfect simplicity. This collection is thus infinitely more relevant than other books of lists that are actually little more than quaint presentations of trivia. In contrast, numbered lists are a central component of human knowledge and experience. This anthology spans the breadth and depth of human history, culture, religion, and science. It is at times fascinating, technical, fun, and arcane.

Numbered lists are also quintessential demonstrations of the principle that the whole is greater than the sum of its parts. For example, the beloved Yuletide song "The Twelve Days of Christmas" tells of twelve gifts presented on twelve successive days. While each day's gift is important in and of itself, the complete group of twelve gifts creates an endearing and memorable expression of love. Another example: Each of the Seven Ancient Wonders of the World is an awesome and historic creation on its own. Collectively, however, they are a superb demonstration of human ingenuity, a living monument to civilizations that have long since perished.

Virtually every category of human endeavor has its own numbered lists. They have been used as vocational tools, memory aids, and sources of entertainment. Early lists were mystical (the Four Elements, the Seven Heavenly Spheres); modern lists are practical (the Three Rs, the Five Ws). Some lists have religious or social significance (the Ten Commandments, the Watergate Seven), while others serve as convenient labels for useful knowledge (the Six Basic Food Groups, the Nine Planets).

The numbered lists presented in this volume represent a wide spectrum of human history, earthly knowledge, and spiritual endeavor. Some are quite common, while others are rare and unusual. Many have their origins in ancient ritual; others are products of modern science and popular culture. Simple and popular lists are included here as well as the profound and complex.

A numbered list may have as few as two items or as many as over a hundred. Naturally, there are many numbered lists that would be impractical to include here, such as the 95 Theses of Martin Luther or the 102 Atomic Elements. For this reason, I have focused my research on lists numbering Three to Twelve. For the more curious, I have also taken the liberty of including a few select lists with more than twelve elements in the chapter titled Thirteen and Up.

It's worth noting that some familiar phrases that sound like numbered lists do not really qualify. For example, ancient proverbs say there are 99 Names of Allah, 72 Secret Names of God, and an Indian goddess called the Thousand-named Kali. These proverbs are intended to deepen the mystery of the deity and do not refer to any actual list of names or characteristics, so they do not qualify for inclusion. Similarly, *The Five Hundred Hats of Bartholomew Cubbins* by Dr. Seuss and the Eleven Thousand Virgins of Saint Ursula have no corresponding enumerations. The Forbes 400 Richest Americans and the Fortune 500 Largest Corporations and other ratings lists are revised every year and do not have the permanence of a true and useful numbered list. There are Thirty-one Flavors of Baskin Robbins ice cream and Fifty-seven Varieties of Heinz sauces; these are promotional slogans, not numbered lists.

Despite the realization that a volume such as this one must remain imperfect and incomplete, it is nevertheless my hope that you will enjoy almost as many hours of pleasure reading it as I found in compiling it.

HOW TO USE THIS BOOK

Each entry is headed by the list's title, such as the Six Immortals. Lists are grouped into chapters according to their number, starting with Threes and proceeding to Thirteen and Up.

Within each chapter, lists are presented alphabetically. Looking at the capped words in a title will point to its place. The second word is often the key: for example, Five **Cities of the Plain** is followed by **Five Civilized Tribes**. However, many lists are alphabetized under a key word that appears later in the title: for example, Four Sides of a **Dreydl**.

Some well-known lists have their key term first—for example, **Big Eight** and **Hollywood Ten**; **Group of Seven**, for example, is found between Seven **Great Towns** and Seven **Hells**.

In a few cases, a suffix is attached to the number, as in the Eightfold **Path of Buddhism.** In such cases the suffix is ignored, and the entry is alphabetized under the second word.

Lists with alternate titles are entered under their most commonly known title. Alternate titles are mentioned in the list's description and usually entered alphabetically as well, with a cross-reference.

In the index, entries refer to list titles. For example, the Five Peers is indexed under "Peers, Five."

THREES

In early mysticism, Three was seen as the compound of One (unity) and Two (diversity), healing that which had been split apart and representing the creative power of the universe. Three symbolized the female element of nature—that which brought forth new life. Three was believed to be the first "real" number, representing beginning, middle, and end. Three also represented the family—mother, father, and child—a symbol of life itself and therefore the most sacred of numbers.

Three symbolized trinities and triads of mystical and religious beings common to the beliefs of people around the world. Trinities held sway in Mesopotamia, Egypt, Babylon, China, and India. In Greece, there were Three Fates; in Rome, Three Fortunae; in Scandinavia, Three Norns; and in central Europe, Three Wyrd Sisters.

The Romans had a particular fondness for triads. When Christianity became the accepted religion, the trinity was made a high tenet of church doctrine. Representing the deity, Three came to be seen as the most perfect of all numbers. Medieval monks, in creating musical notation, used a circle, believed to be the most perfect of all figures, to represent perfect time (three beats per measure). Imperfect time (four beats per measure) was represented by a broken circle resembling the letter C. This musical symbol is still in use today.

Three AGES OF MAN
See Seven Ages of Man.

Three ALLIES
During World War II (1939–45), these nations were united in battle against the Three Axis Powers. *Many other nations joined the Allies to defeat the Axis. See also* Big Three of World War II.

1. Great Britain
2. Soviet Union
3. United States

¡THREE AMIGOS!
This 1986 comedy featured three of the top box-office draws of that year.

1. Steve Martin
2. Chevy Chase
3. Martin Short

Three Rs of ANIMAL RIGHTS
Animal rights activists created these three Rs to help educate the public on the issues of animal rights and animal research. Their threefold goal is as follows:

1. Reduction—in the number of animals used in laboratory research
2. Refinement—of techniques that cause suffering
3. Replacement—of live animals with simulations or cell cultures

Three ARCHANGELS
Also referred to as Three Idols of Mecca in the Qur'an, these were a triad of moon goddesses worshiped in ancient Arabia. The Muslim prophet Mohammed first accepted them as archangels, then rejected them as false idols.

1. Al-Lat or Lata or Lut
2. Manat or Madut
3. Al-Uzza or Aloza or Aza

Threefold AUSTERITY

From the Bhagavad Gita, a Hindu scripture.

1. Austerity of the Body: worship, cleanliness, nonviolence, celibacy
2. Austerity of Speech: truthfulness, using pleasing speech, reciting scripture
3. Austerity of the Mind: simplicity, self-control

Three Types of AVERAGES

These mathematical terms are often used to confuse the public with statistics. The term "average," having three different uses, enables unscrupulous politicians and advertisers to make claims that may be mathematically true but in reality are leaning heavily toward fiction. For example, for the group of numbers 2, 2, 2, 6, 17, 35, 78, 92, 126, 127, and 134: The median is 35, the mean is 66, and the average is 56.4.

1. Median: the point below which there are as many instances as there are above
2. Mean: the point midway between the extremes
3. Average: the sum of the figures divided by the number of figures

Three AXIS POWERS

During World War II (1939–45), these countries were united in battle against the Three Allies. Bulgaria, Croatia, Czechoslovakia, Hungary, and Romania also fought for the Axis.

1. Germany
2. Italy
3. Japan

Three Bs of MUSIC
Three composers learned as the Three Bs by students of Western classical music.

1. Johann Sebastian Bach (1685–1750)
2. Ludwig van Beethoven (1770–1827)
3. Johannes Brahms (1833–97)

Three Pillars of BAHA'I
See Eleven Beliefs.

Three BALTIC STATES

1. Estonia
2. Latvia
3. Lithuania

Three BASKETS OF THE LAW (BUDDHISM)
Three basic Buddhist texts dating from the second millennium B.C.E.; also called the Tripitaka.

1. Abhidharma (doctrine) written by Kashyapa
2. Vinaya Pitaka (law) written by Upali
3. Sutta Pitaka (parables) written by Ananda

Three Vows of BENEDICTINE MONKS
The Benedictines were founded about 529 by Saint Benedict in Italy. These were the original vows of the order.

1. To remain at the monastery
2. To labor till death in order to attain perfection
3. To obey one's superiors

BIG THREE

Nickname given to the representatives at the Paris Peace Conference of 1919.

1. Georges Clemenceau, premier of France
2. David Lloyd George, prime minister of Great Britain
3. Woodrow Wilson, president of the United States of America

BIG THREE OF WORLD WAR II

Leaders of the Allies during World War II (1939–45). See also Three Allies.

1. Winston Churchill, prime minister of Great Britain
2. Franklin Delano Roosevelt, president of the United States of America
3. Joseph Stalin, premier of the Soviet Union

BIG THREE IN AUTOMOBILES

In U.S. auto manufacturing.

1. GM (General Motors: Chevrolet, Oldsmobile, Pontiac, Buick, Cadillac)
2. Ford (Lincoln, Mercury, Merkur)
3. Chrysler (Dodge, Plymouth, Jeep, Eagle)

BIG THREE IN GOLF

These pros made the game into the popular pastime it is today.

1. Ben Hogan (1912–1997)
2. Byron Nelson (b. 1912)
3. Sam Snead (b. 1912)

BIG THREE IN LONG-DISTANCE TELECOMMUNICATIONS
The giants of telecommunications, based in the United States.

1. AT&T (American Telephone and Telegraph)
2. MCI Telecommunications Corporation (formerly Microwave
    Communications, Inc.)
3. Sprint

BIG THREE IN RODEO
Annual events.

1. Cheyenne Frontier Days
2. Calgary Stampede
3. Pendleton Roundup

BIG THREE UNIVERSITIES
Ivy League universities.

1. Harvard
2. Princeton
3. Yale

Three Factors of BLUFFING
According to master gambler Edwin Silberstang, one should not attempt to bluff unless at least two of these three factors are on your side.

1. Your opponent: It is easier to bluff a strong player than a weak one.
2. Your position in the game: It is easier to bluff a big loser than a big winner.
3. Money: The bigger the stakes, the easier it is to bluff.

Three BODILY FUNCTIONS THAT COMPLETELY TAKE OVER
YOUR AWARENESS
While one experiences these, one's entire body is momentarily taken over (a medically accurate list).

1.   Laugh
2.   Sneeze
3.   Orgasm

Three BODY TYPES
Identified by psychologist William H. Sheldon (1899–1977) in his first major work, The Varieties of Human Physique *(1940). In his second work,* The Varieties of Human Temperament *(1941), he found a general correlation to psychological types (in many cases, this correlation was not true). Many years later he added the Balanced Physique, a combination of all three, but professional references to Sheldon's Three Body Types are still common.*

	Body Type	Description	Corresponding Psychological Type	Description
1.	Ectomorph	slender and asthenic ("thin")	cerebrotonia	sensitive, nervous, loves intellectual stimulation
2.	Endomorph	short and powerful ("round")	viscerotonia	of goodwill, tolerant, loves food
3.	Mesomorph	athletic ("just right")	somatotonia	assertive, callous, loves exercise

Three BRANCHES OF THE U.S. GOVERNMENT
These three divisions of government were laid out in the U.S. Constitution in 1787 and were designed to limit the powers of government by giving each branch one area in which it oversees another.

1.   Executive: the president, who can sign or veto laws

2. Legislative: Congress, which can create laws and override a presidential veto
3. Judicial: the Supreme Court, which reviews laws

Three BRONTË SISTERS
Three sisters who produced some of the greatest novels in English literature.

		Pen Name	*Major Work*
1.	Charlotte Brontë (1816–55)	Currer Bell	*Jane Eyre* (1847)
2.	Emily Brontë (1818–48)	Ellis Bell	*Wuthering Heights* (1848)
3.	Anne Brontë (1820–49)	Acton Bell	*Agnes Grey* (1848)

Three BROWNIE Bs
American Brownie Girl Scouts, ages 5–8, are taught these three principles.

1. Be Discoverers
2. Be Ready Helpers
3. Be Friend-Makers

Three CARDINAL VIRTUES
See Three Graces (Christian).

Three CAULDRONS
According to Norse mythology, these Three Cauldrons hold the power of creation.

1. Odrerir
2. Són
3. Bodn

Three CHIPMUNKS
Recording stars with Liberty Records, these animated characters also had their own TV show in the 1960s.

1. Alvin
2. Simon
3. Theodore

Three CHRISTIAN DIVISIONS
See Four Branches of Christianity.

Three CHRISTIAN VALUES
See Three Graces (Christian).

Three CLASSES OF SOCIETY (HOPI)
From traditional Hopi culture; the three classes are listed here in order from highest to lowest.

1. Mong-cinum (leaders of kivas, priests, and high priests)
2. Pavun-cinum (members of society; hold no office but take part in ceremonies)
3. Sukaving-cinum (not members; do not take part in ceremonies)

Three CLEFS
Musical symbols that tell performers what musical notes appear in what positions on the staff. The drum clef is often included as the fourth clef.

Name	Alternate Names	Symbol
1. G-clef	treble clef, violin clef	
2. F-clef	bass clef	
3. C-clef	alto clef, viola clef (called tenor clef when on fourth line)	

Three Kinds of CLOSE ENCOUNTERS
See Four Kinds of Close Encounters.

Three Ships of COLUMBUS
One of the earliest numbered lists introduced to schoolchildren. Christopher Columbus (1451–1506) sailed to the New World with this fleet of three ships in 1492.

1. *Niña*
2. *Pinta*
3. *Santa María* (the flagship)

Three Steps of COMPETITION

1. Look
2. Learn
3. Stomp

Three Rs of CONSERVATION
These three Rs were created as a guideline to help consumers care for the environment by reminding them to reduce the amount of goods they consume, reuse items instead of throwing them out, and recycle items that cannot be reused. Some conservationists list a fourth R: Restore what has been destroyed or damaged in nature.

1. Reduce
2. Reuse
3. Recycle

Three-tiered CROWN OF THE POPE
According to Roman Catholic tradition, the pope's three-tiered crown represents his supremacy in three spheres of power. Medieval folklore had it that the three crowns represented the three (known) parts of the world: Europe, Asia, and Africa.

1. Spiritual Power
2. Temporal Power
3. Ecclesiastical Power

Three Types of DECAFFEINATED COFFEE
Decaffeinated coffee is manufactured by these three different methods.

1. Sparkling Water: Carbon dioxide pulls caffeine from moistened green coffee beans
2. Ethyl Acetate: This natural plant chemical pulls caffeine out of green beans soaked in hot water; flavor elements, also pulled out, are returned by a spray-on process.
3. Methylene Chloride: Similar to Ethyl Acetate, but absorption of caffeine takes longer; this method is least expensive and most popular with distributors.

Three DEGREES OF BURNS
Students of first-aid techniques must learn this list.

1. First degree: skin pink, not serious
2. Second degree: skin red, blisters form; serious
3. Third degree: skin black, very serious

Three Stages of DEVELOPMENT
According to Austrian psychoanalyst Sigmund Freud (1856–1939), children pass through three stages of development in the formation of their sexuality. Freud also identified specific behavioral developments in each stage that may lead to concerns: sucking during oral stage, potty training during the anal-sadistic stage, and penis envy during the phallic (genital) stage.

1. Oral: the infant understands the world through the lips and mouth
2. Anal-sadistic: the child is fascinated by feces and the anus
3. Phallic (Genital): the child discovers the penis (or clitoris) as the center of sexual sensation

Three DIMENSIONS

Three dimensions recognized by geometricians. Theoretical scientists posit a fourth dimension, time.

1. First dimension: a line with no width
2. Second dimension: a plane ("flatland")
3. Third dimension: common objects

Three DIRAE

See Three Furies.

Three DIRECTIONS OF MOVEMENT

These three terms apply to the movements of watercraft, aircraft, and spacecraft.

1. Roll: to dip, rocking to the side
2. Pitch: to angle, nosing the craft up or down
3. Yaw: to turn, swinging the craft on its vertical axis

Three Books of the *DIVINE COMEDY*

The Divine Comedy, *by Italian poet Dante Alighieri (1265–1321), is a philosophical poem in one hundred cantos recounting a journey through hell, purgatory, and heaven. It is considered a masterpiece of world literature. The* Inferno *is the most famous of the three books.*

1. Cantica 1: *L'Inferno* (Hell)
2. Cantica 2: *Il Purgatoria* (Purgatory)
3. Cantica 3: *Il Paradiso* (Heaven)

The "DOLLARS" TRILOGY

A trilogy of popular "spaghetti westerns" starring Clint Eastwood.

1. *A Fistful of Dollars* (1964)

2. *For a Few Dollars More* (1965)
3. *The Good, The Bad, and The Ugly* (1967)

Three DONENESS LEVELS
Terms used in cooking meat.

1. Rare: red
2. Medium: pink
3. Well: brown

Three Divisions of DRUIDISM
Druidism, a term that has been loosely used to refer to the pagan religion of the British Isles, particularly Wales, at one time organized its leaders into these three divisions.

1. Ministers; wear white, act as ministers
2. Bards; wear blue, stand for harmony and truth; poets and musicians
3. Ovates; wear green, stand for learning; physicians and astrologers

Three Bones of the EAR
One of the first numbered lists memorized by anatomy students.

1. Hammer
2. Anvil
3. Stirrup

Three ERRORS OF LEADERS (SUN TZU)
According to legendary Japanese philosopher Sun Tzu, author of The Art of War.

1. Hobbling the Force: calling for an advance when the Force is unable to advance, or the same for a retreat
2. Creating Doubtfulness: aligning the Force along political lines
3. Creating Skepticism: aligning the Force with appointed officials

Three ESTATES

Three divisions of social classes during feudal times in Europe. In addition, the sovereign is not among any of the three classes but stands alone. The term Fourth Estate, for the press, was created by British statesman Edmund Burke (1729–1797) when he so referred to journalists seated in the gallery at Parliament.

1.	First Estate	Lords Spiritual	(the clergy): archbishops, bishops
2.	Second Estate	Lords Temporal	(the nobility): dukes, marquesses, earls, viscounts, and barons (see *Five Peers*)
3.	Third Estate	Commons	(the masses): others

Three EUMENIDES

See Three Furies.

THE THREE FACES OF EVE

Film (1957) starring Joanne Woodward. Three personalities in one woman, each had her own name.

1. Eve White
2. Eve Black
3. Jane

Three FATES

Also known as the Three Moirae or the Three Parcae, these deities were believed to control the destinies of human beings. They are related to the Three Norns *of Norse mythology and the three* Wyrd Sisters *of Saxon mythology.*

Three Fates of Greek Mythology

1. Clotho: spinner
2. Lachesis: drawer-off of the thread
3. Atropos: cutter of the thread

Three Fortunae of Roman Mythology

1. Nona: spinner
2. Decuma: drawer-off of the thread
3. Morta: cutter of the thread

Three FENCING WEAPONS

1. Épée
2. Foil
3. Saber

THREE FLASHES
See Hoboken Four.

Three FOREHEAD MARKS
The small dot in the center of the forehead indicates the marital status of Hindu women. The mark is located in the center of the forehead because it represents the third eye.

1. Black: unmarried
2. Red: married
3. None: widowed

Three FORTUNAE
See Three Fates.

Three FOSSIL FUELS

1. Coal
2. Oil
3. Gas

Three FRANCISCAN ORDERS
Founded by St. Francis of Assisi in the 1200s.

1. Friars Minor: missionaries and educators
2. Poor Clares: founded 1212, woman's order named for Saint Clare
3. Brothers and Sisters of Penance, also called the Third Order

Three Degrees of FREEMASONRY
Officially founded in 1717, Freemasonry is a secret organization whose origins are lost in antiquity. Master masons are also eligible for higher degrees. See also Thirty-two Degrees of Freemasonry.

1. Entered Apprentice
2. Fellowcraft
3. Master Mason

Three Components of a FULFILLING LIFE (FREUD)
According to Austrian psychoanalyst Sigmund Freud (1856–1939).

1. Love
2. Work
3. Play

Three FURIES
In Greek mythology, the Three Furies were said to be the punishers of wrongdoers. They were also known as the Three Dirae, the Three Erinyes ("angry ones"), the Three Eumenides ("kindly ones," a euphemism), and the Three Solemn Ones. Sometimes Greek writers made reference to the Four Fates, which then included Nemesis (vengeance).

1. Alecto: envy
2. Megaera: slaughter, grudge
3. Tisiphone: rage, retaliation, destruction

Three Gs

A saying from folklore holds that these three things made America great.

1. God
2. Guns
3. Guts

Three Gs

Actor Dennis Dun (TV Guide, 1990) described the limited roles available to Asians in these terms.

1. Geeks: intellectuals, advanced students
2. Gooks: enemy soldiers
3. Gangsters: criminals, villains

Three GATES TO HELL

From the Bhagavad Gita, a Hindu scripture.

1. Lust
2. Anger
3. Greed

Three Sizes of GENITALIA

The Kama Sutra, a Hindu scripture, states that marriages should be made, in part, based on matching these.

Man—Size of Lingam:

1. Hare
2. Bull
3. Horse

Woman—Depth of Yoni:

1. Deer
2. Mare
3. Elephant

GIANT TRIPLET

As expounded by Dr. Martin Luther King, Jr., these are the unconquerable forces that will be in place after profits become more important than people.

1. Racism
2. Materialism
3. Militarism

Three GODS

The universal appeal of the number three is shown with these lists of deities, which appear as triads and/or trinities in the religions of many different cultures. For more trinities and triads, see Three Archangels, Three Fates, *and* Three Pure Ones.

BABYLONIAN

Ancient Babylonians recognized many divine triads, but this was the chief group. Occasionally Ishtar, the mother goddess, was substituted for Ramman.

1. Ramman: thunder god
2. Sin: moon god
3. Shamash: sun god

BUDDHIST

The Buddhist sect known as Mahayana recognizes the following trinity, wherein each person is seen as encompassing these three aspects of the Buddha.

1. Transformation
2. Bliss
3. Dharma

CELTIC

The Celtic peoples of Europe and the British Isles honored these three goddesses representing the three stages of womanhood:

1. Macha: virgin
2. Morrighan: mother
3. Badhbh: crone

CHRISTIAN

As mentioned in Matthew 28:19. The Holy Trinity, as it is called, did not become an official Christian doctrine until a vote was taken by the bishops at the Council of Nicaea in 325.

1. God the Father: Creator
2. God the Son, Jesus Christ: Redeemer
3. God the Holy Ghost or Holy Spirit: Sustainer or Giver of Life

EGYPTIAN

The Egyptian pantheon survived for many centuries and experienced many changes and variations from place to place and era to era. Seven different trinities are presented here, with location and era noted.

Memphite Triad (worshiped at Memphis—early version)

1. Ptah
2. Sekhmet (goddess of war)
3. Nefertem

Memphite Triad (worshiped at Memphis—later version)

1. Ptah
2. Sekhmet (goddess of war)
3. Imhotep

Theban Triad (worshiped at Thebes)

1. Amen-Ra or Amon
2. Mut (consort of Amen-Ra)
3. Khonsu, son of Amen-Ra and Mut

Abydosan Triad (worshiped at Abydos, Philae, and Edfu—early version)

1. Osiris
2. Isis (goddess of creation, wife and sister of Osiris)
3. Horus, son of Isis and Osiris

Abydosan Triad (worshiped at Abydos, Philae, and Edfu—later version)

1. Osiris
2. Isis (goddess of creation)
3. Harpocrates

Edfuan Triad (worshiped at Edfu)

1. Horus
2. Hathor (goddess of love, cow goddess, mother of Pharaoh)
3. Harsomatus or Horus the Younger

Elephantine Triad (worshiped at Elephantine)

1. Khnum
2. Anukis (goddess of fertility and of the Nile)
3. Satis, daughter of Khnum and Anukis

GREEK AND ROMAN

Like the Egyptian pantheon, the gods and goddesses of ancient Greece and Rome occurred in a myriad of changing triads, depending on the place and era. Originally the Greek and Roman pantheons existed as separate groups of deities having a few common characteristics.

Ancient Roman Triad

1. Jupiter, chief god
2. Mars, war god
3. Quirinus: war god, the deification of Romulus

Capitoline Triad (worshiped in classical Rome)

1. Jupiter (emperor of the gods)
2. Juno (goddess of marriage, wife of Jupiter)
3. Minerva (goddess of wisdom)

In a later era, the pantheons of Greece and Rome were merged and the personalities of the various gods and goddesses were altered to match their counterparts in the other culture. The resulting triads reflected these realignments.

Greek and Roman Converged

Greek Name	Roman Name	Kingdom	Symbol
1. Zeus	Jupiter	Earth and sky	Three-forked lightning
2. Poseidon	Neptune	Sea	Three-tined spear (trident)
3. Hades	Pluto	Underworld	Three-headed dog (Cerberus)

Greek Triad of Goddesses

1. Hebe (goddess of dance)
2. Hera (goddess of marriage)
3. Hecate (goddess of learning)

Greek Triad of Moon Deities

1. Hera (goddess of marriage)
2. Artemis (goddess of the hunt)
3. Hermes (messenger god)

Greek Triple Goddess (With Sacred Color)

1. Iambe, maiden (white)
2. Demeter, mother (red)
3. Baubo, crone (black)

HINDU

The Hindu religion is fundamentally monotheistic. God is seen in many different guises with many different names, leading some Westerners to conclude erroneously that Hindus worship many distinct gods. However, Hindu trinities composed of triple aspects do exist and are presented here so the reader may compare the Hindu trinities with those of other religions. (The Hindu deity is often gender neutral, so in the first group the various personalities of God are neither male nor female.)

Trimurti (the trinity)

1. Brahma or Parvati: the Creator
2. Vishnu or Ganesha: the Preserver
3. Siva or Shiva: the Destroyer

Feminine Triad

1. Parvati: virgin
2. Durga: mother
3. Uma: crone

MESOPOTAMIAN AND SUMERIAN

The mythologies of these two ancient cultures were closely related.

Mesopotamian

1. An (sky god)
2. Enlil (earth god)
3. Ninhursaga or Belitili, Ninmah, Dingirmah, Nintur (mountain goddess)

Sumerian

1. Anu (god of heavens)
2. Enlil (earth god)
3. Ea or Enki (water god)

NEO-PAGAN

Sometimes known as the Triple Goddess, this trinity is celebrated by some, but not all, Neo-Pagans. It is symbolic of the three aspects of womanhood. Also listed are the corresponding male versions.

1. Maiden (Virgin); Warrior (Hunter)
2. Mother; Father
3. Crone (Hag); Sage (Guide)

NORSE

Three distinct trinities occur. The first closely resembles the Teutonic *triad, a group of deities that sprang from the same cultural source.*

Norse Trinity

1. Odin, sky god
2. Frigga, wife of Odin
3. Thor, thunder god

Three Aspects of Odin
One Norse myth tells the story of three brothers, each an aspect of the deity Odin, who slew the protogiant Ymir and made the worlds out of his body.

1. Odin (The Mad One)
2. Ve (Holiness)
3. Vili (Will)

Three Gods of the Vanir
In Asatru, the ancient Norse religion of Scandinavia, there is a legend of a great battle between the gods of the Aesir and the gods of the Vanir. The Vanir were ruled by

three primary deities, while the Aesir were ruled by twelve. Generally, the gods of the Vanir are seen as peaceful fertility deities associated with earth, water, and nature, in contrast to the warlike gods of the Aesir, associated with air, fire, and things mechanical. After the great war, however, the two houses were united, and later stories refer to the entire pantheon as the Aesir. See also Twelve Gods of the Aesir.

1. Njord, Njorth, or Niord: sea god, god of trade and prosperity
2. Freya or Freyja: "Lady," goddess of love and fertility, a warrior
3. Frey, Freyr, Ing, Ingwaz, or Yngvi-Freyr: "Lord," god of love, fertility, and joy

ROMAN
See Three Gods: Greek and Roman.

TEUTONIC
Norse and Teutonic (Germanic) cultures sprang from the same source, and the similarity of their mythologies reflects this relationship. Compare Three Gods: Norse.

1. Wotan or Odin (chief god)
2. Thor or Donar (god of thunder)
3. Tiwaz, Tiu, Tyr, or Ziu (god of war)

ZOROASTRIAN
Not precisely a trinity, these three personalities are believed to be three aspects of Ahura Mazda (Ormazd), the primary deity of Zoroastrianism.

1. Ahura Mazda, Creator
2. Ahura Mazda, Preserver
3. Ahura Mazda, Reconstructor

Three GOODS
Three things required of students in contemporary China.

1. Good marks
2. Good health
3. Good spirit

Three GORGONS
In Greek mythology, these three sisters were turned into hideous monsters for claiming that their beauty surpassed that of the gods.

1. Euryale
2. Medusa
3. Stheno

Three GRACES OF CHRISTIANITY
Also known as the Three Virtues, Cardinal Virtues, Theological Virtues, or Christian Values. See also Seven Virtues, Twelve Virtues. *The symbols for each follow in parentheses.*

1. Faith (cross)
2. Hope (anchor)
3. Charity or Love (heart)

Three GRACES OF GREEK MYTHOLOGY
The Three Graces of Greek mythology were often pictured as attendants to Aphrodite, the goddess of love. Some ancient writers described four graces, the fourth being Pasithea (warmth and light). The attributes of each follow in parentheses.

1. Aglaia (beauty, goodness)
2. Euphrosyne (cheerfulness)
3. Thalia (perpetual freshness)

Three Degrees of GRADUATION
These Latin phrases accompany the graduation honors of the highest-achieving students.

1. Cum Laude (with praise)
2. Magna cum Laude (with great praise)
3. Summa cum Laude (with greatest praise)

Three Masters of GREEK TRAGIC ART

Three ancient Greek playwrights. Some of their works are listed here.

1. Aeschylus (c. 525–456 B.C.E.): *The Persians, Prometheus Bound,* the *Oresteia*
2. Sophocles (c. 495–406 B.C.E.): *Oedipus Rex, Antigone, Electra*
3. Euripides (c. 480–406 B.C.E.): *Medea, The Trojan Women, The Bacchae*

Three GUNAS

In Hinduism, three qualities that pervade all living things.

		Definition	*Rank*	*Sacred Color*
1.	Sattva	purity, harmony, intelligence	superior	white
2.	Rajas	activity and passion	intermediate	red
3.	Tamas	dullness, inertia, ignorance	inferior	black

Three HARMONIES (BALI)

According to Agama Tirtha, the primary religion of Bali ("Religion of Holy Water"), an amalgam of Hindu and Buddhist sources mixed with animistic elements.

1. Harmony among all mankind
2. Harmony between man and environment
3. Harmony between God and man

Three HARPIES

In Greek mythology, the harpies were hideous winged creatures who delighted in harassing people.

1. Aello
2. Celeno
3. Ocypete

Three Tenets of IDENTITY

Identity is an American pseudo-religion created by fascists and neo-Nazis. Organizations that espouse Identity include the Church of Jesus Christ Christian; the Covenant, Sword and Arm of the Lord; the Aryan Nations; the Ku Klux Klan; and the Christian Knights.

1. Jews are Satan's children.
2. The Prophesy of a Racist Revolution—a worldwide race war that will leave only whites.
3. White Supremacy (or British-Israelism)—the people of British and northern European ancestry are the true descendants of the Lost Tribes of Israel.

Three IDOLS OF MECCA

See Three Archangels.

IMMORTAL THREE

The three greatest poets to have ever lived, according to English poet laureate John Dryden (1631–1700).

1. Homer (dates unknown), Greece
2. Dante Alighieri (1265–1321), Italy
3. John Milton (1608–74), England

INDIANA JONES TRILOGY

A popular series of films produced by Steven Spielberg, starring Harrison Ford as archaeologist and adventurer Indiana Jones.

1. *Raiders of the Lost Ark* (1981)
2. *Indiana Jones and the Temple of Doom* (1984)
3. *Indiana Jones and the Last Crusade* (1989)

Three JAPANESE ALPHABETS

Japanese writing consists of not one but three distinct alphabets. The alphabets are used interchangeably, and words and phrases appear in all three alphabets throughout a single piece of writing.

Alphabet	Type of Symbols	Description of Characters	Number of Characters
1. Kanji	ideographs	complex	approx. 10,000
2. Hirogana	phonetics	squiggly	52
3. Katakana	phonetics	long and narrow	25

Three JEWELS OF JAINISM

These three virtues of Jainism, an ancient branch of Hinduism, are comparable to the three virtues of other religious belief systems.

1. Right Faith
2. Right Knowledge
3. Right Conduct

Three JEWELS OF TAOISM

Three basic virtues of Taoism.

1. Compassion
2. Moderation
3. Humility or Modesty

Three JOLLY FISHERMEN

See Three Patriarchs.

Three JUDGES OF THE UNDERWORLD

From Roman mythology. A fourth judge, Triptolemus, is sometimes included.

1. Minos, the presiding judge

2. Rhadamanthus, the judge of Asians
3. Aeacus (or Eachus), the judge of Europeans

Three Daughters of KING LEAR

From Shakespeare's play, they are listed here from oldest to youngest.

1. Goneril
2. Cordelia
3. Regan

Three KINGDOMS OF NATURE

These categories are used in the game Twenty Questions, in which one player secretly chooses a familiar object, and the other players are allowed up to twenty yes-or-no questions with which to discover the object. Objects in the game are classified as one of these three categories.

1. Animal
2. Vegetable
3. Mineral

Three KINGDOMS PERIOD

An era of Chinese history (220–65 C.E.) in which the unified empire of the previous Han Dynasty was split into three kingdoms.

1. Wei
2. Shu
3. Wu

Three KINGS
See Three Magi.

KINGSTON TRIO

A popular folk music group of the 1950s and 60s.

1. Dave Guard
2. Nick Reynolds
3. Bob Shane

Three Ranks of the KNIGHTS OF PYTHIAS

Listed in order from lowest to highest.

1. Page
2. Esquire
3. Knight

Three Tenets of the KNIGHTS OF PYTHIAS

A secret society founded in 1864 in Washington, D.C., to promote friendship, charity, and benevolence.

1. Toleration in religion
2. Obedience to law
3. Loyalty to government

Three LAWS OF LOGIC

Also called the Three Laws of Thought.

1. Identity: A = A
2. Excluded Middle or Tertium non Datur: Of two contradictions, one must be true.
3. Contradiction: It is impossible for something both to be and not to be.

Three LAWS OF MOTION

Discovered by English scientist Sir Isaac Newton (1642–1727).

1. Inertia: An object will remain motionless or will move in a straight line unless acted upon by a force.
2. The acceleration of an object is directly proportional to the force acting upon it, and inversely proportional to the object's mass.
3. For every action, there is an equal and opposite reaction.

Three LAWS OF THERMODYNAMICS
Basic principles governing the behavior of heat and energy.

1. Conservation of Energy: In a system where no outside forces act upon it, energy will remain constant.
2. Mechanical work can be derived from the heat in a body only when (1) the body is able to communicate with another at a lower temperature, or (2) all actual spontaneous processes result in an increase of total energy.
3. At the temperature of absolute zero, the entropy of any pure crystalline substance is zero and its derivative with respect to temperature is zero.

Three LAWS OF THOUGHT
See Three Laws of Logic.

Three Divisions of LEARNING
According to English author Francis Bacon (1561–1626) in his Advancement of Learning, *first published in 1605.*

1. Memory: factual data, history
2. Understanding: reason, philosophy, theoretical investigation
3. Imagination: the fine arts

LORD OF THE RINGS Trilogy
This trilogy by J. R. R. Tolkien is considered a masterpiece of fantasy fiction.

1. *The Fellowship of the Ring* (1954)

2. *The Two Towers* (1955)
3. *The Return of the King* (1956)

Three Kinds of LOVE

In English there is only one word for love, but in Greek there are several. Translations of the Bible therefore differ, according to how scholars translate these various terms.

1. Philia: brotherly and sisterly love, friendship, companionship, mutual sharing
2. Agape: self-giving love, love that endures even when it is not returned, kindness, empathy, awareness of the other, sensitivity of others' needs, acceptance, charity
3. Eros: sensual, sexual, romantic, and erotic love

Three MAGI

In Christian mythology, these Three Kings or Three Wise Men followed a star in the east, traveled to the birthplace of Jesus Christ, and brought gifts to the infant. Epiphany in the Christian calendar is sometimes called Three Kings' Day in honor of the Three Magi. Their respective gifts to Jesus follow in parentheses.

1. Kaspar (gold)
2. Melchior (frankincense)
3. Balthasar (myrrh)

Three Parts of MAN

Also called the Three Planes of Existence, the notion of three inseparable concepts exists in nearly every culture and belief system around the world. Here are two versions.

Ancient Greece

1. Body: corporeal form, the instincts
2. Mind: intellect, the impalpable
3. Shadow (ghost): soul or immortal essence, the sentiments

Primitive Christianity

1. Corpus (body)
2. Anima (mind)
3. Spiritus (spirit)

Three States of MATTER
See Four States of Matter.

Three MEN IN A TUB
From an old English nursery rhyme, "Rub a dub dub/Three men in a tub."

1. Butcher
2. Baker
3. Candlestick maker

Three MOIRAE
See Three Fates.

Three MONKEYS
In Chinese folklore, monkeys represent both good (protectiveness, good fortune) and evil (trickery, conceit). Although the Three Monkeys derive from ancient Chinese philosophy and are found in the folklore of Japan as well as English-speaking places, only their Japanese and English names are in common usage. Each of the Three Monkeys represents a denial of evil; the Three Monkeys are pictured as covering either their eyes, ears, or mouth with their hands.

	Japanese Name	*English Name*
1.	Mazaru	Speak No Evil
2.	Mikazaru	Hear No Evil
3.	Mizaru	See No Evil

Three MUSES

In Greek mythology, these were the three goddesses of the arts. They were later expanded to become Nine Muses. *See also the* Five Muses *of Arabic mythology.*

1. Aoide: song
2. Melete: meditation
3. Mneme: remembrance

Three MUSKETEERS

From the novel of the same name by Alexandre Dumas, published in 1844. The Fourth Musketeer and hero of the story is D'Artagnon.

1. Athos
2. Porthos
3. Aramis

Three MYSTERIES

The three greatest mysteries of Christianity, so called because they can not be explained but must be accepted on faith.

1. The Trinity
2. Original Sin
3. The Incarnation

Three MYSTIC MONKEYS
See Three Monkeys.

Three NETWORKS

In American broadcast television, these three networks dominated the airwaves from the 1950s through the 1980s. In addition, the early DuMont Television Network broadcast several popular shows but went out of business in the 1960s. Alongside these commercial networks also exists Public Broadcasting System (PBS), a publicly funded, noncommercial network, and many regional noncommercial networks. In the 1980s, the popularity of pay, cable, and satellite TV, and the proliferation of new commercial broadcast networks, began to erode the supremacy of the big three. A surrogate network, Fox (FBC), gained a foothold by buying limited blocks of time on various stations throughout the country. Paramount (UPN), Warner (WB), and other networks soon began doing the same.

1. ABC   American Broadcasting Corporation
2. CBS   Columbia Broadcasting System
3. NBC   National Broadcasting Corporation

Three Rs of the NEW DEAL

Created by President Franklin D. Roosevelt in 1933, the New Deal was a sweeping plan to combat the devastating effects of economic depression. These three Rs were the foundation of his plan.

1. Relief: programs for the poor
2. Recovery: stabilization of economy
3. Reform: oversight of financial institutions

Three Islands of NEW ZEALAND

Most tourists, having heard only of North and South Island, are surprised to learn that New Zealand is composed of three islands. Here are the English and Maori names of the islands. A Maori legend tells of the ancient god Maui, who went out in his great canoe and struggled to land an enormous fish. The canoe was overturned, and Maui dropped his anchor stone at that place. The original Maori name and its meaning follow each entry in parentheses.

1. North Island (Te Ika-A-Maui: fish of Maui)
2. South Island (Te Waka-A-Maui: canoe of Maui)
3. Stewart Island (Rakiura: anchor stone, or "the glowing sky")

Three Tactics of NONVIOLENT ACTION

Author and activist Gene Sharp expanded on Mohandas K. Gandhi's Three Principles of Nonviolent Resistance in order to enable Western activists to better put the principles to work.

1. Nonviolent Protest and Persuasion: Legal activities (petitioning, picketing, demonstrating, lobbying, vigiling, leafleting)
2. Nonviolent Noncooperation: Legal but somewhat obstructive activities (boycotting, striking, tax resisting, hunger striking, creating a factory slowdown, running an underground press)
3. Nonviolent Intervention: Illegal but morally defensible activities (physically obstructing, blockading, doing civil disobedience, holding a sit-in, giving sanctuary)

Three Principles of NONVIOLENT RESISTANCE

The philosophy of nonviolent resistance was espoused by Mohandas K. Gandhi (1869–1948) as a means to bring about peaceful change under the oppressive rule of the British in India. While Gandhi is often referred to as advocating "passive resistance," this term is a misnomer. Gandhi advocated "active resistance," an active and dedicated position of refusing to assist in one's own oppression.

1. Satyagraha: openness, honesty, fairness, and truth
2. Ahimsa: refusal to inflict injury on others
3. Tapasya: willingness for self-sacrifice

Three NORNS

In Norse mythology, the Norns were roughly equivalent to the deities of Greek mythology believed to control the fates of humans. See also three Wyrd Sisters, Three Fates.

1. Urdur: time past
2. Verthandi: time present
3. Skuld: time to come

Three OFFICES OF CHRIST
As described in the Bible. See also Fourfold Office of the Lord.

1. High Priest
2. Bridegroom or Prophet
3. King-Judge

Three Ps
See Four Ps.

Three PARCAE
See Three Fates.

Three PARDONS OF GOD
According to Cao Daiism, literally "Reigning God," a religion founded in Indochina by Ngo-van Chieu in 1919. There is no direct English translation for the original term translated here as "Pardon."

1. First Pardon of God: Western religions: Judaism and Christianity
2. Second Pardon of God: Eastern religions: Taoism, Confucianism, and Buddhism
3. Third Pardon of God: Dai Dao Tam Pho Do, a fulfillment of the two previous pardons, the basic tenet of Cao Daiism

Three Basic PARTICLES
Recognized by nuclear physicists as the basic building blocks of atoms.

1. Electron (negative charge: −)
2. Neutron (neutral charge: 0)
3. Proton (positive charge: +)

Three PARTITIONS OF POLAND
The history of Poland is divided by these three events in which parcels of the country were awarded to or taken by various nations.

1. 1772: by treaty, Russia, Prussia, and Austria receive parts
2. 1793: by invasion, Russia and Prussia occupy parts
3. 1795: following the unsuccessful Polish revolution, Russia, Prussia, and Austria take remaining parts

Three PATRIARCHS
Three of the seven founders of Judaism. A humorous folk song tells of the Three Patriarchs in simple language, calling them Three Jolly Fishermen. See also Four Matriarchs.

1. Abraham
2. Isaac
3. Jacob

Three PLANES OF EXISTENCE
See Three Parts of Man.

Three Types of PLAY
One of the first numbered lists drama students learn. The plays of Shakespeare are often categorized accordingly.

1. Tragedy: The hero(es) dies.
2. Comedy: The hero(es) doesn't die.
3. History: The hero(es) is indistinguishable from the villain(s).

Three Literary POINTS OF VIEW
Literature is often described as being in first person or third person in reference to who is the narrator of the story. These are the three possible points of view.

1.	First person	I, we
2.	Second person	you
3.	Third person	he, she, they

Three PRIMARY COLORS OF LIGHT

Many people familiar with the Three Primary Colors of Paint are not aware that the three primary colors of light are different. When it comes to mixing light waves, colors react quite differently. This list is used in the television industry and among technicians who deal in similar areas.

1. Blue
2. Green
3. Red

Three PRIMARY COLORS OF PAINT

Most students learn this list before they begin mixing paints. By using these three colors, along with white and black, any desired color or shading can be achieved. See also Three Secondary Colors.

1. Blue
2. Red
3. Yellow

Three Parts of the PSYCHE

According to Austrian psychoanalyst Sigmund Freud (1856–1939), these are the three basic divisions of the human psyche. Each is followed by the term used in Transactional Analysis and a brief description.

1. Id (child): immature, irrational
2. Superego (adult): enforces moral standards
3. Ego (parent): mediates between the other two

Three Rs of EDUCATION

Considered by some educators to be the basic subjects for all students, this list is credited to Sir William Curtis, mayor of London in the early 1800s. During the years 1954–57, a Sunday morning television show in the United States called The Fourth R *included Religion. Reasoning has also been called the Fourth R. In recent years, with the advent of sex education and condoms in the schools, the Fourth R has jokingly become Rubbers.*

1. Reading
2. 'Riting (writing)
3. 'Rithmetic (arithmetic)

Three Steps of the RECORDING PROCESS

In the days of the LP and the record player, average consumers did not need to know this list. With the advent of the compact disk and the rerelease of old analog recordings in new digital formats, knowledge of these three steps became essential to distinguish low- from high-quality recordings. Compact disk packages contain a three-letter code indicating the recording format used in each of these three steps. The code appears as AAD, ADD, or DDD, the letter A representing analog and the letter D representing digital. The digital format is generally considered superior.

1. Session recording: original recording
2. Mixing and editing: technical manipulation of original tapes
3. Mastering: final recording or transcription

Three REICHS

Three empires of Germany, as described by Adolf Hitler.

1. The First Reich (771–1806): Holy Roman Empire, founded by Charlemagne
2. The Second Reich (1871–1918): German Empire, founded by Otto von Bismarck
3. The Third Reich (1933–1945): Nazi Germany, founded by Adolf Hitler

Three REVOLUTIONS
The three primary shapers of our present civilization.

1. Agricultural Revolution (c. 10,000 years ago); cultivation of crops
2. Industrial Revolution (since the 1700s); mechanical and electrical devices
3. Informational Revolution (since the 1930s); rapid communications devices

Three RHINEMAIDENS
Mythical characters found in the epic Niebelungenlied. See also Four Operas of the Ring Cycle, Nine Valkyries.

1. Woglinde
2. Wellgunde
3. Flosshilde

Three RINGS OF SATURN
Listed from the outermost to the innermost. In addition to the three major rings, two very narrow rings, called the E Ring and the F Ring, exist just beyond A. See also Four Rings of Neptune, Nine Rings of Uranus.

1. A Ring
2. B Ring
3. C Ring

Three RIVERS OF QUEBEC
A city in Quebec, Trois Rivières, was founded in 1634 by Champlain, and got its name since it was located at the juncture of these three rivers.

1. Saint Lawrence
2. Saint Maurice (first tributary)
3. Saint Maurice (second tributary)

Three RIVERS OF THE U.S. ARMY
The nickname of the 278th Armored Cavalry Regiment derives from these three rivers.

1. Tennessee
2. Holston
3. French Broad

Three Laws of ROBOTS
Author Isaac Asimov described these three laws in his landmark novel I, Robot. *Many authors have since incorporated these three laws into their own visions of the future.*

1. A robot may not injure a human being or, through inaction, allow a human being to come to harm.
2. A robot must obey the orders given it by human beings except where such orders would conflict with the First Law.
3. A robot must protect its own existence as long as such protection does not conflict with the First or Second Law.

Three Types of ROCK
Three basic kinds of rock found on the earth. This list is fundamental to knowledge of geology and mineralogy.

1. Igneous; originating in volcanic lava
2. Sedimentary; fragments of rock deposited in distinct strata
3. Metamorphic; created by heat, pressure, or chemical change

Triumvirates of ROME
Three rulers who shared supreme power.

First Triumvirate (60–53 B.C.E.)

1. Pompeii
2. Julius Caesar
3. Crassus

1. Marc Antony (Marcus Antonius)
2. Marcus Aemilius Lepidus
3. Octavian (later became known as Augustus Caesar)

Three SACRED COLORS

These three colors hold significant symbolic positions in many cultures and religions. Below are listed the symbology of the Triple Goddess of Neo-Paganism (see Three Gods), and the three canonical ranks of Christianity.

		Triple Goddess	*Canonical Rank*	*Symbolizing*
1.	White	maiden	first	innocence, purity, and faith
2.	Red	mother	second	suffering, martyrdom, and sacrifice
3.	Black	crone	third	death and mourning on Good Friday

Three Countries of SCANDINAVIA

Three sovereign nations on the Scandinavian peninsula. While not located on the peninsula, Denmark (which includes Greenland) and Iceland also have a Scandinavian culture.

1. Finland
2. Norway
3. Sweden

The ABCs of SCIENCE FICTION

Three of the most popular exponents of science fiction literature.

1. Isaac Asimov
2. Ray Bradbury
3. Arthur C. Clarke

Three SEASONS
In the calendar of ancient Egypt, only three seasons were recognized.

1. Akhet: sowing
2. Pert: growing
3. Shemu: inundation

Three SECONDARY COLORS
Made by mixing combinations of two of the Three Primary Colors of Paint.

1. Green: blue + yellow
2. Orange: red + yellow
3. Purple: blue + red

Three Stages of SEX IN MARRIAGE
A saying from American folklore.

1. Honeymoon Sex: For the first few years, you can't wait to have sex with each other.
2. Holiday Sex: For the next several years, you only have sex on special occasions.
3. Hallway Sex: After about twenty years, you pass each other in the hallway and say, "Fuck you."

Three SIRENS
In Greek mythology, sirens were beautiful sea nymphs whose lovely voices mesmerized sailors, causing them to wreck their ships on the rocks.

1. Leucosia
2. Ligea
3. Parthenope

THREE SISTERS

A famous play by Russian playwright Anton Chekhov (1860–1904). The main characters are the three sisters of the Prozorov family.

1. Olga
2. Masha
3. Irina

Three SKI SLOPE SYMBOLS

These symbols are posted in ski areas to warn novice skiers away from the more difficult and dangerous slopes.

1. Beginner: green circle
2. Intermediate: blue square
3. Expert: black diamond

Three Stages of SMOG ALERT

1. Stage 1: up to .20 parts per million (caution to those with heart and respiratory conditions)
2. Stage 2: up to .35 parts per million (caution against strenuous exercise)
3. Stage 3: over .35 parts per million (emergency—schools close, people remain indoors)

Three SOLEMN ONES

See Three Fates.

Three SOPRANOS

See Three Tenors.

Three SPHERES OF THE EARTH

Earth is divided by biologists into Three Spheres or distinct areas in which life exists. The entire zone of life is known as the biosphere and includes all three spheres.

1. Lithosphere (solid earth); includes the inner core (5,000 miles [center of the Earth]), outer core (3,000 miles), lower mantle (1,600 miles), upper mantle (560 miles), and crust (9 miles)
2. Hydrosphere (surface water)
3. Atmosphere (gaseous envelope); includes the troposphere (10 miles), stratosphere (30 miles), mesosphere (50 miles), thermosphere (300 miles), and exosphere (beyond 300 miles)

Three STOOGES

This group of American slapstick comedians made its first film in 1930. Over the years, several substitutions were made in the original cast: In 1948, Shemp Howard replaced Curly; in 1955, Joe Besser replaced Shemp; and in 1958, Joe de Rita replaced Joe Besser.

1. Larry (Larry Fine)
2. Curly (Curly Howard)
3. Mo (Mo Howard)

Three Parts of a SYLLOGISM

In the study of rational thought, the syllogism represents the most pure and basic form of logical deduction. A syllogism consists of one each of these three statements. (Examples in parentheses.)

1. Major Premise (All elephants are pink.)
2. Minor Premise (Bessie is an elephant.)
3. Conclusion (Therefore, Bessie is pink.)

Three TENORS

Impresario Tibor Rudas brought together the world's three most famous tenors in 1994. Their success on stage and in recordings spawned several imitations.

Three Tenors

1. Placido Domingo
2. José Carreras
3. Luciano Pavarotti

In order to capitalize on the success of the Three Tenors, RCA Victor released the following tenors on CD in 1996.

Legendary Three Tenors (1900–1950)

1. Enrico Caruso
2. John McCormack
3. Beniamino Gigli

Three Tenors of the Golden Age (1940s–1950s)

1. Mario Lanza
2. Jussi Bjoerling
3. Jan Peerce

Rudas brought together three young American sopranos in 1996. All were award-winning operatic sopranos who also performed modern American and Latin songs.

Three Sopranos

1. Kathleen Cassello
2. Kallen Esperian
3. Cynthia Lawrence

Three THEOLOGICAL VIRTUES
See Three Graces of Christianity

Three Tenets of THEOSOPHY

A mystical religion founded in 1875 by Helena Petrovna Blavatsky when she had a vision of Tsong-kah-pa, an incarnation of Buddha.

1. To form a nucleus of the Universal Brotherhood of Humanity, without distinction of race, creed, sex, caste, or color.
2. To encourage the study of comparative religion, philosophy, and science.
3. To investigate unexplained laws of nature and the powers latent in Man.

TRIATHLON

A three-in-one Olympic event; participants complete these three feats in this order.

1. Swimming (2.4 miles)
2. Bicycling (112 miles)
3. Running (full marathon, 26.2 miles)

TRIMURTI

See Three Gods: Hindu.

TRIPITAKA

See Three Baskets of the Law.

TRIPLE ALLIANCE

Unions of European countries.

Formed against France in 1668

1. England
2. Sweden
3. Netherlands

Formed 1717 (see Quadruple Alliance*)*

1. England
2. France
3. Netherlands

Formed 1882 (see Triple Entente*)*

1. Germany
2. Austria-Hungary
3. Italy

TRIPLE CROWN of Baseball
Awarded to any major league baseball player simultaneously holding the annual record in these three categories.

1. Highest Batting Average (BA)
2. Most Home Runs (HR)
3. Most Runs Batted In (RBI)

TRIPLE CROWN of Harness Racing
Awarded to any horse winning these three harness races in one year.

1. Little Brown Jug, Delaware, Ohio
2. William H. Cane Futurity, Yonkers Raceway, Yonkers, N.Y.
3. Messenger Stakes, Roosevelt Raceway

TRIPLE CROWN of Thoroughbred Racing
Awarded to any horse winning these three thoroughbred races in one year.

1. Kentucky Derby, Louisville, KY.
2. Preakness, Pimlico Track, Baltimore, MD.
3. Belmont Stakes, Belmont, N.Y.

TRIPLE ENTENTE

Formed in opposition to the Triple Alliance *of 1882, this loose diplomatic agreement between three powerful European nations existed from 1907 to 1917.*

1. France
2. Great Britain
3. Russia

TRIPLE GODDESS

See Three Gods: Greek and Roman *(Greek Triple Goddess) and* Three Gods: Neo-Pagan.

TRIPLE THREAT

A description often given to performers who are capable of mastering a range of skills or working successfully in different media.

Skills

1. Singing
2. Dancing
3. Acting

Media

1. Movies
2. Theater
3. Records

TRIUNE CAUSE

A term used in nineteenth-century America to describe the three great struggles for human rights being waged in the country. Temperance, which later grew into the Prohibition movement, was seen as a human rights issue because the abuse of alcohol often destroyed families and left women and children destitute.

1. Abolition: immediate end to slavery

2. Suffrage: equal rights for women
3. Temperance: moderation of the use of alcohol

TRIVARGA

The Trivarga, or Three Worldly Attainments, are the three basic goals of life listed in the Kama Sutra and other sacred Hindu texts.

1. Dharma (virtue): right conduct, natural law (similar to the Tao)
2. Artha (wealth): accumulation of material goods
3. Kama (pleasure or love): fulfillment of sexual desire

Three Kinds of TURQUOISE

Jewelry manufacturers often include turquoise stones in silver settings in imitation of Native American jewelry. However, consumers might not be aware that turquoise comes in three distinct types, one of which contains none of the actual mineral in question.

1. Genuine Turquoise: Identified by the streaks or specks of rock or other minerals, called matrix. Genuine turquoise is also known as real, solid, or pure turquoise. The most valuable of the three types.
2. Reconstituted Turquoise: Contains turquoise but is not as valuable as genuine turquoise. Made by grinding up turquoise and mixing it with epoxy, a clear substance that hardens to a strong, stonelike finish. May or may not contain matrix.
3. Stabilized Turquoise: Completely artificial; contains no turquoise but might be marketed as turquoise. Made of blue-green epoxy. Unofficially called tofu turquoise. Of no value as a mineral.

Three Precepts of the UNIVERSAL LIFE CHURCH (ULC)

An American religion founded by freethinkers in California. A salient feature of the ULC is that they will ordain anyone who wishes to become a ULC minister.

1. Freedom. Every living thing on this earth fights for its freedom. . . .
   The ULC is the active advocate of freedom for everyone, as long as that freedom does not infringe on the rights of others.

2. Food
3. Sex. The ULC recognizes sexuality as a positive force in our lives. If you deny your desire for sex, then you deny life itself.

Three Types of VEGETARIAN

1. Seafood group: will not eat beef, pork, lamb, chicken, or other meat but will eat seafood, fish, dairy foods, and eggs
2. Lacto-Ovo group: will not eat meat or seafood but will eat dairy foods or egg
3. Vegans: will not eat meat, seafood, dairy foods, or egg

Three Speeds of VIDEOCASSETTE RECORDERS
Most videocassette recorders (VCRs) have three speeds of operation. While most machines match this list, some use a different set of initials for the three speeds, such as SP, EP, and SLP (for superlong play), and some have only two speeds (SP and EP).

1. SP: standard play (two hours)
2. LP: long play (four hours)
3. EP: extended play (six hours)

Three Types of VOLCANO
As classified by vulcanologists.

1. Active
2. Dormant
3. Extinct

Three WISE MEN
See Three Magi.

Three WISE MONKEYS
See Three Monkeys.

Three WORLDLY ATTAINMENTS
See Trivarga.

Three WORLDS OF POLITICS AND ECONOMICS
These terms were devised by French intellectuals in the 1950s to describe the three different grades of civilization found in different countries throughout the world. These terms are now seen by some as hopelessly Eurocentric and obsolete. An additional term, "Fourth World," has been used since the 1970s to designate nations forcefully incorporated into states that maintain a distinct political culture but are internationally unrecognized, such as Native Americans, Catalonians, Bavarians, Palestinians, and the people of Tibet.

1. The First World: The West (Europe, America, and later Japan)
2. The Second World: The Soviet bloc (including China, North Korea, North Vietnam, and parts of Eastern Europe)
3. The Third World: The poor, politically unstable nations of the South (newly decolonized, economically disadvantaged states)

Three WORLDS OF SPIRITUAL THOUGHT
The concept of these three places wherein human souls dwell is found throughout many cultures and religions.

1. Heaven, the Celestial World, symbolized by the Sky
2. Earth, the Terrestrial World, symbolized by the Land
3. Hell, the Infernal World, symbolized by the Underworld

WYRD SISTERS
From Saxon mythology. The Wyrd Sisters, from whose name we get the word "weird," correlate to the Three Fates *of Greek mythology and the* Three Norns *of Norse belief.*

1. Wyrd
2. Verthandi
3. Skadi

FOURS

Early mystics recognized Four Directions and built their views of the cosmos on this pattern. Four was found in the basic beliefs of many ancient religions, demonstrated by such widespread concepts as *Four Mystic Animals, Four Sacred Mountains, Four Sacred Rivers,* and Four Pillars of the World (which has no corresponding list). Tetrads, or groups of four powerful deities, were plentiful, though not as numerous as triads.

In the West, mystics recognized *Four Elements* and saw Four as a symbol of the material world. Four represented the cosmos, the totality of space and time, and the soul of the world. Paired with Three as the female element, Four symbolized the male element of life.

Four represented that which brought order out of chaos. In astrology, when planets were square (ninety degrees or one-fourth of a circle apart) it was believed to indicate restless energy and creative tension. Swiss psychologist Carl Jung (1875–1961) believed the appropriate symbol for the deity was a quaternity, or fourfold structure, as opposed to a trinity.

Four AGES
Part of the mythology of Hinduism. It is believed that one complete cycle of the Four Ages, 4,320,000 years, occurring one thousand times constitutes one "day" of Brahma. One thousand complete cycles again constitutes one night. Brahma lives one hundred "years" of these "days" and then dies, having a life of 311,040,000,000,000 years.

1. Satya Yuga: 1,728,000 years when virtue, wisdom, and religion abound
2. Treta Yuga: 1,296,000 years when vice introduced
3. Dvapara Yuga: 864,000 years when vice increases
4. Kali Yuga: 432,000 years when vice (the present age) is abundant

Four ARCHANGELS

According to the holy texts of Islam. In addition to these four, the fallen angel Azazil became the devil Eblis.

1. Gabriel
2. Michael
3. Azrael
4. Israfil or Uriel

BIG FOUR

The four most powerful countries in the world at the time of the Dumbarton Oaks Conference in 1944, dealing with international security and peace.

1. China
2. Great Britain
3. Soviet Union
4. United States

The four countries that occupied parts of Germany after World War II.

1. France
2. Great Britain
3. Soviet Union
4. United States

BIG FOUR IN THE CABINET

The four most important posts in the U.S. president's cabinet.

1. Attorney General
2. Secretary of State
3. Secretary of Defense
4. Secretary of the Treasury

Four BIORHYTHMIC CYCLES
Four internal cycles identified by proponents of biorhythm theory. Each cycle begins at birth and follows a set number of days throughout a person's life.

1. Physical Cycle (23 days)
2. Emotional Cycle (28 days)
3. Intellectual Cycle (33 days)
4. Intuitional Cycle (38 days)

Four BLOOD TYPES
Each blood type is subdivided by Rh factor, either positive (+) or negative (-). The most common blood type is O+; the second most common is A+. AB- is the rarest.

1. O+, O-
2. A+, A-
3. B+, B-
4. AB+, AB-

Four Basic BRAIN WAVES
Researchers of human sleep patterns sometimes classify their subjects according to the characteristics of the brain waves being experienced at a given moment. See also Four Stages of Sleep.

1. Alpha (7–13 waves per second): relaxed, meditative
2. Beta (13 or more waves per second): awake and active
3. Delta (1–4 waves per second): sleep
4. Theta (4–7 waves per second): deep sleep

Four Cs (DIAMONDS)

Jewelers determine the value of diamonds by factoring in these four measurements.

1. Cut
2. Carat
3. Clarity
4. Color

Four Cs (SILENT FILMS)

Early silent comedy films followed this formula, known as the Four Cs.

1. Confrontation
2. Chase
3. Chaos
4. Conquest

Four CANOPIC JARS

In the ancient Egyptian science of mummification, there were four special jars into which four specific organs were stored. Each organ was protected by a genius, or "Son of Horus," and each jar was fashioned in the shape of one of four deities. Each jar also corresponded to one of the Four Directions *and had a protective goddess and symbol.*

	Organ	Genius	Deity Shape	Direction	Protective Goddess	Symbol
1.	Lungs	Hapi (fertility)	ape	south	Isis (creation)	throne
2.	Stomach	Duamutef (funerary god)	jackal	north	Nephthys (the dead)	house and lady
3.	Liver	Imsety (prosperity)	man	east	Neith (teaching, war, domestic arts)	shield and arrows
4.	Intestines	Qebsennuef (mumification)	falcon	west	Selket (conjugal union)	scorpion

Four CARDINAL POINTS
See Four Directions.

Four CARDINAL VIRTUES
See Four Virtues of Christianity.

Four CHILDREN OF PASSOVER
Also known as the Four Sons of Passover, these are four symbolic characters in the liturgy of this Jewish holiday.

1. The Wise Child
2. The Wicked Child
3. The Simple Child
4. The Ignorant Child (The Child Who Does Not Ask)

Four Branches of CHRISTIANITY
The four major divisions of Christianity. In the U.S., lists of the major divisions of Christianity often include only three, overlooking Orthodox Christianity because its main areas of population are in Africa, Asia, Europe, and the Middle East. Listed in chronological order, the oldest first.

1. Roman Catholic
2. Orthodox
3. Protestant
4. Mormon (Church of Jesus Christ of Latter-day Saints)

Four CLASSES OF INDIAN SOCIETY
Ancient Hindu social customs decreed that each member of society belong to the class into which he or she was born. Each of these classes was further divided into castes.

1. Brahmans: priests
2. Kshatriyahs: warriors, royalty

3. Vaisyas: traders, farmers
4. Sudras: workers, servants

Four CLASSES OF JAPANESE SOCIETY

Ancient Japan was divided into discrete social classes, listed here in order of most to least important.

1. Samurai (warriors)
2. Farmers
3. Artisans
4. Traders

Four CLEFS

See Three Clefs

Four Kinds of CLOSE ENCOUNTERS

UFO enthusiasts list four kinds of close encounter.

1. Close Encounters of the First Kind: sighting aliens or alien spacecraft
2. Close Encounters of the Second Kind: recovering alien artifacts or concrete proof
3. Close Encounters of the Third Kind: meeting aliens
4. Close Encounters of the Fourth Kind: visiting the aliens' own world

Four-leaf CLOVER

From the popular 1927 song "I'm Looking over a Four-leaf Clover" by Harry Woods and Mort Dixon. Each leaf of the tiny plant is assigned a symbolic association.

1. Sunshine
2. Rain
3. Roses that grow in the lane
4. Somebody I adore

Four COLLEGE DEGREES

In the United States, college students generally work toward earning one of four degrees. Each degree is listed with the approximate number of years required for completion.

1. Associate (2)
2. Bachelor (4)
3. Master (6)
4. Doctor (8)

Four COLLEGE LEVELS

College students are frequently referred to by these labels, indicating their current year of college. The same terms are also used for high school students.

1. Freshman
2. Sophomore
3. Junior
4. Senior

Four COLORS OF THE DIRECTIONS

Many religions place importance on the Four Directions *and assign symbolic associations to each direction, including color. East is often considered the predominant direction, due to the daily appearance of the sun in that quarter, so it is listed first. Here are several different variations on this nearly universal system of symbology.*

		Hopi	*Cree*	*Apache*	*Aztec/ Mayan*	*China*	*Tibet*	*Ireland*
1.	East	white	yellow	black	red	green	white	purple
2.	South	blue (or red)	red	white	green	red	blue	white
3.	West	yellow (or blue)	black	yellow	blue	white	red	brown
4.	North	black (or yellow)	white	blue	yellow	black	yellow	black

FOUR CORNERS
The nickname given to the only place in the United States where four states meet at a single point.

1. Arizona
2. Colorado
3. New Mexico
4. Utah

Four Precepts of CREATIVITY
An American religious belief system founded by white supremacists in opposition to Christianity.

1. Antisemitism: hatred of Jews
2. Racism: hatred of blacks, Asians, and other minorities
3. Homophobia: hatred of gays
4. Anti-Christianism: Hatred of Christians—the belief that Christianity is mass insanity, a Jewish hoax calculated to destroy the White race.

Four CROSS-QUARTER DAYS
See Four Sabbaths of Pagans.

Four CROWN PRINCES OF HELL
From the Satanic Bible by Anton Szandor La Vey. Each of the Four Princes corresponds to one of the Four Directions *and the* Four Elements.

		Origin of Name	*Direction*	*Element*	*Represents*
1.	Satan	Hebrew	south	fire	adversary
2.	Lucifer	Roman	east	air	enlightenment
3.	Leviathan	Hebrew	west	water	the ocean
4.	Belial	Hebrew	north	earth	independence

FOUR CROWNED

These four early Christian martyrs, Roman citizens executed as Christians under the emperor Diocletian, are known by the Roman Catholic church as the Four Crowned.

1. Carpophorus
2. Severianus
3. Severus
4. Victorinus

FOUR DAUGHTERS

The first film (1938) in a popular series of films made during the Golden Age of Hollywood. The four women who played the daughters also starred in Four Wives *(1938) and* Four Mothers *(1939).*

1. Ann Lemp (Priscilla Lane)
2. Thea Lemp (Lola Lane)
3. Kay Lemp (Rosemary Lane)
4. Emma Lemp (Gale Page, the only nonsister of the group)

Four DEAD IN OHIO

This line appears in the rock hit "Ohio" written by Neil Young and performed by Crosby, Stills, Nash, and Young. The four were students at Kent State University in Kent, Ohio, who were killed on May 4, 1970, when national guardsmen opened fire on a campus protest.

1. Allison Krause
2. Jeffrey Miller
3. Sandra Scheuer
4. William Schroeder

Four DIRECTIONS

Also known as the Four Cardinal Points of the compass. The Four Directions are cel-ebrated, symbolized, personified, and deified by nearly every culture and religious sys-tem in the world. See also Four Colors of the Directions, Five Directions.

1. North
2. South
3. East
4. West

Four Bases of DNA

Deoxyribonucleic acid (DNA), the molecule that carries the genetic information in liv-ing organisms, is structured as two side-by-side strands, each strand made up of a sequence of chemicals; the whole structure is a double helix or spiral. There are only four chemicals in DNA. Each chemical pairs up with only one other chemical, so there are only two possible pairs. DNA molecules are able to divide and create replicas of themselves because of this pairing of chemical bases.

Pair

1. A (adenine)
2. T (thymine)

Pair

3. C (cytosine)
4. G (guanine)

Four Sides of a DREYDL

A dreydl is a four-sided spinning toy similar to a top. There is a Hebrew letter on each side. The traditional dreydl game consists of players taking turns spinning the dreydl and either placing coins in the pile or taking them out depending on how the dreydl falls. When dreydls are made in Israel, the letter on the fourth side is changed to pé, which stands for "po," meaning "here."

Letter Name	Hebrew Word	Translation	Play	Symbol
1. Noon	Ness	Miracle	none	נ
2. Gimmel	Gadol	Great	win pile	ג
3. Hé	Haya	Happened	win half	ה
4. Shin	Sham	There	put in one piece	ש

Four DWARFS

Four characters in Norse mythology who hold up the celestial skull of Ymir. For a similar construct, see Four Gods. Each character is listed with its respective "direction."

1. Austri (east)
2. Vestri (west)
3. Nordri (north)
4. Sudri (south)

Four ELEMENTARY TRUTHS

See Four Noble Truths.

Four ELEMENTS

The ancient belief that all material in the universe is composed of one of these four elements formed the basis of medieval alchemy. Similar beliefs appear in many cultures; see Five Elements *and* Six Elements. *(The discovery of the molecular composition of matter led to the discovery of 92 naturally occurring elements.)*

1. Air: gas
2. Fire: power to change (chemical reaction)
3. Water: liquid
4. Earth: solid

This belief system is so fundamental to so many religions and mythologies that the four elements have acquired numerous intertwining and mystical correspondences. Here are a few of the more interesting or unusual groups of correspondences. See the Four Gospels.

	Directions	Temperaments	Stages of the Moon
1. Air	east	sanguine	crescent moon
2. Fire	south	nervous (choleric)	full moon
3. Water	west	lymphatic (phlegmatic)	waning moon
4. Earth	north	bilius (melancholic)	new moon

	Seasons	Stages of Life	Times of Day
	spring	infancy	dawn
	summer	youth	midday
	autumn	middle age	evening
	winter	old age	night

Mystic Animals (Orient)	Mystic Animals (Occident)	Elemental Beings
blue dragon	lion	sylphs and giants
red bird	eagle	salamanders
white tiger	peacock	undines and mermaids
black tortoise	ox	gnomes and dwarves

Elements of Life (Hindu)	Tarot Suits
breath	swords
vital heat	wands
blood	cups
flesh	pentacles

Four ERAS OF NATURAL HISTORY

Paleontologists divide the history of the planet Earth into four eras, each of which is subdivided into periods. The periods of the Cenozoic are further subdivided into epochs. Some scientists group the Mississippian and Pennsylvanian into one period known as the Carboniferous. Biological development for each era and period follows each entry.

1. Pre-Cambrian Era
   a. Azoic Period (no life)
   b. Archaeozoic Period (no life)
   c. Proterozoic Period (no life)

2. Paleozoic Era
    a. Cambrian Period (primitive marine life)
    b. Ordovician Period (fish)
    c. Silurian Period (land plants)
    d. Devonian Period (amphibians)
    e. Mississippian Period (scale trees)
    f. Pennsylvanian Period (insects)
    g. Permian Period (reptiles)
3. Mesozoic Era
    a. Triassic Period (dinosaurs)
    b. Jurassic Period (birds)
    c. Cretaceous Period (mammals)
4. Cenozoic Era
    a. Tertiary Period (mammals dominate)
        i. Paleocene Epoch
        ii. Eocene Epoch
        iii. Oligocene Epoch
        iv. Miocene Epoch
        v. Pliocene Epoch
    b. Quaternary Period (modern mammals)
        i. Pleistocene Epoch
        ii. Recent Epoch

Four ESTATES
See Three Estates.

Four EVANGELISTS
See Four Gospels.

Four Fs
This German gymnastic club takes its name from its four basic goals.

1. Frisch (healthy)
2. Fromm (godfearing)
3. Fröhlich (cheerful)
4. Frei (free)

Four Fs

In the world of journalism, the Four Fs is a nickname for what some male editors think are the only topics women are interested in.

1. Food
2. Fashion
3. Family
4. Furnishings

FAB FOUR

Nickname for the British rock band the Beatles.

1. John Lennon (rhythm guitar)
2. Paul McCartney (bass)
3. George Harrison (lead guitar)
4. Ringo Starr (drums)

FANTASTIC FOUR

A group of crime-fighting superheroes in a popular comic series by Stan Lee and Jack Kirby. Each character's "real" name follows each entry.

1. Mr. Fantastic (Reed Richards)
2. Human Torch (Johnny Storm)
3. The Thing (Ben Grimm)
4. Invisible Girl (Sue Storm Richards)

Four FATES

See Three Fates, Three Furies.

Four Types of FIRE

Firefighters and fire extinguisher manufacturers use these definitions and symbols (letters and shapes) when discussing different types of fire and the correct method of extinguishing each. Fire extinguishers are marked as to what type of fire they are designed to extinguish.

1. Wood, paper, cloth, or rubber: A, triangle
2. Oil, gas, or grease: B, square
3. Electrical equipment: C, circle
4. Heavy metals, sodium, or magnesium: D, star

Four Basic FOOD GROUPS

This fundamental categorization of food types has, for the most part, been eclipsed by the more complex Food Guide Pyramid (see Six Basic Food Groups). Some nutritionists also expound on a related list, the Four Evil Food Groups: salt, sugar, cholesterol, and fat.

1. Cereal: breads and cereals
2. Vegetable: fruits and vegetables
3. Meat: meat and protein
4. Milk: dairy products

Four Basic FORCES

Natural forces identified in the field of particle physics. These four forces bind matter together and direct the motion of all matter, from atomic particles to planets and stars.

1. Gravity
2. Electromagnetic force
3. Strong nuclear force
4. Weak nuclear force

Four FORCES OF FLIGHT
The aviation industry is based on the invention of flying machines that solve the equation of equalizing and adjusting for these four forces.

1. Lift: upward motion
2. Thrust: forward motion
3. Weight: downward motion
4. Drag: backward motion

Four FORMS
From the Jain religion, an ancient branch of Hinduism. Jains base their public conduct on the following four guidelines.

1. To perform a kind act without expectation of a reward.
2. To rejoice at the well-being of others.
3. To sympathize with distressed people and to relieve their sufferings.
4. To pity criminals.

Four FREEDOMS
President Franklin D. Roosevelt outlined these in a famous speech delivered on January 6, 1941. These basic freedoms formed the foundation of his public service administration.

1. Freedom of Speech and Expression
2. Freedom of Religion
3. Freedom from Want
4. Freedom from Fear

Four Classes of GALAXY
The four types of galaxy identified by astronomer Edwin P. Hubble in 1925. Our galaxy, the Milky Way, is a spiral galaxy.

1. Elliptical: elliptical disk with no spiral arms
2. Spiral: nucleus with arms spiraling outward

3. Barred Spiral: a spiral galaxy with a bright bar through the nucleus
4. Irregular: other types

Four GALILEAN SATELLITES
See Sixteen Moons of Jupiter.

GANG OF FOUR (CHINA)
Four top leaders of the Chinese Communist Party who attempted to seize power on the death of Mao Tse-tung, during China's Cultural Revolution of 1966–76. They were defeated and imprisoned. The leader of the group, Jiang Qing, was Mao's wife. After the death of Mao, a triumvirate of Hua Guofeng, Ye Jianying, and Li Xiannian led the nation for a short period of time until Deng Xiaoping came to power.

1. Jiang Qing (Chaing Chi'ing or Madame Mao), sentenced to life in prison; committed suicide in 1991
2. Wang Hongwen (Wang Hung-wen), the youngest of the gang; sentenced to life in prison, died of a liver ailment in 1992
3. Yao Wenyuan, propagandist for the Gang of Four; served 15 years in prison and was released in 1996
4. Zhang Chunqiao (Chang Ch'un-ch'iou), sentenced to life imprison; is still alive

GANG OF FOUR
A popular British rock group during the 1960s.

1. Hugo Burnham
2. Andy Gill
3. Jon King
4. Sara Lee

Four GATES OF LONDON

These historic gates in the ancient walls surrounding the city of London, England, are cited in numerous ancient texts. By 1133, at the beginning of the reign of Henry II, three more were in place—Newgate, Bishopsgate, and the Postern—but the Four Gates remain the most common reference.

1. Aldgate in the East
2. Aldersgate in the North
3. Ludgate in the West
4. Bridgegate over the Thames to the South

Four Organic GEMSTONES

Jewelers recognize only four organic substances as gemstones; all other precious and semiprecious gems are considered minerals.

1. Amber (petrified tree sap)
2. Coral (calcareous skeleton of certain sea animals)
3. Pearl (shiny inner lining of certain seashells)
4. Ivory (elephant tooth or tusk)

Four Postulates of GEOMETRY

See Five Postulates of Geometry.

Four Attributes of GLORIFIED BODIES

From the traditional teachings of the Roman Catholic church.

1. Subtility
2. Agility
3. Luminosity
4. Immortality

FOUR GODS OF BABYLON

These were known as the Four Corner Gods in the religion of ancient Babylon. Two of these deities also appear in the Babylon trinity; see Three Gods: Babylonian. *For a similar construct, see* Four Dwarfs.

1. Shamash (east)
2. Sin (west)
3. Nergal (north)
4. Ninib (south)

FOUR GODS OF ROME

Known as the Four Gods of the Household in ancient Rome, these deities oversaw every area of the private residence.

1. Janus: god of the house
2. Lar: god of the farm and harvest
3. Penate: god of the storeroom
4. Vesta: goddess of the hearth

Big Four in GOLF

These are the four tournaments of the men's Professional Golfers Association (PGA) Tour. Winning all four of these tournaments in one year is called a Grand Slam.

1. United States Open
2. Masters (held at Augusta National Golf and Country Club)
3. PGA Championship
4. British Open

Four GOSPELS

The following are believed to be the authors of the first four books of the Christian New Testament, describing the life and death of Jesus of Nazareth. They are also called the Four Evangelists. Each of these persons has also been assigned an animal symbol and symbolic meaning; see Four Mystic Animals.

1. Matthew (winged man); resurrection
2. Mark (lion); ascension
3. Luke (ox); passion
4. John (eagle); incarnation

Four GRACES OF GREEK MYTHOLOGY
See Three Graces of Greek Mythology.

Four Hs
The Four-H (or 4-H) Club exists in numerous chapters across the U.S., focusing on agricultural skills. Members live mostly in rural areas. The name of the club is based on the four main parts of the Four-H Club Pledge: "I pledge my head to clearer thinking, my heart to greater loyalty, my hands to larger service, and my health to better living, for my club, my community, and my country."

1. Head
2. Heart
3. Hands
4. Health

Four Chambers of the HEART

1. Right atrium
2. Left atrium
3. Right ventricle
4. Left ventricle

Four HEAVENLY KINGS
Four Buddhist deities that guard the Four Directions; *see also* Four Colors of the Directions.

1. Mo-Li Ch'ing (the east)
2. Mo-Li Hung (the south)

3. Mo-Li Hai (the west)
4. Mo-Li Shou (the north)

Four HELMS OF RANK

In the customs of British heraldry, or the science of hereditary coats of arms, there are four distinct and symbolic armorial helmets that appear in heraldic designs.

1. Sovereign: gold, full-faced
2. Peer: silver with gold grill, turned
3. Baronet and knight: silver, full-faced
4. Esquire and gentleman: silver, turned

Four HESPERIDES

In Greek mythology, the Hesperides were four nymphs, daughters of the Titan Atlas and Nyx, goddess of the night. They lived in a beautiful garden in which grew a tree with golden apples that Gaia (Gaea) had given as a wedding present to the goddess Hera. The garden was guarded by Ladon, a dragon with a hundred heads. See also Twelve Labors of Hercules.

1. Aegle
2. Arethusa
3. Erythia
4. Hesperia

HOBOKEN FOUR

A popular singing group in the 1930s. Before Frank Sinatra joined the group, it was known as the Three Flashes.

1. James Petrozelli
2. Patty Principi
3. Frank Sinatra
4. Fred Tamburro

Four HORSEMEN OF THE APOCALYPSE
Mentioned in Revelation 6:1–8, each of these horse-and-rider pairs appears in turn upon the breaking of the seals. (See Seven Seals.)

	Color	*Symbol*	*Object Carried by Rider*
1.	White	Christ	crown
2.	Red	War	sword
3.	Black	Famine	scales
4.	Pale	Death	(nothing)

Four HORSEMEN OF NOTRE DAME
During the years 1922–25, these four football stars came to be so known due to their outstanding performance in the game. Seven linemen also became quite well known; see Seven Mules of Notre Dame.

1. Harry Stuhldrehr (quarterback)
2. Elmer Layden (fullback)
3. Dom Miller (halfback)
4. Jim Crowley (halfback)

Four Sons of HORUS
See Four Canopic Jars.

Four HOURS OF THE DAY
See Eight Canonical Hours.

Four HUMORS
Believed by early alchemists to be the four basic liquids of the body.

1. Black Bile
2. Yellow Bile
3. Phlegm
4. Blood

Four Symbols of the I CHING

The ancient Chinese mysticism of the I Ching or Book of Changes derives its method-
ology from these four symbols. They are constructed out of each possible combination of
the Two Primal Forms, yang (represented by a solid line) and yin (represented by a
broken line). These Primal Forms, when combined in groups of three, produce the Eight
Trigrams, *and from the Trigrams are derived the 64 Hexagrams (groups of six), used*
in divination and prophesy.

1. ══
2. ═══
3. ══
4. ══

IMMORTAL FOUR

Nickname of the four greatest poets of Italy.

1. Dante Alighieri (1265–1321)
2. Francesco Petrarch (1304–74)
3. Lodovico Ariosto (1474–1533)
4. Torquato Tasso (1544–95)

Four Families of INSTRUMENTS

Music students learn this list. Each group, except percussion, contains four instruments that
function more or less as the "four voices" in vocal music. In the woodwind group, however,
only the bassoon makes a good match to the bass voice; the other three instruments have
ranges approximately equal to each other. The instruments are listed here in order from
high (soprano) to low (bass). Orchestras are normally arranged by this grouping; but the
list Five Classes of Instruments *groups instruments by specific qualities.*

1. String: violin, viola, cello, bass
2. Woodwind: flute, oboe, clarinet, bassoon
3. Brass: french horn, trumpet, trombone, tuba
4. Percussion

Big Four in JAPANESE MOTORCYCLE COMPANIES
These four corporations dominate the world of Japanese motorcycle manufacturing.

1. Kawasaki
2. Yamaha
3. Suzuki
4. Honda

Four JARS
See Four Canopic Jars.

Four JOVIAN MOONS
See Sixteen Moons of Jupiter.

Four JUDGES OF THE UNDERWORLD
See Three Judges of the Underworld.

Four KURAHITS
In the religion of Sikhism, these are the four forbidden acts. A Sikh becomes a "fallen one" if he or she indulges in any of the Four Kurahits. See also Five Kakars.

1. Trimming of the Keshas (unshorn hair and beard) on the body
2. Use of tobacco or intoxicants
3. Eating meat prepared according to Muslim rites
4. Adultery

Four Levels of LEARNING
A general theory held by those in education; listed in ascending order of usefulness.

1. Unconscious Incompetence: you don't know what you don't know
2. Conscious Incompetence: you know what you don't know

3. Conscious Competence: you know you know
4. Unconscious Competence: you've stopped learning

Four LUCAN CANTICLES
Based on the biblical text found in Luke 1 and 2, these have often been set to music by classical composers.

1. Magnificat: Luke 1:46–55
2. Benedictus: Luke 1:67–79
3. Gloria in Excelsis Deo: Luke 2:13–14
4. Nunc Dimitis: Luke 2:28–32

Four MARX BROTHERS
See Five Marx Brothers.

Four MARYS
One of the most popular ballads in the English language is "The Four Marys." It exists in many variations, and many versions give the names of the four differently. The most widely published version of the ballad lists Mary Beaton, Mary Seton, Mary Carmichael, and Mary Hamilton (the last two Marys are fictional); the real Marys' names are given here. The ballad tells the tale of Mary Hamilton, who kept her pregnancy a secret, killed her baby, and was hanged for the deed. The real Four Marys were ladies-in-waiting to Mary Stuart, Queen of Scots (1542–87).

1. Mary Beaton
2. Mary Seton
3. Mary Fleming
4. Mary Livingston

Four Parts of the MASS

According to the prescriptions of the Second Vatican Council, the Roman Catholic Mass is composed of four parts. The two main parts are bracketed by introductory rites and concluding rites.

1. Introductory Rites
   Antiphon at the Entrance
   Salutation (Greeting) of Altar and People
   Penitential Act
   Appeal for Mercy (Kyrie)
   Gloria in Excelsis (Praise)
   Collect
2. Liturgy of the Word
   Scripture Readings
   Responsorial Psalm of Gradual
   Alleluia
   Homily
   Profession of Faith (Creed)
   Prayer for the Faithful (General Intercession or Bidding Prayer)
3. Liturgy of the Eucharist
   Preparation of the Gifts
   Eucharistic Prayer
       Thanksgiving
       Acclamation
       Epiclesis
       Institution Narrative and Consecration
       Anamnesis
       Oblation
       Intercessions
       Doxology
   Communion Rite
       Lord's Prayer
       Rite of Peace
       Breaking of Bread
       Commingling
       Agnus Dei

Private Preparation of the Priest
Invitation
Distribution of Communion
Singing at Communion
Pause
Postcommunion
4. Concluding Rites
Blessing of the People
Dismissal

Four MATHEMATICAL FUNCTIONS

1. Addition (+)
2. Subtraction (-)
3. Multiplication (x)
4. Division (÷)

Four MATRIARCHS

Also known as the Four Matrons, these four women are celebrated in Jewish tradition as four of the seven founders of Judaism. See also Three Patriarchs.

1. Sarah
2. Rebecca
3. Rachel
4. Leah

FOUR MATRONS

See Four Matriarchs.

Four States of MATTER
The first three states have been known since the dawn of history, but the fourth state was added to the list only in the twentieth century. A fifth state, ether, exists in theory, but some scientists do not consider it an actual possibility.

1. Liquid
2. Gas
3. Solid
4. Plasma

Four Levels of MEANING
Four different methods of interpreting a piece of literature, particularly scripture.

1. Historical (Literal)
2. Allegorical
3. Moral
4. Anagogical

Four Sacred MOUNTAINS
From Navajo mythology. See also Four Colors of the Directions.

		Direction	Adornment	Fastened to Earth with	Covered with	Dwellers there
1.	Sisnajinni	east	white shell	bolt of lightning	sheet of daylight	Dawn Youth and Dawn Maiden
2.	Tsodsichl	south	turquoise	knife of stone	blue sky	Turquoise Youth and Turquoise Maiden
3.	Doko-oslid	west	haliotis shell	sunbeam	yellow cloud	Twilight Youth and Haliotis Maiden

| 4. | Depenitsa | north | cannel coal (a sacred black gemstone) | rainbow | covering of darkness | Youth of Cannel Coal and Darkness Maiden |

Four MOVEMENTS OF A DANCE SUITE

A dance suite is traditionally a four-part piece of instrumental music in which the composer is free to choose four styles of dance, although many dance suites contain five or even six movements. Around 1650, the dance suite became standardized and was expected to contain these four movements, but over time, dance suites became less rigid and included other dances, including the bourrée, the gavotte, the minuet, and the air.

1. Allemande
2. Courante
3. Sarabande
4. Gigue

Four MUSKETEERS
See Three Musketeers.

Four MYSTIC ANIMALS
Symbologies from around the world show evidence of ancient systems of Four Mystic Animals. Here are six versions. See also Four Elements: Correspondences; Four Gospels; *and* Tetrachord.

Chinese

1. Dragon
2. Phoenix or Bird
3. Unicorn or Tiger
4. Turtle or Tortoise

Mesopotamian

1. Lion
2. Eagle
3. Ox
4. Peacock

Four Totems of Asshur (Assyrian)

1. Lion
2. Eagle
3. Bull
4. Man

Four Totems of the Directions (Babylonian)

1. Lion
2. Eagle-headed Dragon
3. Bull
4. Man-like being

Christian

1. Lion
2. Eagle
3. Ox or bull
4. Man or winged man

Greek (from Plato)

1. Sheep
2. Cock
3. Horse
4. Man

Four NOBLE TRUTHS

According to Buddhism, these are the basic truths with which one may reconcile one's life. Also known as the Four Elementary Truths of Zen (a branch of Buddhism).

1. The Nature of Existence: Life is vain; birth and death bring grief.
2. The Nature of Causation: Indulgence of desire causes vanity and grief.
3. Ultimate Freedom in Perfect Existence: End desire; bring surcease from grief.
4. The Way of Supreme Life: End desire by living wisely.

Four OCEANIDES

In Greek mythology, these were the messengers of the gods.

1. Amphitrite
2. Clymene
3. Doris
4. Metis

Fourfold OFFICE OF THE LORD

Isaiah 32:22 describes the Fourfold Office of the Lord in these terms. See also the Three Offices of Christ.

1. Judge
2. Lawgiver
3. King
4. Savior

Four OLODUS

From Ifa, an African Yoruba religion. The Olodus are the first elders who were present at the creation of the universe.

1. Ogbe
2. Oyeku

3. Iwori
4. Idi

Four ORDERS

In architecture, the four styles of column, including base, shaft, capitol, and entablature, are called orders. Historically, there are four, as well as the Composite, which contains elements of more than one.

1. Corinthian
2. Doric
3. Ionic
4. Tuscan

The Four Ps

A short play by English epigrammatist John Heywood (c. 1497–1580) in which four characters compete to see who can tell the biggest lie.

1. Palmer
2. Pardoner
3. Potecary
4. Pedlar

Four Ps

A philosophy of business marketing. The first three items are sometimes known as the Three Ps.

1. The right Product
2. At the right Price
3. In the right Place
4. With the right Promotion

Four PHASES OF THE MOON

See Eight Phases of the Moon.

Four Causes of a PLANE CRASH

Plane crashes may be categorized into one of these four types.

1. Human error
2. Mechanical failure
3. Force of nature
4. Sabotage

Four Sacred PLANTS

From Navajo mythology. These four plants figure prominently in the ceremonies of Native Americans of the southwest.

1. Corn
2. Squash
3. Beans
4. Tobacco

Four Positions in POLO

Polo teams consist of four players on horseback. As in other organized sports, each player position has a specific name and function.

Forwards

1. Number One Forward
2. Number Two Forward

Backs

3. Number Three Back
4. Number Four Back

Four Major PROPHETS OF THE OLD TESTAMENT

The books of the Old Testament Bible have been divided by scholars into five distinct groups, placing these, the twenty-third, twenty-fourth, twenty-sixth, and twenty-seventh books, respectively, in the group known as the Four Major Prophets. See also Five Books of Moses.

1. Isaiah
2. Jeremiah
3. Ezekiel
4. Daniel

Four PROTOCOLS

As discussed in the film The Fourth Protocol *(1984), these are four progressively more disruptive techniques of espionage.*

1. Secrecy
2. Conspiracy
3. Sabotage
4. Utter destruction

QUADRUPLE ALLIANCE

A mutually beneficial diplomatic alliance between four countries. Two such pacts have been known as such. The first was formed in 1718 out of the Triple Alliance of England, France, and the Netherlands to oppose Spain (see Triple Alliance*).*

1. England
2. France
3. Netherlands
4. Austria

The second was formed in 1814 to oppose Napoleon of France.

1. Great Britain
2. Russia

3. Prussia
4. Austria

Four QUARTETS

A long poem by British author T. S. Eliot (1888–1965) consisting of four individual poems set in four different places. They were first published during 1936–1942. Each poem combines realistic and mystical imagery and correlates to one of the Four Elements.

1. *Burnt Norton* (air)
2. *East Coker* (earth)
3. *The Dry Salvages* (water)
4. *Little Gidding* (fire)

Four Rs

See Three Rs of Conservation.

Four RACES OF APARTHEID

Under the South African system of apartheid, which ended in 1993, four distinct races were legally recognized, each with distinct rights. Because South Africa traded with Japan, Japanese citizens were classified White (called Honorary Aryans) while other orientals were classified Asian.

1. African
2. Asian
3. Coloured
4. White

Four Operas of the RING CYCLE

This group of four operas, also called the Ring des Niebelungen, *composed by German composer Richard Wagner during 1853–74, tells epic tales based on Teutonic archetypes. See also* Three Rhinemaidens, Nine Valkyries.

1. Das Rheingold (The Rhine Gold)
2. Die Walküre (The Valkyries)
3. Siegfried (Siegfried)
4. Götterdämmerung (Twilight of the Gods)

Four RINGS OF NEPTUNE

Listed from the outermost to the innermost. See also Three Rings of Saturn, Nine Rings of Uranus.

1. Main Ring
2. Inner Ring
3. Plateau (a broad, diffuse ring of fine material)
4. Inside Diffuse Ring

Four RIVERS

Many differing mythological systems refer to the Four Rivers. Here are four lists.

Four Rivers of the World (Buddhist)

1. Ganges
2. Indus
3. Nile
4. Oxus

The following four mystical rivers are said to originate on Mount Meru (Sumeru), the Buddhist Axis of the World. Each river also has many mystical correspondences.

Four Rivers of Mount Meru (Buddhist)

		Liquid	*Process*	*Humor*	*Direction*
1.	Blue-black	water	nigredo (blackening)	black bile	south
2.	White	milk	albedo (whitening)	phlegm	east
3.	Yellow	honey	citrinitas	yellow bile	north
4.	Red	wine	rubedo	blood	west

	Element	Quality	Precious Gem or Mineral
1. Blue-black	fire	hot	lapis lazuli or sapphire
2. White	air	dry	crystal, silver, or diamond
3. Yellow	earth	cold	gold
4. Red	water	wet	ruby

In Greek mythology, four rivers meet at the entrance to the underworld. Some versions of the myths describe five, including Lethe (forgetfulness, oblivion). Meanings and qualities are listed here also.

Four Rivers of Hades

1. Phlegethon or Pyriphlegethon: fire, blazing like fire (hot)
2. Cocytus: lamentation, shrieking, wailing (dry)
3. Styx: death, hatred (cold)
4. Acheron: darkness, gloom, grief, woe (wet)

Also called the Four Rivers of Paradise, the following are mentioned in Genesis 2:10–14. (Locations in parentheses.)

Four Rivers of Eden (Judeo-Christian)

1. Pishon or Pison, in the land of Havilah
2. Gihon, in the land of Cush (Ethiopia)
3. Tigris or Hiddekel, east of Assyria
4. Euphrates, in the fertile crescent

Four ROYAL STARS

In astrology these four stars are given special honor due to their locations in the constellations.

1. Aldebaran: "Eye of the Bull," in Taurus
2. Regulus: "Heart of the Lion," in Leo
3. Antares: "Heart of the Scorpion," in Scorpio
4. Fomalhaut: "Mouth of the Southern Fish," in Pisces

Four SABBATHS OF PAGANS

Also known as the Four Cross-quarter Days, these holidays are celebrated by some, but not all, Neo-Pagans who are reviving the ancient Celtic religion of the British Isles. Brigid and Lugh are two deities of the old religion. See also Eight Holy Days of Pagans.

1. Samhaim (Halloween, All Hallow E'en, Feast of the Dead, November Eve, Hallowmas) October 31
2. Imbolc (Candlemas, Olmelc, Surrounding the Belly, Brigid's Night, Winter Purification) February 2
3. Beltane (May Eve, Roodmas, Walpurgis, Walpurgisnacht) April 30
4. Lughnassad (August Eve, Lammas, Games of Lugh) July 31 or August 1

Four SCALES OF BAROQUE MUSIC

These four scales, or basic groups of notes related by specific intervals, are the basic scales in which nearly all baroque and classical music was composed. Students of music theory are required to learn this list. The melodic minor scale changes as the melody descends, as shown in parentheses. Notes are in the key of C.

1. Major scale   C D E F G A B C
2. Pure Minor scale   C D Eb F G Ab Bb C
3. Melodic Minor scale   C D Eb F G A B C (Bb Ab G F Eb D C)
4. Harmonic Minor scale   C D Eb F G Ab B C

Four SCALES OF JAPANESE MUSIC

Known as the Four Sen, these scales are used in the composition of Japanese classical music. Optional tones are shown in parentheses. Western note values are given.

1. Ryo-sen   D E F# (G#) A B (C#) D
2. Ritsu-sen D E (F) G A B (C) D
3. Yo-sen   D F G A C D
4. In-sen   D Eb G A Bb D

Four Colors of SCRIPT REWRITES
Scripts for film and television productions often go through many rewrites, each rewrite being done on a specific color paper.

1. White: original
2. Blue: first change
3. Pink: second change
4. Yellow: third change

Four SEAS
The waters surrounding the Isle of Britain are known as the Four Seas.

1. North Sea (north)
2. German Ocean (east)
3. English Channel (south)
4. Irish Sea, Scottish Sea, and St. George's Channel (west)

Four SEASONS
See also Four Solar Festivals.

1. Spring
2. Summer
3. Autumn (Fall)
4. Winter

Four SEN
See Four Scales of Japanese Music.

Four Phases of SEXUAL INTERCOURSE
From the landmark book Human Sexual Response *by William Howard Masters and Virginia E. Johnson (1966). The researchers also discovered a fifth physiological*

phase, experienced only by men, the Refractory Period, in which the body is unrespon-
sive to sexual stimulation.

		Male	Female
1.	Excitement	Penis erection, secretion of lubricating fluid	Increased heart rate, breasts and labia swell, clitoris engorged, moistening of vagina
2.	Plateau	Increased heart rate, testes enlarge	Clitoris retracts, vaginal walls thicken
3.	Orgasm	Ejaculation	Rhythmic contractions of vaginal muscles (various patterns possible)
4.	Resolution	Loss of erection, heart rate normalizes	Heart rate normalizes

Four Precepts of SHAKERISM

The United Society of Believers in Christ's Second Appearing, popularly known as Shakers, was a nineteenth-century American religion in which participants communed with the deity through deep prayer, shaking, and speaking in tongues.

1. Celibacy
2. Confession of all sin
3. Brotherhood
4. Community ownership of property

Four Stages of SLEEP

Based on sleep research. Two additional stages, called prestages, include the awake stage and the relaxed (eyes closed) stage. (Descriptions of brain waves follow in paren-theses.) Light sleep is also known as rapid eye movement (REM) or dreaming sleep. See also Four Basic Brain Waves.

1. Light Sleep (small and irregular)
2. Sleep Spindles (spikes)

3. Deeper Sleep (some delta waves)
4. Deep Sleep (mostly delta waves)

Four SOLAR FESTIVALS

These four astronomical events occur every year, on or about the same dates. They represent the beginnings of the Four Seasons *and are celebrated as holidays by many cultures. See* Eight Holy Days of Pagans.

1. Winter Solstice (shortest day of the year): December 20–23
2. Spring or Vernal Equinox (day and night are same length): March 20–23
3. Summer Solstice (longest day of the year): June 20–23
4. Autumn or Harvest Equinox (day and night are same length): September 20–23

Four Parts of a SONATA

Music students are required to memorize these successive elements of a sonata, an extended composition for one or two instruments. The sonata form is also the pattern typically used in the first movement of a symphony.

1. Exposition or Introduction
2. Development
3. Recapitulation
4. Coda

Four SONS OF PASSOVER

See Four Children of Passover.

Four SPIRITS

A belief of alchemy holds that there are Four Spirits, *or magical substances, with which one may create.*

1. Mercury (quicksilver)
2. Orpiment (trisulfide of arsenic)
3. Salammoniac (ammonium chloride)
4. Brimstone (sulfur)

Four SUITS

The standard deck of playing cards has 52 cards, containing four suits of thirteen each. However, it was not always so; it has evolved since before the Middle Ages into its present form. The names of the suits have differed in different versions (the tarot is perhaps the next most familiar) and carry mystical correspondences. See also Four Elements: Correspondences.

	Suit	*Tarot Name(s)*	*Element*	*Element of Life*
1.	Spades	Swords	air	breath
2.	Hearts	Cups, Goblets, or Chalices	water	blood
3.	Diamonds	Disks, Circles, or Wheels	earth	flesh
4.	Clubs	Wands, Scepters, Staves, Maces, Truncheons, or Rods	fire	heat

Four Steeds of the SUN'S CHARIOT

From Greek mythology. Sol, god of the sun, was believed to drive his chariot across the sky every day.

1. Eous or Erythreos (red)
2. Ethon (hot)
3. Phlegon (earth-loving)
4. Pyrois (luminous)

Four SYMBOLS OF CHRISTIANITY

These four formularies of doctrine are known as the Four Symbols by the Roman Catholic church.

1. Apostles' Creed; attributed to the Twelve Apostles

2. Nicene Creed; Council of Nicaea (325 C.E.)
3. Symbol of Constantinople; based on the Nicene Creed (331 C.E.)
4. Athanasian Creed; attributed to Athanasius (670 C.E.)

Four TASTES

Despite opinions to the contrary, humans are only able to distinguish four different tastes. Note that "hot," or "spicy," is not among them, for this "flavor" is caused by acid burning the tongue. (Locations of taste buds in parentheses.)

1. Sweet (front of the tongue)
2. Sour (sides of the tongue)
3. Salty (front and sides of the tongue)
4. Bitter (back of the tongue)

Four TEENAGE MUTANT NINJA TURTLES

Successful cartoon characters created by Peter A. Laird and Kevin B. Eastman. The Turtles' mentor is a rat known as Splinter, their close friend among the human population is April O'Neil, and their arch-enemy is Shredder.

		Color of Headband	*Weapon of Choice*	*Description*
1.	Leonardo	blue	two swords	serious, the leader
2.	Donatello	purple	bo stick	sensitive, the gadget guy
3.	Raphael	red	sais	hot-headed
4.	Michelangelo	orange	numchucks	goofy

Four TEMPERAMENTS

Corresponding to the Four Elements.

1. Choleric: irritable, aggressive (fire)
2. Melancholic: thoughtful, unsuccessful (earth)
3. Phlegmatic: lazy, peaceful (water)
4. Sanguine: successful, active, outward-focused (air)

Big Four in TENNIS

The four most important tennis tournaments. Winning all four in one year is called a Grand Slam.

1. United States Open, held at Forest Hills, NY
2. British Open, held at Wimbledon, London
3. French Open
4. Australian Open

TETRACHORD

In music theory, the first four notes of the major scale are called the Tetrachord. These four notes, while being basic to Western music, have also been associated with the Four Mystic Animals *and have acquired some mystical symbolism. See also* Seven Notes of the Major Scale.

1. Do (lion): valor and strength
2. Re (ox): sacrifice and duty
3. Mi (man): faith and incarnation
4. Fa (eagle): elevation and prayer

TETRAGRAMMATON

The Tetragrammaton is the holy name of God, which—according to ancient Jewish tradition—must never be spoken aloud. It is called the Tetragrammaton because it is composed of four letters. Because ancient Hebrew has no vowels, scholars disagree as to what the correct pronunciation should be. The name, when transliterated into the characters of the English alphabet, appears as YHWH, which is frequently interpreted as Yahweh, and also as Jehovah. The Tetragrammaton has also been interpreted as having mystical correlations to many religious traditions. The name of God occurs in many languages as a four-letter word—for example: Deus (Greek and Latin), Dieu (French), Dios (Spanish), Adat (Assyrian), Alla (Arabic), Agla (Cabalistic), Gott (German), Soru (Persian), Deva (Sanskrit), and Odin (Scandinavian). Here are the Hebrew letters with their English transliterations.

1. yod; Y   יֹ

2. he'; H ך

3. vau; W ה

4. he'; H ↙

Four THINGS TO DO TO BE A MAN

As espoused by American author Ernest Hemingway (1899–1961).

1. Write a book
2. Plant a tree
3. Fight a bull
4. Have a son

FOUR TOPS

A popular Motown group in the 1960s.

1. Renaldo "Obie" Benson
2. Abdul "Duke" Fakir
3. Lawrence Payton, Jr.
4. Levi Stubbs

Four TOTEMS OF ASSHUR

See Four Mystic Animals.

Four TOTEMS OF THE DIRECTIONS

See Four Mystic Animals.

Four Types of TRIAD

A numbered list from music theory. A triad is a chord composed of three notes, either the first, third, and fifth notes of the scale or a similar group of related notes. The notational symbol and musical notes follow each entry.

1. Major (C): C, E, G
2. Minor (Cm): C, Eb, G
3. Diminished (C° or Cdim): C, Eb, Gb
4. Augmented (C+ or Caug): C, E, G#

Four VEDAS

The Vedas are chief among the sacred books of Hinduism.

1. Rig Veda
2. Sama Veda
3. Yajur Veda
4. Atharva Veda

Four VIRTUES OF CHRISTIANITY

The Roman Catholic church maintains this list, often labeling it the Four Cardinal Virtues. See also Seven Virtues, Twelve Virtues.

1. Fortitude
2. Justice
3. Prudence
4. Temperance

Four VIRTUES OF DAKOTA RELIGION

The Dakotas, Native Americans of the Great Plains, hold that there are four virtues for men and four for women.

	Men	*Women*
1.	courage	ability
2.	endurance	hospitality
3.	generosity	fidelity
4.	honor	fertility

Four VOICES

The standard division of singers in a choir. Each voice group may be further divided into two subgroups, yielding eight voices or eight subdivisions.

1. Soprano (soprano and mezzo-soprano)
2. Alto (alto and contralto)
3. Tenor (countertenor and tenor)
4. Bass (baritone and bass)

Four WATCHES OF THE NIGHT

See Eight Canonical Hours.

Four WINDS

While many people know the west wind is called Zephyr, not everyone knows there are names for all the winds of each of the Four Directions. *There are also names for the winds of the four directions in between. (Alternate names in parentheses.)*

Winds of the Four Directions

1. Boreas: north (Volturnus, bise, mistral, aquila, aquilo, tramontane)
2. Notus: south (Auster, Africus)
3. Eurus: east (Aurora, Solanus, Eos, leventer)
4. Zephyr: west (Zephyrus, Favonius, Ireieus, stannus)

The Four Directions in Between

1. Euroauster: southeast
2. Afer: southwest (kite-wind)
3. Caurus: northwest
4. Euroclydon: northeast (Euroaquila, Tehuantepecer, gregale)

Four WORLDS

From Navajo mythology. The Navajo creation myth tells of the first people and their emergence from the first world. Each world also relates to one of the four directions and carries other mystical correspondences.

		English Name	Direction	Color	Tree or Plant
1.	Tokpela	First World	west	yellow	muha (little four-leafed plant)
2.	Tokpa	Underworld	south	blue	salavi (spruce)
3.	Kuskurza	Middle World	east	red	piva (tobacco)
4.	Túwaqachi	Our Own World	north	white	kneumapee (juniper)

Bird	Animal	Mineral
wisoko (fat-eating bird)	káto'ya (snake with big head)	sikyásvo (gold)
kwáhu (eagle)	kolíchiyaw (skunk)	qöchásiva (silver)
angwusi (crow)	chöövio (antelope)	palásiva (copper)
mongwau (owl)	tohopko (mountain lion)	sikyápala (mixed)

Four WORLD-QUARTER GODS

From Pawnee mythology. As in many other complex belief systems, these four deities carry many symbolic correspondences.

	World-quarter God	Guardian Beast	Season	Weather Element	Kind of Corn	Tree
1.	Black Star	black bear	autumn	thunder	black	cotton-wood
2.	Yellow Star	mountain lion	spring	lightning	yellow	elm
3.	White Star	wildcat	winter	clouds	white	willow
4.	Red Star	wolf	summer	winds	red	box-elder

FIVES

Five was the lucky number of Chinese philosophy. Eastern philosophers recognized *Five Elements* and *Five Directions,* as opposed to Four as was common in the West. As the sum of Two (the first even compound) and Three (the first odd compound), Five was seen as the great mystic number of the universe. Five figured prominently in Muslim belief and appeared in many other theologies as well.

Early Greek mystics believed Five symbolized alteration and new direction. In Western philosophy, Five represented sex and marriage. It was the sacred number of the goddesses Athena, Ishtar, and Venus, and of the Virgin Mary. Five was also seen as a natural or cyclical number because of its frequent occurrence in nature; for example, in petals, leaves, fingers and toes.

Five ADVANTAGES (SUN TZU)
From The Art of War *by Chinese philosopher Sun Tzu. Those who master these will triumph.*

1. To know when to challenge and when not to challenge.
2. To recognize how to use the numerous and the few.
3. To agree on superior and inferior objectives.
4. To prepare to lie in wait for the unprepared.
5. To lead without interference from a ruler.

Five AGES OF MAN

From the landmark work (1965) of the same name by psychologist Gerald Heard.
Also known as the Five Crises. Heard also correlated the Five Ages to psychology and
mystical belief systems. See also Five Elements.

	Age	Stage of Individuality	Stage of Self
1.	Coconscious	preindividual	nonpersonal group constituent
2.	Heroic	protoindividual	self-assertive
3.	Ascetic	midindividual	self-accusing
4.	Humanic	total individual	self-sufficient
5.	Leptoid	postindividual	from the Greek *lepsis,* "leap"

	Description	Mystery
1.	creature of a spoken tradition	earth
2.	protesting that stifling tradition	water
3.	person of self-blame	air
4.	individual of objectivity	fire
5.	individual objectively aware of own subjectivity	ether (finer fire)

	Mental Age Group	Type of Insanity
1.	infancy	womb-recessionalism
2.	childhood	paranoia
3.	adolescence	schizophrenia
4.	first maturity	manic-depressive insanity
5.	second maturity (the veterine)	involutional melancholy

	Therapy	Initiation
1.	burial and resurrection	rebirth
2.	immersion and catharsis	catharsis
3.	breathing and auditory suggestion	inspiration
4.	infrared radiation	illumination
5.	construction of a fivefold society	transformation

Five AHKAM

Ahkam, or orders, are the five kinds of decrees authorized under Islamic law.

1. Wajib: compulsory
2. Mustahab: without obligation
3. Muharram: forbidding
4. Makruh: disapproving but not forbidding
5. Halal: legalizing and allowing

Five ALTARS

From Dianic witchcraft. Among the modern practitioners of the old religions there are countless variations, and no one system is considered more or less correct than another. Worship takes on a very individual nature based on the knowledge and experience of those participating. Therefore these may differ greatly from the altars used by other worshipers. See also Five Mythic Tigers.

	Location/direction	Goddess(es)	Color	Element
1.	Center	Diana		
2.	East	Astarte	white, purple	air
3.	South	Vesta, Esmerelda, Pele	yellow, red	fire
4.	West	Isis	blue, green	water
5.	North	Demeter	tan, black, brown, orange	earth

Five BALKAN STATES

Countries situated on the Balkan peninsula in southeastern Europe.

1. Albania
2. Bulgaria
3. Greece
4. Turkey (partial)
5. Yugoslavia (partial)

Five Positions of BALLET

The fundamental placings of the feet that form the basis of all ballet movements.

1. First Position: heels together, toes turned out, feet in a straight line
2. Second Position: feet about twelve inches apart, parallel, weight evenly distributed
3. Third Position: heel of one foot against instep of other foot, feet perpendicular
4. Fourth Position: feet about twelve inches apart, perpendicular, weight evenly distributed
5. Fifth Position: feet pressed together, heel of each foot against toes of the other foot

Five BASKETBALL PLAYER POSITIONS

These player positions have different names in amateur games, but these are the terms used in the National Basketball Association.

1. Center
2. Power forward
3. Small forward
4. Shooting guard
5. Point guard

Five BELOVED ONES (SIKHISM)

The Panj Piaras, or Five Beloved Ones, were the first five Sikhs to be initiated into the Khalsa Panth, the Brotherhood of the Pure, by Guru Gobind Singh on Baisakhi Day in 1699. The last three died fighting in the battle of Chamkaur in 1704, and the second may have also died in the battle or lived until 1708. Sikhs hold an annual holiday in celebration of the memory of the Five Beloveds.

1. Bhai Daya Singh Ji (1669–1708)
2. Bhai Dharam Singh Ji (1666–1708?)
3. Bhai Mohkam Singh Ji (1663–1704)
4. Bhai Sahib Singh Ji (1662–1704)
5. Bhai Himmat Singh Ji (1661–1704)

BIG FIVE (HOLLYWOOD)
In the Golden Age of Hollywood (1930s–1950s), these giants were known as the Big Five. All were major film production companies that also owned theaters.

1. Metro-Goldwyn-Mayer (MGM)
2. Paramount
3. Radio-Keith-Orpheum (RKO)
4. 20th Century-Fox
5. Warner Bros.

Five BODIES (ANCIENT EGYPT)
An ancient Egyptian myth states that human beings have not one but five bodies.

1. Aufu (physical body)
2. Ka (double)
3. Haidit (shadow)
4. Khu (magical body)
5. Sahu (spiritual body)

Five BOOKS OF THE LAW
See Five Books of Moses.

Five BOOKS OF MOSES
Also known as the Five Books of the Law, the Five Scrolls (Rolls), and the Pentateuch, these are the first five books of the Old Testament, held in highest esteem by followers of Judaism. See also Four Major Prophets of the Old Testament, Twelve Minor Prophets of the Old Testament, Five Poetical Books of the Old Testament *and* Twelve Historical Books of the Old Testament.

1. Genesis
2. Exodus
3. Leviticus
4. Numbers
5. Deuteronomy

Five Cs

In the credit industry, these Five Cs are used to determine whether a given customer is a good credit risk.

1. Credit: How has customer paid bills in the past?
2. Capacity: Is customer able to repay loan?
3. Character: What is customer's reputation?
4. Capital: What is customer putting into his/her business?
5. Collateral: How can customer cover debt?

Five CALVINIST BELIEFS

The five chief points of Calvinism, a Christian theological system devised by French divine John Calvin (1509–64), published in his Institutes of the Christian Religion *in 1536.*

1. Predestination: man's salvation or damnation has already been determined
2. Irresistible grace: men are saved by unmerited grace from God
3. Original sin: the total depravity of man and the absence of free will
4. Particular redemption: the necessity of Christ for man's redemption
5. Final perseverance of the saints

Five CHANNEL ISLANDS

In Great Britain, these five islands have individual identities and their cultures differ somewhat from the culture of the main island.

1. Alderney
2. Guernsey
3. Herm
4. Jersey
5. Sark

Five CIVILIZED TRIBES

This confederation of Native Americans was formed in the 1830s and for a short time was granted some autonomy by the U.S. government. The confederation continues to exist today but wields little power other than as a protector of Native American culture.

1. Cherokee
2. Chickasaw
3. Choctaw
4. Creek
5. Seminole

Five CLASSICS

These are the sacred texts of Confucianism. The books are attributed to K'ung Fu-tse (Master Kung), whose Western name was Confucius. Over the centuries, more books (Chinese "king" or "ching") were added to the liturgy to create a list of Six Classics, then Thirteen Classics.

1. Shih Ching: Book of Odes (containing 305 ancient ballads and songs)
2. Shu Ching or Shang Shu: Book of History or Book of Records
3. I Ching or Chou I: Book of Changes
4. Li Chi: Book of Rites
5. Ch'un Ch'iu: Spring and Autumn Annals

Five Basic Levels of CONCEPTUAL ABILITY

Harvard psychologist Richard Herrnstein found that the first four levels can be found in almost any species.

	Ability	Definition	Example
1.	Discrimination	telling one object from another	apple/orange
2.	Categorization by Rote	memorizing the individual members of a class	state capitals

3.	Open-ended Categorization	grouping objects according to some observable similarity	all acorns
4.	Concepts	open-ended categories whose constituents bear no outward similarity	crib, diapers, and baby
5.	Abstract Relations	ability to sort the same group of objects by any concept	shape, color, number of letters in name

Five CRISES
See Five Ages of Man.

Five CRUSADES
See Nine Crusades.

DAVE CLARK FIVE
A popular British music group of the 1960s.

1. Dave Clark
2. Lenny Davidson
3. Rick Huxley
4. Denis Payton
5. Michael Smith

DIONNE QUINTUPLETS
The Dionne quintuplets were born in Canada on May 28, 1934.

1. Annette
2. Cecile
3. Emilie

4. Marie
5. Yvonne

Five DIRECTIONS
Ancient Chinese philosophy, strongly governed by the number five, recognized these.

1. North
2. South
3. East
4. West
5. Center

Five ELEMENTS
The Four Elements *of alchemy are familiar to Western readers. In the far east, however, systems recognizing five elements have also existed. See also* Six Elements.

Five Elements of Ancient Chinese Buddhism

1. Earth (yellow)
2. Wood (green)
3. Fire (red)
4. Metal (white)
5. Water (black)

Also known as the Five Pancha Boothas or the Five Pancha Tattwas, the following are described in the Taittirya Upanishad, Hindu scripture.

Five Tattvas (Hindu)

	Hindu Name	Manifestation	Symbol
1. Ether, Spirit, Void	Akasha	space	white crescent ☾
2. Air	Vayu	gas	blue circle ◉

3.	Fire	Agni, Tejas	light	red triangle ▲
4.	Water	Jala, Apas	liquid	yellow diamond ◇
5.	Earth	Prithivi	solid	black oval ⬤

FAB FIVE
Nickname of the rock band Duran Duran.

1. Simon LeBon
2. Nick Rhodes
3. Andy Taylor
4. John Taylor
5. Roger Taylor

FAB FIVE (BASKETBALL)
Nickname of the five freshman players on the University of Michigan basketball team, the Wolverines, during the 1991–92 season.

1. Juwan Howard
2. Ray Jackson
3. Jimmy King
4. Jalen Rose
5. Chris Webber

Five FIFTHS OF IRELAND
Ireland was divided into five regions, known as Fifths, during the Celtic era.

	Gaelic Name	English Name	Modern Name	Capital
1.	Coiced Uloth	the Uliti	Ulster	Emain Macha
2.	Coiced Connacht	the Connachta	Connaught	Cruachain
3.	Coiced Lagan Tuad-Gabair	the Lageni North	North Leinster	Temuir

115

| 4. | Coiced Lagan Des-Gabair | the Lageni South | South Leinster | Dinn Rig |
| 5. | Coiced Muman | the Muma | Munster | Temuir Erann |

Five FINGERS

The five fingers of the hand are given names in every land, and they have many different names in different cultures. They are also numbered in different ways by pianists and violinists.

		For Pianists	*For Violinists*
1.	Thumb	1	
2.	Index finger, forefinger, pointer finger	2	1
3.	Middle finger	3	2
4.	Ring finger	4	3
5.	Little finger, pinky	5	4

Five Basic FUNCTIONS OF LIFE (BIOLOGY)

The five biological functions that define life.

1. Respiration
2. Reproduction
3. Ingestion
4. Digestion
5. Excretion

Five Precepts of FUNDAMENTALISM

Published in a series of books, The Fundamentals *(1910–15), these five beliefs underlie fundamentalist Christian thought. Two sects of Christian fundamentalism divide along the lines of Premillenialism (Jesus will return before a thousand years of peace) and Postmillenialism (Jesus will return after a thousand years of peace).*

1. Infallibility of the Bible: The Bible is truth.
2. Virgin Birth: Mary was a virgin.

3. Substitutionary Atonement: Jesus died for our sins.
4. Literal Resurrection: Jesus was resurrected from the dead.
5. Second Coming: Jesus will return to Earth.

Five Postulates of GEOMETRY

Greek mathematician Euclid (fl. 300 B.C.E.) devised these five basic postulates, or assumptions that need not be proven, that serve as the basis of standard geometry. Four-Postulate Geometry is based on the first four of these. Systems of geometry known as non-Euclidean do not rely on these assumptions.

1. A straight line segment can be drawn joining any two points.
2. Any straight line segment can be extended indefinitely in a straight line.
3. Given any straight line segment, a circle can be drawn having the segment as radius and one end point as center.
4. All right angles are congruent.
5. If two lines are drawn that intersect a third in such a way that the sum of the inner angles on one side is less than two right angles, then the two lines inevitably must intersect each other on that side if extended far enough.

Five GREAT LAKES (AFRICA)

Five massive bodies of water in the Great Rift Valley of eastern Africa. Lake Victoria is the largest lake in Africa and, after Lake Superior, the second largest freshwater lake in the world.

1. Lake Albert (Lake Mobutu Sese Seko): between Uganda and Zaire
2. Lake Nyasa (Lake Malawi): Malawi
3. Lake Rudolf: Kenya
4. Lake Tanganyika (Lake Tanzania): between Tanganyika and Zaire
5. Lake Victoria: between Tanganyika, Uganda, and Kenya

Five GREAT LAKES (NORTH AMERICA)

The Great Lakes of North America constitute the largest freshwater lake system in the world. An easy way to help remember their names is with the acronym HOMES.

1. Lake Huron
2. Lake Ontario
3. Lake Michigan
4. Lake Erie
5. Lake Superior

Five HOLY BEINGS

From Jainism, an ancient branch of Hinduism.

1. Monks
2. Teachers
3. Religious leaders
4. Enlightened masters (Arihants or Jinas)
5. Liberated souls (Siddhas)

IMMORTAL FIVE

See Russian Five.

Five Classes of INSTRUMENTS

Musical instruments are usually placed into four major groups (see Four Families of Instruments), *but this system groups them according to how they create sound rather than how they are arranged in a standard orchestra.*

1. Chordophones: stringed instruments
2. Aerophones: wind instruments
3. Idiophones: percussion other than drums
4. Membranophones: drums
5. Electrophones: electronic instruments

Five IROQUOIS NATIONS

Also known as the Iroquois League, Iroquois Confederacy, and the Five Iroquois Nations, this confederation of tribes was founded about 1570 by Onandaga chief Hiawatha. They were eastern tribes living in northern and northeastern New York and parts of Ohio, Michigan, and Ontario. The Tuscarora joined the confederation in 1722, whereupon the group was known as the Six Nations.

1. Cayuga
2. Mohawk
3. Onandaga
4. Oneida
5. Seneca

Five Precepts of ISLAM

Also known as the Five Pillars, these are the five duties required of Muslims.

1. Shahadah (witness): believing that God is the one God and Mohammed is his prophet
2. Salat (prayer): praying five times a day
3. Zakat (alms): charity, giving alms to the poor
4. Sawm (fasting): fasting during Ramadan during daylight hours
5. Hajj (pilgrimage): traveling at least once to the holy cities Mecca and Medina

JACKSON FIVE

A popular 1970s recording group of five brothers. Three other siblings were later added to the group: Randy Jackson, LaToya Jackson, and Maureen Jackson Brown.

1. Jackie Jackson (1951–)
2. Tito Jackson (1954–)
3. Jermaine Jackson (1955–)
4. Marlon Jackson (1957–)
5. Michael Jackson (1958–)

Five Branches of JUDAISM

The five major divisions of Judaism.

1. Orthodox
2. Conservative
3. Reformed
4. Reconstructionist
5. Humanistic

Five KAKARS (SIKHISM)

Also called the Five Ks, these are five essential symbols of Sikh faith and identity that must be worn at all times. See also Four Kurahits.

1. Keshas: unshorn hair and beard
2. Kangha: a comb in the hair
3. Kara: a steel or iron bracelet on the right wrist
4. Kachhaira: specially tailored (short) underwear
5. Kirpan: a sword

Five KALYANAS (JAINISM)

In the Jain religion, an ancient branch of Hinduism, the Tirthankaras or major prophets are each believed to have experienced these five religiously significant life events. See Twenty-four Tirthankaras.

1. Conception
2. Birth
3. Renunciation
4. Attainment of omniscience
5. Nirvana

KEATING FIVE

Five U.S. senators accused of illegal actions in connection with crooked savings and loan activities leading to a major nationwide savings and loan crisis in 1989–90.

Charles Keating, head of Lincoln Savings and Loan, had meetings with these five senators before the crisis struck.

1. Alan Cranston (D, California)
2. Dennis De Concini (D, Arizona)
3. John Glenn (D, Ohio)
4. John McCain (R, Arizona)
5. Donald Riegle (D, Michigan)

Five Ranks of the LEGION OF HONOR

France's only military order, the Legion of Honor, was founded in 1802 by Napoleon Bonaparte. The five ranks are listed in order from greatest to least.

1. Grand Cross
2. Grand Officer
3. Commander
4. Officer
5. Chevalier

Five Classes of LIFE (JAINISM)

This belief of Jainism (an ancient branch of Hinduism) underlies the practice of avoiding the taking of life of any kind.

1. Having intelligence, sight, smell, taste and touch: gods, humans, higher animals
2. Having sight, smell, taste and touch: larger insects—wasps, butterflies
3. Having smell, taste and touch: smaller insects—ants, fleas
4. Having taste and touch: worms, shellfish, tiny animals
5. Having touch: vegetation and all "inanimate" objects

Five MARX BROTHERS

These showbiz brothers became famous on the vaudeville stage prior to making a series of comedy films in the 1930s. They were the sons of Minnie Marx Palmer, a popular vaudeville star, who functioned as their manager. They appeared in vaudeville under many names before they took their act to Hollywood, minus the fifth brother, Milton. Harpo, originally named Adolph, changed his name to Arthur while he was fairly young.

1. Chico (Leonard): 1886–1961
2. Harpo (Arthur): 1888–1964
3. Groucho (Julius): 1890–1977
4. Zeppo (Herbert): 1901–1979
5. Gummo (Milton): 1893–1977

Five Parts of the Human MICROCOSM

Hildegard of Bingen (c. 1098–1179) identified the physical human being as a microcosm consisting of five corresponding groups of five parts each: five senses, five bodily members, five fingers, height (five feet), and girth (five feet).

	Senses	*Bodily Members*	*Fingers*
1.	Eyes	Head	Forefinger
2.	Ears	First arm	Middle finger
3.	Nose	Second arm	Ring finger
4.	Mouth	First leg	Pinky
5.	Hands	Second leg	Thumb

Five Phases of MITOSIS

Basic information learned by biology students.

1. Prophase: cell gets ready
2. Metaphase: chromosomes line up
3. Anaphase: chromosomes split
4. Telophase: two groups of chromosomes form two new cell nuclei
5. Interphase: resting stage; two new cells wait before dividing again

Five MOVEMENTS OF THE MASS

German composer Johann Sebastian Bach (1685–1750) used these five movements in his compositions; they have since become standard, though many variations on this basic structure exist.

1. Kyrie (Lord)
2. Gloria (Glory)
3. Credo (I Believe)
4. Sanctus (Holy)
5. Agnus Dei (Lamb of God)

Five MOVIE RATINGS

Developed by the American motion picture industry, these ratings are designed to aid parents in selecting appropriate movies for their children. Ratings are set by the motion picture rating board and take into account strong language, violence, sex, nudity, and other factors. Two extinct ratings, GP (similar to present PG) and X (similar to the present NC-17) may be seen on older films.

1. G (General audiences)
2. PG-13 (Parental Guidance suggested for children under thirteen)
3. PG (Parental Guidance suggested)
4. R (Restricted. No children under seventeen unless accompanied by an adult)
5. NC-17 (No Children under seventeen admitted)

Five MUSES (ARABIC)

The Nine Muses of Greek mythology may or may not be related to these muses of Arabic culture.

1. el-Sabh
2. el-Qadr
3. el-Asar
4. el-Maghreb
5. el-Leil

Five Elements of MUSIC
According to Western music theory, these are the five elements that define music.

1. Melody
2. Rhythm
3. Harmony
4. Form
5. Interpretation (timbre or color)

Five MYTHIC TIGERS (CHINA)
This ancient Chinese system incorporates the same elements as other systems found throughout the world. See also Five Altars *and* Five Elements.

		Kingdom	*Season*	*Element*
1.	Red Tiger	south	summer	fire
2.	Black Tiger	north	winter	water
3.	Blue Tiger	east	spring	wood
4.	White Tiger	west	autumn	metal
5.	Yellow Tiger	center		earth

Five NATIONS
See Five Iroquois Nations.

Five Levels of NEEDS (PSYCHOLOGY)
Also known as Maslow's Hierarchy of Needs, this list of fundamental, instinctual needs was developed by psychologist Abraham Maslow in the 1970s. Before Maslow, psychology consisted of behaviorism and psychoanalysis. He added a third alternative by creating psychological humanism. Beyond these five levels of basic needs, higher levels of needs exist, including needs for understanding, esthetic appreciation, and spiritual fulfillment.

1. Biological, physiological (oxygen, food, comfortable temperature)
2. Safety (security, order, protection)

3. Love, affection, belongingness (membership, acceptance)
4. Esteem, ego status (prestige, ability to display competence, self-respect)
5. Self-actualization (autonomy, ability to prove self)

Five Boroughs of NEW YORK CITY

1. Manhattan (New York County)
2. Brooklyn (Kings County)
3. Bronx (Bronx County)
4. Queens (Queens County)
5. Staten Island (Richmond County)

Five OCEANS
Geographers recognize five major bodies of water known as oceans.

1. Atlantic
2. Pacific
3. Arctic (North Polar Sea)
4. Indian
5. Antarctic (Southern Ocean)

Five OLYMPIC RINGS
The five rings of the Olympic symbol represent the five continents participating in the games (America is counted once). The colors of the rings represent not the continents but the colors in the flags of the participating nations; each national flag carried at the Olympics has at least one color in common with the Olympic flag. The black ring is sometimes shown as a white ring on a black background.

1. Black
2. Blue
3. Green
4. Red
5. Yellow

Five PANCHA BOOTHAS (PANCHA TATTWAS)
See Five Elements.

Five PATRIARCHS OF CHRISTIANITY
The five most powerful archbishops of the Roman Empire had these seats.

1. Antioch
2. Jerusalem
3. Alexandria
4. Constantinople
5. Rome

Five PEERS
The nobility of England consists of five levels of peerage. Nobles are called peers of the realm because symbolically they are equal in power to the king. Dukes are the highest level. Peers of the second, third, and fourth ranks are addressed as Lord (or Lady). Below the rank of baron are three lesser ranks: Knights of the Garter, Baronets, and all other Knights. (The title for a woman holding equivalent rank, shown in parentheses, is the same as that for the wife of a man of that rank.)

1. Duke (Duchess)
2. Marquess or Marquis (Marchioness)
3. Earl (Countess)
4. Viscount (Viscountess)
5. Baron (Baroness)

PENTATEUCH
See Five Books of Moses.

PENTATHLON
A five-in-one athletic event, one of the earliest in the history of Olympic competition. The pentathlon has been composed of five different events in the past and currently con-

sists of different events for men and women. *See also* Heptathlon *(among the Sevens)* and Decathlon *(in the Tens).*

Ancient Greece

1. Leaping
2. Foot racing
3. Wrestling
4. Discus
5. Spear

Former Olympics

1. Running broad jump
2. Javelin
3. 200-meter dash
4. Discus
5. 1,500-meter run

Modern Olympics (Men)

1. Horseback riding (5,000-meter steeplechase with 30 jumps)
2. Shooting (target shooting at 25 meters)
3. Fencing (épée)
4. Swimming (300-meter freestyle race)
5. Running (4,000-meter cross-country run)

Modern Olympics (Women)

1. 100-meter hurdles
2. Shot put
3. High jump
4. Long jump
5. 200-meter dash

Five PILLARS OF ISLAM
See Five Precepts of Islam.

Five POETICAL BOOKS OF THE OLD TESTAMENT
The books of the Old Testament Bible have been divided by scholars into five distinct groups, including this one, which consists of the eighteenth through the twenty-second books. See also Five Books of Moses.

1. Job
2. Psalms
3. Proverbs
4. Ecclesiastes
5. Song of Solomon (Canticles or the Canticle of Canticles)

Five POLITICAL LABELS
Terms used to describe individuals and political parties in relation to their general stand on the issues.

1. Reactionary: extremely conservative
2. Conservative: right-leaning
3. Moderate: fence-sitting
4. Liberal: left-leaning
5. Radical: extremely liberal

Five PROOFS
See Five Ways.

Five PYTHAGOREAN SOLIDS
Greek mathematician Pythagoras (c. 570–500 B.C.E.) discovered the principle that there are only five three-dimensional shapes whose sides are composed of equal, regular polygons. These five solids are often used in the designs of special multisided dice.

1. Cube (6): square
2. Tetrahedron (4): equilateral triangle
3. Octahedron (8): equilateral triangle
4. Icosahedron (20): equilateral triangle
5. Dodecahedron (12): pentagon

Five QUADRILATERALS

Geometry students learn that quadrilaterals are defined by their sides and angles, and that only five different basic types exist. The parallelogram has two subtypes: the rhombus, which has four equal sides, and the rhombus, which has unequal sides.

1. Square: four right angles and four equal sides
2. Rectangle: four right angles and two pairs of equal sides
3. Parallelogram: a pair of angles less than 90° and a pair of angles greater than 90°
4. Trapezoid: unequal angles and two parallel sides
5. Concave: one angle greater than 180°

Five QUESTIONS OF LIFE

Students of theology and comparative religion learn that the great religious systems of the world are formed out of the struggle to answer these five basic philosophical questions.

1. Cosmology: Who or what is in charge?
2. Epistemology: How do I know what I know?
3. Eschatology: What happens after death?
4. Ontology: Who am I?
5. Soteriology: What is the purpose of life?

Five RANKS OF GENERAL AND ADMIRAL

The five top ranks in the U.S. armed forces. The U.S. Army includes the rank of five-star general, and the Navy includes the five-star admiral, but these positions are only filled during wartime or other national emergencies. Civilians who know that a major outranks a lieutenant are often surprised to learn that a lieutenant general outranks a major general.

		Army	Navy
1.	Five Stars	General of the Army	Admiral of the Fleet
2.	Four Stars	General	Admiral
3.	Three Stars	Lieutenant General	Vice Admiral
4.	Two Stars	Major General	Rear Admiral Upper Half (previously Rear Admiral)
5.	One Star	Brigadier General	Rear Admiral Lower Half (previously Commodore)

Five Classes of RAYAHS

A rayah is a peasant subject of a Muslim ruler or an unbeliever who pays a poll-tax. This system, once widespread throughout Muslim nations, was abolished after World War I.

1. Roum milleti: Greek
2. Ermeni milleti: Armenian
3. Ermeni gatoliki milleti: Catholic Armenian
4. Roum gatoliki milleti: Latin Christian
5. Yahoudi milleti: Jewish

Five REPUBLICS OF FRANCE

These periods in the history of France mark the times when that nation was not ruled by an emperor or unstable regime. (Originating events in parentheses.)

1.	First Republic	(French Revolution)	1792–1804
2.	Second Republic	(rise of Napoleon III)	1848–52
3.	Third Republic	(fall of Napoleon III)	1879–1940
4.	Fourth Republic	(end of World War II)	1946–58
5.	Fifth Republic	(election of Charles de Gaulle)	1958–present

Five RIVERS OF HADES
See Four Rivers.

Five RIVERS OF THE PUNJAB
These five tributaries of the Indus River flow through the Punjab, an area whose name means "Land of the Five Rivers." The ancient names given here (in parentheses) were the names of the rivers in the time of Alexander the Great (356–23 B.C.E.)

1. Jhelum (Hydaspes)
2. Chenab (Acesines)
3. Ravi
4. Beas (Hyphasis)
5. Sutlej (Zaradrus)

Five ROLLS
See Five Books of Moses.

RUSSIAN FIVE (MUSIC)
Also known as the Immortal Five, these were composers who created a national Russian musical style in the last quarter of the nineteenth century. Borodin functioned as the leader of the group. Composer Peter Ilich Tchaikovsky (1840–93), whose music was extremely popular, was not considered Russian enough by some to be a member of the group.

1. Mili Balakirev (1837–1910)
2. Alexander Borodin (1833–87)
3. César Cui (1835–1918)
4. Modest Mussorgsky (1839–81)
5. Nikolai Rimski-Korsakov (1844–1908)

SAVOY BIG FIVE (BASKETBALL)
Five basketball players who became famous in Chicago in 1927. They were the original members of the group that later came to be known as the Harlem Globetrotters.

1. Byron "Fats" Long
2. Al "Runt" Pullins
3. Willie "Kid" Oliver
4. Andy Washington
5. Walter "Toots" Wright

Five Steps of the SCIENTIFIC PROCESS
The standard method used by scientists and researchers.

1. Identify the question
2. Formulate a theory
3. Test the theory
4. Analyze the results
5. Publish the findings

Five SENSES
In addition to the standard five senses, the term "Sixth Sense" is often used to refer to psychic or extrasensory abilities such as clairvoyance and precognition. An old folk belief holds that beyond the five senses there exist two more: animation and emotion.

1. Sight
2. Hearing
3. Smell
4. Taste
5. Touch

Five SCROLLS
See Five Books of Moses.

Five Seats of SIKH POWER
Locations in India of the five major Sikh centers of worship.

1. Sri Akal Takhat Sahib, Amritsar (Punjab)

2. Sri Harimandir Sahib, Patna Sahib (Bihar)
3. Sri Kesgarh Sahib, Anandpur Sahib (Punjab)
4. Sri Dam Dama Sahib, Sabo-Ki-Talwandi (Punjab)
5. Sri Hazur Sahib, Nanded (Maharashtra)

Five STAGES OF GRIEF

Elisabeth Kubler-Ross identified these five stages in her landmark work, On Death and Dying *(1969). She found that the same stages are experienced both by the terminally ill who must deal with the knowledge of their own death and by persons who experience the death of a close friend or loved one.*

1. Denial
2. Anger
3. Bargaining
4. Depression
5. Acceptance

Five SULLIVAN BROTHERS (WORLD WAR II)

Five American brothers lost on the morning of November 13, 1942, when a Japanese submarine sank the U.S.S. Juneau *in the Battle of Guadalcanal. Their sister, Genevieve Marie, also served in the U.S. Navy during the war. The loss of the five brothers was the biggest blow to any single family in U.S. wartime history, and led to the passage of the Sullivan Law, preventing brothers from serving on the same ship. In April 1943, the navy launched a new destroyer, christened by Mrs. Sullivan, the U.S.S.* The Sullivans. *The convention center in the family's hometown, Waterloo, Iowa, is named Five Sullivan Brothers in their honor.*

1. George Thomas Sullivan (1914–42)
2. Francis Henry Sullivan (1916–42)
3. Joseph Eugene Sullivan (1918–42)
4. Madison Abel Sullivan (1919–42)
5. Albert Leo Sullivan (1922–42)

Five TATTVAS
See Five Elements.

Five THUNDERBIRDS
The U.S. Air Force maintains this crack team of highly trained pilots who perform spectacular stunts and precision maneuvers at air shows, exhibitions, and other recruitment venues. The aircraft are arranged into five specific positions, each with its own name and its own flight path in various patterns.

1. Leader
2. Left Wing
3. Right Wing
4. Solo
5. Slot

TORAH
See Five Books of Moses.

Five TRIANGLES
Geometry students learn that triangles are defined by their angles, and that only five different basic types exist.

1. Equilateral: three equal sides and three equal angles.
2. Isosceles: two equal sides and two equal angles.
3. Obtuse: one angle greater than 90°
4. Right: one angle equal to 90°
5. Scalene: no equal sides and no equal angles

Five Permanent Members of the UNITED NATIONS
In order to provide stability among nations, the United Nations charter established these five great powers as permanent members.

1. China
2. France
3. Russia
4. United Kingdom
5. United States of America

Five VICES
According to the Sikh religion. See also Six Vices, Seven Deadly Sins.

1. Lust
2. Anger
3. Greed
4. Attachment
5. Ego

Five VOWELS
In the English language, these five letters are known as the five vowels. The letters Y and W are sometimes called "near-vowels" because they often take on vowel-like characteristics.

1. A
2. E
3. I
4. O
5. U

Five Ws
Journalism students learn the principle that a good news story answers these in the first paragraph.

1. Who
2. What
3. When

4. Where
5. Why

Five WAYS (THOMAS AQUINAS)

Thomas Aquinas (c. 1225–74), Christian saint, used Aristotelian logic to devise these five "proofs" that God exists.

1. The Unmoved Mover or the Argument from Motion: Whatever is in motion is moved by another thing; this other thing also must be moved by something; to avoid an infinite regression, one must posit a "first mover," which is God.
2. Efficient Causality or the Watchmaker Argument: Nothing is caused by itself; there must be a "first cause," which is God.
3. The Cosmological Argument or the Argument of Possibility and Necessity: Since all things come into being and go out of existence, and since time is infinite, there must be some time at which none of these things existed; therefore, there must always have been at least one necessary thing that is eternal, which is God.
4. Degrees of Perfection or the Argument from Perfection: Objects in the world have differing degrees of qualities, such as perfection; speaking of more or less perfection makes sense only by comparison with what is the maximum perfection, which is God.
5. The Teleological Argument or the Argument from Design: Things in the world move toward goals, just as an arrow moves toward its goal by an archer's directing it; therefore there must be an intelligent designer who directs all things to their goals, which is God.

Five WITS

An old English folk belief holds that there are five wits, besides the five senses, that are used to gather knowledge about the world. The five wits are mentioned by William Shakespeare in Much Ado About Nothing *and appear in other notable works.*

1. Common sense: the outcome of the five senses
2. Imagination: the wit of the mind

3. Fantasy: imagination united with judgment
4. Estimation: sense of the absolute, such as time, space, and locality
5. Memory: the wit of recalling past events

Five Types of WOUND
Students of first-aid techniques, as well as medical care professionals, must learn this list. First-aid techniques and risk of infection differ according to the type of wound.

1. Abrasion (skin and/or tissue has been rubbed)
2. Cut
3. Laceration (skin and/or tissue has been torn)
4. Puncture
5. Scratch

Five YAJÑA (BALI)
From Agama Tirtha, the primary religion of Bali; these are the five rituals through which the Balinese demonstrate their faith.

1. Dewa Yajña: sacrifices to the gods
2. Buta Yajña: sacrifices to the elements
3. Manusia Yajña: rites of passage, including naming, tooth filing, and marriage
4. Pitr Yajña: offerings to the dead
5. Rishi Yajña: consecration of priests

Five Books of the ZENDAVESTA
Holy scriptures of Zoroastrianism. The Zendavesta, coupled with the Larger Avesta and the Twenty-one Nasks (books), is the most sacred writing of this Persian religion.

1. The Yasna; 72 chapters
2. The Vispered; 24 karde (chapters)
3. The Vendidad; 22 fargard (chapters)
4. The Yashts; 21 invocations
5. The Khorda Avesta; short prayers

Five ZENER SYMBOLS

Zener cards are used in the testing and evaluation of suspected psychic or clairvoyant powers. Each card shows one of five symbols. Each Zener deck consists of 25 cards, with five of each type. Subjects are asked to name the symbol on a given card without seeing the card.

1. Circle ⭕
2. Cross ✖
3. Square ◼
4. Star ☆
5. Three wavy lines ≋

SIXES

Greek mathematician Pythagoras (fl. 500 B.C.E.) believed Six to be the first perfect number because it was formed from both the sum and product of One, Two, and Three. Six symbolized the Greek goddess Aphrodite and, to Pythagoras, reflected the basic structure of the cosmos, signified by two triangles representing the spiritual and material planes of existence.

In the mystical belief system of the Tarot, Six (the hexad) was the principle of harmony, since it was composed of both separation (the dyad) and joining (the triad) and was interpreted as conquering and uniting the two. Six was also seen as the product of Two (the feminine) and Three (the masculine), thus representing love and triumph. Astrologers assigned significance to the sextile (two planets at a 60-degree angle, equaling one-sixth of a circle) as it was believed to predict fortune and opportunity.

In the Bible, Six symbolized the creation of the world. The six days of creation were named the Hexameron, a term also used to refer to any six continuous days. In the book of Revelation, however, a triple Six (666) was assigned to the beast, a character believed to represent the antichrist. This negative association with Six explains the lessened frequency of Sixes in Western Bible-based cultures.

Les SIX (MUSIC)

Also called the Group of Six, these six twentieth-century French composers created the musical style known as ultramodern. They were given the name Les Six by French critic Henri Collet in 1920. Arthur Honegger functioned as the leader of the group.

1. Georges Auric (1899–1983)
2. Louis Durey (1888–1979)
3. Arthur Honegger (1892–1955)
4. Darius Milhaud (1892–1974)
5. François Poulenc (1899–1963)
6. Germaine Taillefere (1892–1983)

Big Six in ACCOUNTING

The six major international accounting firms. Once known as the Big Eight; two additional companies, Arthur Young, and Touche, Ross and Co., were each folded into one of these six.

1. Arthur Anderson
2. Coopers & Lybrand
3. Deloitte & Touche
4. Ernst & Young
5. K.P.M.G. Peat Marwick
6. Price Waterhouse

Six Attributes of AHURA MAZDA

Ahura Mazda, also called Ormazd, is the chief deity of Zoroastrianism, an ancient Persian religion. Each of the six attributes is illustrated with an example.

1. Love—the good mind
2. Plan of Grace—righteous order
3. Khshathra—divine noble government
4. Armaiti—piety or holy character
5. Haurvatat—health of mind and body
6. Immortality—perpetual life

Six Branches of the ARMED FORCES

The U.S. armed forces are divided into these six branches, each having active and reserve troops.

1. Army
2. Navy
3. Air Force
4. Marines
5. National Guard
6. Coast Guard

Six ARTICLES (ANGLICAN CHURCH)

Created by Henry VIII of England (1491–1547), these six tenets formed the basis of the Anglican church (Church of England) in its break with the Roman Catholic church.

1. The real presence of Christ in the Eucharist.
2. The sufficiency of communion in one kind.
3. The celibacy of the priests.
4. The obligation of vows of chastity.
5. The expediency of private masses.
6. The necessity of auricular confession.

Six States of AUSTRALIA

Along with these six states, Australia has two territories: Northern Territory and Australian Capital Territory.

1. New South Wales
2. Queensland
3. South Australia
4. Tasmania
5. Victoria
6. Western Australia

Six AWARD RIBBONS

The blue ribbon for first place is a familiar and common symbol, but there is a standard arrangement of colors for award ribbons that extends as far as sixth place.

1. First Place (blue)
2. Second Place (red)
3. Third Place (white)
4. Fourth Place (yellow)
5. Fifth Place (green)
6. Sixth place (pink)

Six Principles of the General Six-Principle BAPTISTS

This sect was founded in Rhode Island in 1653; their creed was based on Hebrews 4:1–2.

1. Repentance
2. Faith
3. Baptism
4. Laying on of hands
5. Resurrection of the dead
6. Eternal judgment

Six Stages of BEHAVIOR DEVELOPMENT

Behavioral psychologists rely on this six-step process to understand human behavior.

1. A need arises.
2. Tension results.
3. Activity ensues to resolve tension.
4. Satisfactory resolution is made.
5. A habit is formed.
6. Habit becomes drive.

BIG SIX (DIRTY WORDS)
See Dirty Seven.

BIG SIX (EUROPEAN AUTO MAKERS)
The six major European auto makers.

1. Fiat
2. Ford
3. General Motors
4. Peugeot
5. Renault
6. Volkswagen

Six CITIES OF REFUGE
According to Deuteronomy 4:43 and Joshua 20:1–8, these cities were set apart at the command of God as places where anyone might flee for refuge who had inadvertently killed another person.

Three Cities east of Jordan (set apart by Moses)

1. Bezer
2. Ramoth
3. Golan

Three Cities west of Jordan (set apart by Joshua)

1. Hebron
2. Shechem
3. Kedesh

Six CLASSICS OF CONFUCIANISM
Also known as the Liu Ching, the sacred scriptures of Confucianism at one time consisted of these six books attributed to Confucius. The sacred literature was later expanded to include Thirteen Classics. *The original group is known as the* Five

Classics. *The sixth, the Yüeh Ching (Book of Music), was lost circa 200 B.C.E. and was never recovered. It was replaced by the Chou Li or Chou Kuan (Rites of Chou).*

1. Shih Ching: Book of Odes (containing 305 ancient ballads and songs)
2. Shu Ching or Shang Shu: Book of History or Book of Records
3. I Ching or Chou I: Book of Changes
4. Li Chi: Book of Rites
5. Ch'un Ch'iu: Spring and Autumn Annals
6. Yüeh Ching: Book of Music

Six COLORS EMITTED BY A BLACK-BODY RADIATOR
British physicist William Thomson, Lord Kelvin (1824–1907), proposed the absolute scale of temperature measurement that was named for him. He also discovered the doctrine of the convertibility of heat and work and determined how heat moves within a solid body. His scale of six colors, listed here from lowest to highest heat, has become standard knowledge in the field. Note that the familiar "white hot" is actually surpassed by the color blue.

1. Red
2. Brighter red
3. Orange
4. Yellow
5. White
6. Blue

Six CONDITIONS THAT AFFECT DRIVING
Automobile drivers need to be aware of these six conditions and adjust their driving habits when adverse conditions threaten safety. Each condition is accompanied by examples.

1. Light: nighttime, glare
2. Weather: rain, fog, ice
3. Road: gravel, asphalt
4. Traffic: rush hour, gridlock

5. Automobile: one headlight, no brakes
6. Driver: visually impaired, angry, upset

Six COUNTIES
The counties of Northern Ireland under dispute between the British government and the Irish Republican Army.

1. Antrim
2. Armagh
3. Down
4. Fermanagh
5. Londonderry
6. Tyrone

Six EGYPTIAN FESTIVALS
The six great festivals of the ancient Egyptians and the deities honored.

1. Bubastis: the goddess of the moon
2. Busiris: the goddess Isis
3. Sais: the god of wisdom
4. Heliopolis: the sun
5. Butis: Buto, the goddess of night
6. Papremis: the god of war

Six ELEMENTS (BUDDHISM)
From the beliefs of Shingonshu, a form of Japanese Buddhism founded by Kobo Daishi (774–835). See also Four Elements, Five Elements.

1. Earth
2. Water
3. Fire
4. Wind
5. Space
6. Consciousness

Six ENEMIES OF MANKIND (HINDUISM)
The Hindu scripture Kama Sutra lists these six items as the Enemies of Mankind. They correspond roughly to the Seven Deadly Sins of Western thought.

1. Lust
2. Anger
3. Avarice
4. Spiritual ignorance
5. Pride
6. Envy

Six Points for ETHICAL BEHAVIOR
From author and philosopher Harry Emerson Fosdick. When one is considering a course of action, one should ask these questions to determine whether it is truly ethical.

1. Is it reasonable?
2. Is it responsible?
3. Is it fair?
4. Will I think well of myself?
5. How would my hero do it?
6. Is it honest?

Six Basic FOOD GROUPS
Teaching of the Four Basic Food Groups has been supplanted in recent years by instruction in the Food Guide Pyramid, which lists Six Basic Food Groups. Each group is followed by the recommended number of servings per day.

1. Bread, Cereal, Rice, and Pasta Group (6 to 11)
2. Vegetable Group (3 to 5)
3. Fruit Group (2 to 4)
4. Milk, Yogurt, and Cheese Group (2 to 3)
5. Meat, Poultry, Fish, Dry Beans, Eggs, and Nuts Group (2 to 3)
6. Fats, Oils, and Sweets (use sparingly)

Six GENII OF AHURA MAZDA

Also called the Six Holy Immortals, these genii are the ministering angels of Zoroastrianism, a Persian religion. Ahura Mazda, also called Ormazd, is its principle deity. Two additional genii who do not minister to Ahura Mazda are Geush Urvan, defender of animals, and Sraosha, the genius of obedience. Alternate names and titles or attributes follow.

Three on the Father-side

1. Vohu-Mano: love, the good principle
2. Asha (Ashem, Ashem Vahishtem): truth, the eternal law of God
3. Kshathra (Khshathrem, Khshathrem Vairim): creative service, the kingdom of Ahura Mazda

Three on the Mother-side

4. Armaiti: reverence, piety
5. Haurvatat: perfection
6. Ameretat: immortality

Six GRADES OF MEAT

This is the official list used by the U.S. Department of Agriculture. Prime, sometimes called Grade A, is the only grade legally sold for human consumption.

1. Prime
2. Choice
3. Good
4. Standard
5. Commercial
6. Utility

Six GREAT IDEAS (PHILOSOPHY)

Mortimer J. Adler, the director of the Institute for Philosophical Research in Chicago, argues in his book Six Great Ideas *(1981) that these are the six fundamental ideas of all human philosophy, and points out that five of them are prominent in the basic documents of American history (the Declaration of Independence, the Constitution, and the Gettysburg Address). See also* Ten Philosophical Mistakes.

Ideas We Judge by

1. Truth
2. Goodness
3. Beauty

Ideas We Live by and Act on

4. Liberty
5. Equality
6. Justice

GROUP OF SIX
See Les Six.

Six HAND TYPES
Adherents of palmistry maintain that the shape of the hand reveals much about a person's individuality. These are the six basic types of hand and their respective traits.

1. Elementary: stupidity
2. Square: orderliness
3. Conical: inspirational
4. Spatulate: energetic
5. Pointed: idealistic
6. Mixed: adaptable

Six Positions in HOCKEY

1. Center
2. Left wing
3. Right wing
4. Defense
5. Defense
6. Goalie

Six HOLY IMMORTALS
See Six Genii of Ahura Mazda.

Six Suits of MAH-JONGG
A set of ancient Chinese mah-jongg tiles consists of 144 tiles made up of three similar and three disparate suits. The arrangement of tiles is reminiscent of the Western deck of cards, but the suits and the arrangement of the groups within each suit are vastly different. Each suit is followed by its alternative name, if applicable, and the assortment of tiles.

1. Bamboos (Sticks): 4 each of 1–9
2. Circles (Dots): 4 each of 1–9
3. Characters (Cracks): 4 each of 1–9
4. Honors (Dragons): 4 each of green, red, and white dragons
5. Winds: 4 each of east, south, west, north
6. Flowers and Seasons: either 4 of each or 8 of either

MILWAUKEE SIX
See Dirty Seven.

Six MONTY PYTHONERS
These six comic performers made up the primary cast of the television show Monty Python's Flying Circus. While each member contributed his creative writing and per-

forming talents, Graham Chapman functioned as the artistic director of the group. Terry Gilliam, who mainly appeared in small, odd roles, also created the show's weird animation sequences and went on to become an acclaimed film director.

1. Graham Chapman
2. John Cleese
3. Terry Gilliam
4. Eric Idle
5. Terry Jones
6. Michael Palin

Six NATIONS
See Five Iroquois Nations.

Six NEW ENGLAND STATES
The region of the United States known as New England consists of these six northeastern states.

1. Connecticut
2. Maine
3. Massachusetts
4. New Hampshire
5. Rhode Island
6. Vermont

Six Faces of the NEW FRONTIER
President John F. Kennedy expounded on these six causes during his administration and worked in many capacities to try to bring them about.

1. Peace Corps
2. Space Program
3. Alliance for Progress
4. Civil Rights

5. Freedom
6. Peace

Six NOBEL PRIZES

1. Chemistry
2. Economics
3. Literature
4. Medicine or Physiology
5. Physics
6. Nobel Peace Prize

Six NOBLE GASES

Chemists label these elements the Six Noble Gases because when first discovered, they were found to have no free electrons and were thus unable to combine with other atoms. However, the heavier noble gases, discovered later, do make compounds, so the term is somewhat misleading.

1. Helium (He)
2. Neon (Ne)
3. Argon (Ar)
4. Krypton (Kr)
5. Xenon (Xe)
6. Radon (Ra)

Six Basic NOISE LEVELS

Industrial noise is measured on this scale. Each level is listed in decibels with the corresponding effect and an example following.

1. Up to 69: comfortable—normal conversation
2. 70–84: intrusive (interferes with telephone use)—vacuum cleaner
3. 85–99: very annoying (damages hearing after eight hours of exposure)—lawn mower

4. 100–119: dangerous (regular exposure over one minute risks permanent hearing loss)—chain saw, rock concert
5. 120–124: threshold of sound vibration—boom box
6. 125 and up; beyond threshold of pain—jet takeoff, shotgun firing

Six RATIOS

From the study of trigonometry, or the mathematics of the ratios of the sides of right-angled triangles. Each is followed by its abbreviation, ratio, and reciprocal.

1. Tangent: tan A; a/c; cotangent
2. Sine: sin A; a/b; cosecant
3. Cosine: cos A; c/b; secant
4. Cotangent: cot A; c/a; tangent
5. Cosecant: cosec A; b/a; sine
6. Secant: sec A; b/c; cosine

Six RHYTHMIC MODES

Thirteen-century Western music used these six rhythmic patterns. See also Eight Church Modes.

1. Trochaic |♩ ♩|
2. Iambic |♩♩ |
3. Dactylic |♩. |♩♩ |
4. Anapestic |♩♩ |♩. |
5. Spondaic |♩. |♩. |
6. Tribrachic |♩♩♩|

Six RIVER CLASSES

This is the International Scale of Water Difficulty. It is used to rate the safety risks to small craft upon different rivers. Those marked with an asterisk (*) are not safe or suitable for open canoes.

1. Class I: few or no obstructions
2. Class II: some easy rapids, maneuvering required
3. Class III: rapids, complex maneuvering required
4. Class IV*: turbulent, scouting from shore required
5. Class V*: violent, Eskimo roll required
6. Class VI*: nearly impossible

Six RODEO CONTESTS

These events are the six most basic types of rodeo competition.

1. Saddle Bronc Riding
2. Bareback Riding
3. Calf Roping
4. Bull Riding
5. Steer Wrestling
6. Team Roping

Six Positions for SEXUAL INTERCOURSE

According to zoologist Alfred C. Kinsey, author of Sexual Behavior in the Human Male *(1948) and* Sexual Behavior in the Human Female *(1953), all positions are variations on these six.*

1. Man on top
2. Woman on top
3. Side by side
4. Rear entrance
5. Sitting
6. Standing

Six Attributes of SHAZAM

From the Captain Marvel comics. Shazam was a magic word that when spoken by Billy or Mary Baston would transform them into a superhero. Each letter of the word Shazam represents the greatest attribute of a mythical heroic character.

Billy Baston/Captain Marvel

1. Solomon: wisdom
2. Hercules: strength
3. Atlas: stamina
4. Zeus: power
5. Achilles: courage
6. Mercury: speed

Mary Baston/Mary Marvel

1. Selena: grace
2. Hippolyta: strength
3. Ariadne: skill
4. Zephyrus: fleetness
5. Aurora: beauty
6. Minerva: wisdom

SINISTER SIX
These six villains inhabit the world of Spider Man comics.

1. Dr. Octopus
2. Mystero
3. Vulture
4. Electro
5. Kraven the Hunter
6. Sandman

Six Positions in SOCCER

1. Right wing
2. Left wing
3. Right defense
4. Left defense

5. Center
6. Goalie

Six TELEVISION RATINGS

Created by the American television broadcasting industry in 1996, these ratings are designed to provide guidance for parents in selecting appropriate programs for their children. Ratings are based on strong language, violence, sex, nudity, and other factors. Each rating is followed by its abbreviated description.

1. TV-Y: Young audiences: suitable for all children
2. TV-Y7: Youth age seven or older: may contain mild violence
3. TV-G: General: appropriate for all ages
4. TV-PG: Parental Guidance suggested: may contain sexual or violent content
5. TV-14: Parents Strongly Cautioned: may contain material parents would find unsuitable for children under fourteen
6. TV-M: Mature audiences: program designed to be viewed by adults; may be unsuitable for children under seventeen

Six Flags over TEXAS

The state of Texas is proud that it has existed under the flags of six sovereign nations, including its own. The states and dates follow each entry.

1. Spain: colony/1519–1685 and 1690–1821
2. France: colony/1685–90
3. Mexico: territory/1821–36
4. Texas: independent republic/1836–45
5. Confederate States of America: state/1861–65
6. United States of America: state/1845–61 and 1865–present

Six Languages of the UNITED NATIONS

The six official languages in which the United Nations conducts business. Five languages were adopted immediately on the formation of the United Nations in 1946; Arabic was added by the General Assembly in 1973.

1. Arabic
2. Chinese
3. English
4. French
5. Russian
6. Spanish

Six Organs of the UNITED NATIONS

The Charter of the United Nations created an international organization with these six divisions.

1. General Assembly
2. Security Council
3. Economics and Social Council
4. Trusteeship Council
5. International Court of Justice
6. Secretariat

Six VICES

According to Agama Tirtha, the primary religion of Bali. For comparative lists from other traditions, see Five Vices *and* Seven Deadly Sins.

1. Kama: lust
2. Krodha: anger
3. Lodha: greed
4. Moha: error
5. Mada: intoxication
6. Matsarya: jealousy

Six Ss of WINE TASTING

Wine tasters learn these six techniques for evaluating the fermented grape.

1. See (examine the wine)
2. Smell
3. Sip (Slurp)
4. Savor
5. Spit (or swallow)
6. Swallow

Six WIVES OF HENRY VIII

King Henry VIII of England essentially created the Anglican Church so he could obtain his first divorce.

1. Catherine of Aragon: 1485–1535/died naturally, possibly poisoned
2. Ann Boleyn: 1507–36/beheaded
3. Jane Seymour: 1509–37/died after childbirth
4. Anne of Cleves: 1515–57/died naturally
5. Catherine Howard 1520–42/beheaded
6. Catherine Parr: 1512–48/outlived Henry

Six ZOOGRAPHICAL REGIONS

Zoological geographers divide the globe into six major areas according to climate and vegetation.

1. Palaearctic
2. Nearctic
3. Ethiopian
4. Oriental
5. Neotropical
6. Australasian

SEVENS

Once called the first prime number because it does not divide evenly into 360, Seven has at one time or another represented nearly every being and aspect of creation. The Babylonians, being the first to study and record the stars, identified seven planets; Seven thus became the basis for the number of days in a week.

Some ancient mystics, using Three to represent the spiritual and Four the material, made Seven the symbol of the universe. Others believed Seven to be the perfect culmination of the feminine (Three) and the masculine (Four), symbolic of the most primal aspects of life and death.

To the ancient Greeks, Seven represented the god Apollo, and to the Zoroastrians Seven symbolized Ahura Mazda and his six genii. Buddhists believed there were Seven days between death and rebirth. A Shi'ite Muslim sect known as Ismailis is also known as Seveners because they venerate Ismail, the Seventh Imam.

The appeal of Seven lies at the heart of Theosophy, a mystical religion founded in 1875 by Helen Patrovna Blavatsky when she had a vision of Tsong-kah-pa, an incarnation of Buddha. The belief system of Theosophy includes a concept known as the Septenary Law, manifested in the Seven Primordial Rays that support and influence every action in the universe.

In Judaism, Seven was a holy number. The abundant Sevens of that faith were adopted by the succeeding religions Christianity and Islam and led to the present belief in Lucky Seven in Western culture. The immense popularity of Seven is demonstrated in the model numbers of automobiles, Boeing aircraft, and a myriad other products.

Sir Isaac Newton (1642–1727), the British scientist who discovered gravity, also created the scientific field of optics with his work in the color spectrum. His strong belief in the perfect quality of Seven led him to divide the spectrum into seven colors. An examination of primary and secondary colors reveals only six, but Newton included indigo between blue and purple, thus avoiding the objectionable Six.

A detailed list of mystical associations and correspondences given to Seven is presented in the appendix.

Seven Consistencies of ADAM
According to the Gnostics, early mystical Christians, Adam was composed of these materials.

1. Clay (earth): flesh
2. Dew: blood
3. Sun: eyes
4. Stone: bones
5. Cloud: mind
6. Grass: hair
7. Wind (breath): soul

Seven AGES OF MAN (BALTASAR GRACIAN)
Spanish writer Baltasar Gracian (1601–58) presented his own version of the Seven Ages of Man in his Art of Worldly Wisdom.

1. At 20, a Peacock
2. At 30, a Lion
3. At 40, a Camel
4. At 50, a Serpent
5. At 60, a Dog
6. At 70, an Ape
7. At 80, Nothing at all

Seven AGES OF MAN (SHAKESPEARE)

William Shakespeare's Jaques expounds on these in As You Like It, *act 2, scene 7.*

1. Infant
2. Schoolboy
3. Lover
4. Soldier
5. Justice
6. Pantaloon
7. Second Childishness

Seven ARCHANGELS

The Seven Archangels appear in many versions and many sources in ancient literature, both Christian and Jewish. In the first version of the list, the angel Samael (Chamuel) is Satan. In Jewish tradition, the seven branches of the menorah are said to represent the Seven Archangels. See also Seven Celestial Hierarchies.

Seven Archangels (Traditional Christianity)

1. Gabriel
2. Michael
3. Uriel
4. Raphael
5. Samael (Chamuel)
6. Jophiel
7. Zadkiel

Seven Archangels (According to Enoch)

1. Uriel
2. Raphael
3. Ragual
4. Michael
5. Zerachiel

6. Gabriel
7. Remiel

Seven Angels of the Days of the Week (Early Christianity)

1. Michael (Sunday)
2. Gabriel (Monday)
3. Samael (Tuesday)
4. Raphael (Wednesday)
5. Sachiel (Thursday)
6. Anael (Friday)
7. Cassiel (Saturday)

Archangels of the Seven Spheres (Hebrew)

1. Michael (Sun): the likeness of God
2. Gabriel (Moon): strength
3. Madimiel (Mars): blood, redness
4. Raphael (Mercury): healing
5. Zadkiel (Jupiter): justice
6. Haniel (Venus): splendor
7. Cassiel (Saturn): the keeper of secrets

Seven Angels (according to the mystical book Arbatel of Magick, *London, 1655)*

1. Aratron (Saturn)
2. Bether (Jupiter)
3. Phalec (Mars)
4. Och (Sun)
5. Hagith (Venus)
6. Ophiel (Mercury)
7. Phul (Moon)

Seven BABY BELLS

These regional phone companies were formed by a government-mandated breakup of the Bell Telephone monopoly in 1984. They were quickly nicknamed the Seven Baby Bells.

1. Ameritech (*American Information Tech*nology): Wisconsin, Michigan, Illinois, Indiana, and Ohio
2. Bell Atlantic: Pennsylvania, New Jersey, West Virginia, Virginia, Delaware, and Maryland
3. Nynex (*New York/New England*): New York, Connecticut, Massachusetts, Vermont, New Hampshire, Rhode Island, and Maine
4. Pac Tel (*Pacific Tele*sis): California and Nevada
5. Southern Bell: Kentucky, Tennessee, North Carolina, South Carolina, Louisiana, Mississippi, Alabama, Georgia, and Florida
6. Southwestern Bell: Kansas, Missouri, Oklahoma, Arkansas, and Texas
7. U.S. West: Washington, Oregon, Idaho, Montana, North Dakota, South Dakota, Minnesota, Iowa, Wyoming, Nebraska, Utah, Colorado, Arizona, and New Mexico.

Seven BIBLES

See Seven Sacred Books.

BLAKE'S SEVEN

This popular sci-fi TV show, produced in England during 1978–82 and widely syndicated in the United States, might be described as a future version of the story of Robin Hood, with Blake and his crew of merry men fighting a corrupt galactic government. Their chief adversaries were Servalan (a futuristic Sheriff of Nottingham, played by Jacqueline Pearce) and her henchman Travis (equivalent to Sir Guy of Gisborne, played first by Stephen Greif and later by Brian Croucher). There were many changes in the crew over the series' four years, but these were the original seven. Each character is followed by the name of the actor, a description, and the name of the equivalent character in Robin Hood.

1. Blake (Gareth Thomas): charismatic resistance leader/Robin Hood
2. Jenna (Sally Knyvette): smuggler and top pilot/Maid Marian

3. Avon (Paul Darrow): cold computer genius/Will Scarlet
4. Cally (Jan Chappell): ethical telepath/Friar Tuck
5. Gan (David Jackson): strong and compassionate/Little John
6. Vila (Michael Keating): thief and lockpicker, nervous/Much
7. Zen (Peter Tuddenham): ship's computer, nearly omniscient/Herne

Seven BLIND MEN AND AN ELEPHANT

An old tale tells of seven blind men who examined an elephant. Since each man only touched a small part of the animal, each one "saw" it differently. The moral of the story is one should not draw conclusions without being able to see the whole picture. The following list includes the part of the elephant each felt and what he "saw."

1. Leg: a tree trunk
2. Side: a wall
3. Tail: a rope
4. Ear: a fan
5. Lower Lip: a brush
6. Tusk: a sword
7. Trunk: a snake

Seven BODIES
See Seven Metals.

Seven BOWLS:
See Seven Vials.

Seven BRANCHES OF LEARNING
See Seven Liberal Arts.

SEVEN BRIDES FOR SEVEN BROTHERS

This well-known film is set in 1850s America and concerns the courting difficulties of seven lumberjack brothers. The list includes the name of each character and the actor who played the part.

Seven Brides

1. Milly: Jane Powell
2. Dorcas: Julie Newmeyer (Newmar)
3. Alice: Nancy Kilgas
4. Sarah: Betty Carr
5. Liza: Virginia Gibson
6. Ruth: Ruta Kilmonis (Lee)
7. Martha: Norma Doggett

Seven Brothers

1. Adam: Howard Keel
2. Benjamin: Jeff Richards
3. Caleb: Matt Mattox
4. Daniel: Marc Platt
5. Ephraim: Jacques d'Amboise
6. Frankincense: Tommy Rall
7. Gideon: Russ Tamblyn

Seven CANONICAL HOURS
See Eight Canonical Hours.

Seven CAPITAL (CARDINAL) SINS
See Seven Deadly Sins.

Seven CELESTIAL HIERARCHIES

The symbolism of the planets according to cabala, a mystical Jewish philosophy of the middle ages. See also Seven Archangels.

	Planet	Attribute	Angel	Planet Symbol
1.	Sun	Angel of Light	Michael	☉
2.	Moon	Angel of Hope and Dreams	Gabriel	☾
3.	Mercury	Civilizing Angel	Raphael	☿
4.	Venus	Angel of Love	Anael	♀
5.	Mars	Angel of Destruction	Samael	♂
6.	Jupiter	Administering Angel	Zachariel	♃
7.	Saturn	Angel of Solicitude	Oriphiel	♄

Seven Countries of CENTRAL AMERICA

1. Costa Rica
2. Belize
3. Guatemala
4. Honduras
5. Nicaragua
6. Panama
7. El Salvador

Seven CHAKRAS

From the meditation beliefs of the ancient Hindus. Each chakra is an energy center located at a specific point on the body. Each name is followed by its translation and location.

1. Muladhara (root/support): pelvic floor
2. Svadhisthana (her special abode): genital area
3. Manipura (city of the shining jewel): navel
4. Anahata (the sound "Om"): heart
5. Visuddha (purification): larynx
6. Ajna (command): between the brows
7. Sahasrana (thousand-petaled lotus of light): crown of the head

Seven CHALLENGER ASTRONAUTS

Seven astronauts who perished in the explosion of the U.S. space shuttle Challenger *on January 28, 1986, when the craft exploded 73 seconds after liftoff.*

1. Gregory B. Jarvis: payload specialist 1
2. Sharon Christa McAuliffe: payload specialist 2
3. Ronald E. McNair: mission specialist 3
4. Ellison S. Onizuka: mission specialist 2
5. Judith A. Resnik: mission specialist 1
6. Francis R. "Dick" Scobee: commander
7. Michael J. Smith: pilot

Seven CHAMPIONS OF CHRISTENDOM

The seven national saints of seven major European countries, known as the Seven Champions of Christendom. Their legendary stories were first described by English poet Richard Johnson (c. 1573–1659) in 1592. Each saint is associated to its national affiliation and the corresponding legend.

1. George (England): imprisoned seven years by the king of Morocco
2. Andrew (Scotland): delivered six ladies who had lived seven years as swans
3. Patrick (Ireland): spent seven years in a cell where he dug his own grave
4. David (Wales): slept seven years in the enchanted garden of Ormandine
5. Denis (France): lived seven years in the form of a deer
6. James (Spain): was seven years dumb out of love for a fair Jewess
7. Anthony (Italy): enchanted into a deep sleep by seven magical lamps

CHICAGO SEVEN

This group of antiwar activists was charged with conspiracy to incite a riot at the 1968 Democratic National Convention in Chicago. They were acquitted on February 18, 1970. The group was originally known as the Chicago Eight, but a suspect named Bobby Seale chose to conduct his own defense and ceased to be a member of the group, whereupon it came to be known as the Chicago Seven.

1. Rennie Davis
2. David Dellinger
3. John Froines
4. Tom Hayden
5. Abbie Hoffman
6. Jerry Rubin
7. Lee Weiner

Seven CHURCHES IN ASIA

According to Revelation 1:11, these cities were the principal outposts of Christianity. Over the years, however, all have become Muslim cities, except Laodicea, which no longer exists.

1. Ephesus
2. Smyrna
3. Pergamum
4. Thyatira
5. Sartis
6. Philadelphia
7. Laodicea

Seven CITIES OF BEAUTY

Part of English folklore, these seven cities were believed to be the seven most beautiful cities that ever existed. The Seven Cities of Commerce substituted London for Paris.

1. Athens
2. Babylon
3. Constantinople
4. Egypt
5. Jerusalem
6. Rome
7. Paris

Seven CLASSES OF SOCIETY (INCA)
The ancient Inca civilization was divided into these social classes.

1. Curaco: noblemen
2. Palla: princesses
3. Guaso: farm workers
4. Yanacona: serfs
5. Chino: women of mixed blood
6. Mitimae: conquered races
7. Chuncho: jungle natives

Seven Levels of CLASSIFICATION IN BIOLOGY
These seven terms are memorized by every biology student. In addition to these, subcategories such as superfamily and subclass also exist. Species subcategories include form and breed. Living things are usually described by listing the genus and species name.

1. Kingdom
2. Phylum
3. Class
4. Order
5. Family
6. Genus
7. Species

Seven COLORS OF THE RAINBOW
Science students who must memorize this list often use the mnemonic acronym Roy G. Biv.

1. Red
2. Orange
3. Yellow
4. Green
5. Blue
6. Indigo
7. Violet

Seven CONTINENTS

The seven major land masses recognized by modern geographers. Mythology also tells of Atlantis, the Eighth or "Lost" Continent. The land masses of the earth are traditionally divided into seven, although in reality there are fewer than seven. Europe, which has been accepted as a continent for millennia, is not so much a continent as an oversized peninsula of Asia. Africa and Asia are joined by unbroken land, as are North and South America. However, the Seven Continents is a commonly accepted numbered list.

1. Africa
2. Antarctica
3. Asia
4. Australia
5. Europe
6. North America
7. South America

Seven DAYS OF THE WEEK

Each day is followed by its namesake.

1. Sunday: the Sun
2. Monday: the Moon
3. Tuesday: Tyr, Norse god of war, or Tiu, the equivalent Teutonic deity
4. Wednesday: Odin (Wodin), chief Norse god, or Wotan, the equivalent Teutonic deity
5. Thursday: Thor, Norse god of thunder, equivalent to the Teutonic deity Donar
6. Friday: Freya, Norse goddess of love and fertility, or Frigga, Norse sky goddess
7. Saturday: Saturn, Roman god of the harvest

Seven DEADLY SINS

Also known as the Seven Capital (Cardinal) Sins or Vices, Seven Peccatas (Seven Ps), or Seven Roots of Sinfulness. They do not appear in Christian scriptures but were first expounded by Saint Thomas Aquinas (c. 1225–74) and are among the traditional doctrines of the Roman Catholic church. See also Five Vices, Six Enemies of Mankind, and Six Vices. Each sin is followed by its description or alternative names.

1. Pride: selfish indifference to others
2. Envy: jealousy, resentment, fear
3. Avarice: covetousness, greed, acquisitiveness
4. Sloth: laziness, idleness, cowardice, complacency, lack of imagination
5. Wrath: anger, ill temper, vindictiveness, violent indignation
6. Gluttony: self-indulgence, wanton pursuit of pleasure
7. Lust: perversion, desire

Seven Precepts of DEISM

Deism is a theological view common among many religions, often defined as a belief in a nonpersonal God. Charles Darwin and Voltaire, often vilified as antireligious, were actually Deists.

Beliefs

1. There is one God, supreme over the universe in power, wisdom, and goodness, but he cannot reveal himself to Man.
2. The world is ordered for the best; therefore the end will be good.
3. Immortality is assured, for God loves his creation.
4. God is a constant, powerful stimulant to the highest virtue, not simply an intellectual conviction.

Canons

5. It is the right and duty of every man to think for himself.
6. All knowledge of God is partial, defective, and insignificant; but such knowledge can be increased and refined by the use of reason, conscience, and love.
7. All knowledge of God must be based on immutable facts in Nature. No beliefs are to be at variance with science.

Seven DEMONS

Cast out of Mary Magdalene by Jesus (Luke 8:2 and Mark 16:9), these were once believed to be the seven greatest tempters of mankind.

1. Lucifer
2. Beelzebub
3. Satan
4. Astaroth
5. Leviathan
6. Elimi
7. Baalbarith

Seven DIRECTIONS OF SPACE

1. Up: zenith
2. Down: nadir
3. Forward: north
4. Backward: south
5. Right: east
6. Left: west
7. Center: center

DIRTY SEVEN

Stand-up comedian George Carlin, who has often been harassed for telling jokes about these "banned" words, created or at least popularized this list. He was fined $150 in 1972 for using these words during his performance in Milwaukee, and for a short time they were known as the Big Six or the Milwaukee Six ("fuck" and "motherfucker" were counted as one word). Carlin capitalized on the event and because of his famous routine the expression has become a household term.

1. Cocksucker
2. Cunt
3. Fuck
4. Motherfucker

5. Piss
6. Shit
7. Tits

Seven Classifications of DOGS

The American Kennel Club, which regulates canine pedigrees and breeding standards in the United States, recognizes nearly 200 breeds in these seven distinct groups.

1. Herding dogs
2. Hounds
3. Nonsporting dogs
4. Sporting dogs
5. Terriers
6. Toys
7. Working dogs

Seven DOOMS

From the New Testament, Revelation 17:1–20:15. See also Seven Sevens of the Book of Revelation.

1. Doom of Babylon ("confusion")
2. Doom of the Beast
3. Doom of the False Prophet
4. Doom of the Kings
5. Doom of Gog and Magog (the "prince" of the northern areas and his "kingdom")
6. Doom of Satan
7. Doom of the Unbelieving Dead (the Last Judgment)

Seven DWARFS

The Seven Dwarfs were given cute names and exaggerated character traits for the Disney film Snow White and the Seven Dwarfs, *but they actually originated in an old European folktale. The story was also dramatized for cable television by the Faerie*

Tale Theatre, and the dwarfs were given different names in this production. This nickname was also given to the seven men vying for the Democratic nomination in the presidential election of 1988.

Snow White and the Seven Dwarfs (Disney)

1. Bashful
2. Doc
3. Dopey
4. Grumpy
5. Happy
6. Sleepy
7. Sneezy

Faerie Tale Theatre

1. Bubba
2. Barnaby
3. Boniface
4. Bruno
5. Balwin
6. Botrum
7. Bernard

Presidential Election of 1988

1. Bruce Babbitt, former governor of Arizona
2. Joseph Biden, senator from Delaware
3. Michael Dukakis, governor of Massachusetts
4. Richard Gephardt, congressman from St. Louis, Missouri
5. Albert Gore, senator from Tennessee
6. Jesse Jackson, minister from Chicago, Illinois
7. Paul Simon, senator from Illinois

Seven EMIRATES
Seven independent states, each ruled by an emir, that form the United Arab Emirates.

1. Abu Dhabi
2. Ajman
3. Dubai
4. Fujairah
5. Ras al-Khaimah
6. Sharjah
7. Umm al-Qaiwain

Seven FACES OF DR. LAO
From the film of the same name starring Tony Randall as Dr. Lao (pronounced "Loh"), who played all these "faces" except the last.

1. Dr. Lao, a Chinaman
2. Merlin the Magician
3. Pan, a satyr
4. Abominable Snowman
5. Medusa, a hideous Greek monster
6. Apollonius the Seer
7. Loch Ness Monster

G-7
Also known as the Group of Seven, this name is given to the seven major industrial nations of the world.

1. Canada
2. France
3. Germany
4. Great Britain
5. Italy
6. Japan
7. United States

Seven GATES OF LONDON
See Four Gates of London.

Seven GODS

Mythological systems with seven major gods exist all over the world. Here are four examples. The three Western lists also give correlations to the Seven Planets *and the* Seven Days of the Week.

Babylonian

1. Shamash/Sun/Sunday
2. Sin/Moon/Monday
3. Nergal/Mars/Tuesday
4. Nabu (Nebo)/Mercury/Wednesday
5. Marduk/Jupiter/Thursday
6. Ishtar/Venus/Friday
7. Ninib/Saturn/Saturday

Greek

1. Helios/Sun/Sunday
2. Artemis/Moon/Monday
3. Ares/Mars/Tuesday
4. Hermes/Mercury/Wednesday
5. Zeus/Jupiter/Thursday
6. Aphrodite/Venus/Friday
7. Cronos/Saturn/Saturday

Roman

1. Sol/Sun/Sunday
2. Luna/Moon/Monday
3. Mars/Mars/Tuesday
4. Mercury/Mercury/Wednesday
5. Jove/Jupiter/Thursday

6. Venus/Venus/Friday
7. Saturn/Saturn/Saturday

Seven Gods of Luck
From the mythology of ancient Japan: the deities and their respective kingdoms.

1. Bishamon: war, victory
2. Ebisu: fisherman's luck
3. Fukurokujin: prophesy, miracles
4. Daikoku: wealth, happiness
5. Benten: art, literature
6. Hotei: wisdom
7. Jurojin: longevity

Seven GREAT TOWNS
From an old bit of doggerel: "Seven great towns on Earth, 'tis said, claimed Homer's birth when he was dead, through which, when living, he begged his bread."

1. Argos
2. Athens
3. Chios
4. Colophon
5. Rhodes
6. Salamis
7. Smyrna

GROUP OF SEVEN (ART)
These were Canadian painters who created a new expressionistic style. They traveled all over Canada producing abstract paintings of the rugged wilderness. The founding member of the group was Lawren Harris; their first exhibition was held in 1920. Tom Thomson (1877–1917) was a precursor whose style influenced them a great deal. Three later artists to joint the group were A. J. Casson (1898–1992), LeMoine Fitzgerald (1890–1956) and Edwin Holgate (1892–1977).

1. Franklin Carmichael (1890–1945)
2. Lawren Harris (1885–1970)
3. Alexander Y. Jackson (1882–1974)
4. Frank Johnston (1888–1949)
5. Arthur Lismer (1885–1969)
6. J. E. H. MacDonald (1873–1932)
7. Frederick Horsman Varley (1881–1969)

GROUP OF SEVEN (ECONOMICS)
See G-7.

Seven HABITS OF HIGHLY EFFECTIVE PEOPLE
From the popular self-help book (1989) by Stephen R. Covey, who with it created a program to help people replace self-defeating behavior with a principle-centered approach to problem solving.

1. Be proactive (use initiative).
2. Begin with the end in mind (express and follow your vision).
3. Put first things first (prioritize).
4. Think win/win (find solutions that are mutually beneficial).
5. Seek first to understand, then be understood (the method for working toward a win/win solution).
6. Synergize (find creative new solutions).
7. Sharpen the saw (practice what you've learned).

Seven Foods that Cause HEARTBURN
These are the most common foods that cause indigestion. Interestingly, spicy food, which is often blamed for heartburn, is not medically responsible for it.

1. Citrus juices
2. Chocolate
3. Peppermint
4. Nicotine

5. Alcohol
6. Fatty foods (such as goose, duck, cheese)
7. Caffeine

Seven HELLS
According to Muslim belief, the guilty reside in their separate hells.

1. Muslems
2. Christians
3. Jews
4. Sabaeans
5. Magi
6. Idolators
7. Hypocrites

HEPTATHLON
This seven-in-one Olympic event, in which women compete in seven different track and field sports on two days, was created in 1981. See also Pentathlon *(among the Fives) and* Decathlon *(in the Tens).*

1. 100-meter hurdles
2. High jump
3. Shot put
4. 200-meter dash
5. Long jump
6. Javelin throw
7. 800-meter run

Seven HILLS OF ROME
The city of Rome rests on more than seven hills; therefore, there are many different versions of the list. Since the legendary brothers Romulus and Remus are said to have chosen the Palatine Hill and the Aventine Hill, respectively, on which to found a city, these two are always included in the list.

1. Aventine or Collis Dianae (site of the Temple of Diana)
2. Cælian
3. Capitoline or Mons Tarpeius, Mons Saturni (site of the Temple of Jupiter Capitolinus)
4. Esquiline
5. Palatine
6. Quirinal or Cabalinus (site of two marble statues of a horse)
7. Viminal (site of the Temple of Jupiter Viminalis)

Seven Gifts of the HOLY GHOST

From the traditional doctrines of the Roman Catholic church. The last three gifts are ranged in three steps, knowledge being the highest level of the three.

1. Counsel
2. Fear of the Lord
3. Fortitude
4. Piety
5. Understanding
6. Wisdom
7. Knowledge

Seven INTELLIGENCES

Author Howard Gardner, a psychologist, expounded the concept of multiple intelligences in his book Frames of Mind *(1983). According to him, intelligence tests that do not test all these areas do not provide adequate information on a subject's abilities.*

1. Linguistic: sensitivity to language and the relations among words
2. Logical-mathematical: abstract thought, precision, counting, organization, logical structure
3. Personal 1: sensitivity to others
4. Personal 2: sensitivity to oneself
5. Spatial: observation, mental images, metaphor, gestalt
6. Musical: sensitivity to pitch, rhythm, timbre, the emotional power and complex organization of music

7. Bodily-kinesthetic: control of one's body and objects, timing, trained responses that function like reflexes

Seven JOYS OF MARY
From the traditional doctrines of the Roman Catholic church. See also Seven Sorrows of Mary.

1. Annunciation
2. Visitation
3. Nativity
4. Adoration of the Magi
5. Presentation in the Temple
6. Finding of the Lost Child Jesus
7. Assumption

Seven Parts of the KAMA SUTRA
One of the holy scriptures of Hinduism, the Kama Sutra is divided into these seven major parts. The topics and authors of each part follow.

1. Sadharana: general topics (Charayana)
2. Samprayyogika: embraces, etc. (Suravnanabha)
3. Kanya Samprayuktaka: union of males and females (Ghotakamukha)
4. Bharydhikarika: one's wife (Gonardiya)
5. Paradarika: others' wives (Gonikaputra)
6. Vaisika: courtesans (Dattaka)
7. Aupamishadika: seduction, tonics, etc. (Kuchamara)

Seven KINGDOMS OF IRELAND
These seven kingdoms existed from 500 to 900 C.E. Corresponding contemporary regions follow.

1. Ailech (Donegal)
2. Airgaille (Londonderry, Armagh, Monaghan)

3. Ulaid (Antrim, Down)
4. Connachta (Connaught)
5. Muma (Munster)
6. Mide and Brega (Meath)
7. Laigin (Leinster)

Seven Principles of KWANZAA

The holiday of Kwanzaa was created in 1960 for Americans who wish to get more in touch with their African heritage and roots. The name Kwanzaa and the other terms and symbols of the holiday are based on common customs among the cultures of Africa. Contrary to popular belief, Kwanzaa was not created as a replacement for Christmas or other holidays at the end of the year, but as a supplemental celebration. Each principle is described by its African word, the day of celebration, and the color and its meaning.

1. Unity/Umoja/December 26/black, black togetherness
2. Self-determination/Kujichagulia/December 27/red
3. Collective work/Ujima/December 28/red
4. Cooperative economics/Ujamma/December 29/red, struggle for freedom
5. Purpose/Nia/December 30/green
6. Creativity/Kuumba/December 31/green
7. Faith/Imani/January 1/green, the future

Seven LAST WORDS OF CHRIST

Title of an important work by German composer Franz Joseph Haydn (1732–1809), in which he set to music these quotations from the New Testament. Several other composers have also set these words to music.

1. "Father, forgive them, for they know not what they do." (Luke 23:34)
2. "My God, my God, why have you forsaken me?" (Matthew 27:46)
3. He said to his mother, "Woman, behold your son!" Then he said to the disciple, "Behold your mother!" (John 19:26–27)
4. "I thirst!" (John 19:28)
5. "Truly, I say to you, today you will be with me in Paradise." (Luke 23:43)

6. "It is finished!" (John 19:30)
7. "Father, into thy hands I commit my spirit." (Luke 23:46)

Seven LIBERAL ARTS
Also known as the Seven Branches of Learning, the Seven Pillars of Wisdom, and Sophia's Seven Daughters, these fields of learning were once considered basic to a classical education.

The Trivium

1. Grammar
2. Logic or Dialectic
3. Rhetoric

The Quadrivium

4. Arithmetic
5. Geometry
6. Astronomy
7. Music

Seven LIVELY ARTS
Term used to describe seven basic areas of human artistic performance. There are many versions of the list; here are two.

Traditional

1. Music
2. Dance
3. Poetry
4. Storytelling
5. Drama
6. Mime
7. Singing

According to Author Gilbert Seldes (1924)

1. Movies
2. Popular Songs
3. Jazz
4. Comic Strips
5. Dialect Humor
6. Vaudeville and Burlesque
7. The Columnist

Seven LOKAS (HINDUISM)

According to Hinduism, lokas are levels of existence. (Descriptions follow.)

1. Bhurloka: Earth
2. Bhuvarloka: space between Earth and Sun
3. Swarloka: heaven of Indra
4. Mahaloka: abode of the saints
5. Janaloka: upper abode of the saints
6. Taparloka: abode of the minor deities
7. Brahmaloka (Satyaloka): abode of Brahma

The MAGNIFICENT SEVEN

A 1960 Hollywood remake of The Seven Samurai, *directed by John Sturges and set in Mexico. Each character is followed by the name of the actor who played the part.*

1. O'Reilly (Charles Bronson)
2. Chris (Yul Brynner)
3. Chico (Horst Bucholz)
4. Britt (James Coburn)
5. Harry Luck (Brad Dexter)
6. Vin (Steve McQueen)
7. Lee (Robert Vaughn)

Seven Parts of MAN (THEOSOPHY)

From Theosophy, a mystical religion founded in 1875 by Helena Petrovna Blavatsky, which contains the belief that each person has seven bodies or selves.

1. Atman (universal self)
2. Buddhi (intellectual)
3. Manas (mental)
4. Kama (desire)
5. Prana (vitality)
6. Linga-sarira (astral body)
7. Stula-sarira (physical body)

Seven MARTYRS

The Roman Catholic church honors over 20 thousand saints and martyrs, too numerous to be presented here. These two lists are representative samples.

SEVEN MARTYRS OF PERSIA

These six men and one woman were martyred in 341–80 by Sapor, the king of Persia.

1. Azade, Sapor's chief eunuch
2. Acepsimas, an Assyrian bishop
3. Joseph, priest of Bethcatuba
4. Aithala, deacon of Bethcatuba
5. Tarbula, sister of the archbishop of Seleucia
6. Milles, a Persian soldier turned bishop
7. Barsabias, bishop of Susa

SEVEN MARTYRS OF SAMOSATA

These seven martyrs died in the year 297 under the rule of Roman emperor Maximian. The first two were magistrates; the others were nobles and senators.

1. Hipparchus
2. Philotheus
3. James

4. Habibus
5. Lollianus
6. Paragrus
7. Romanus

Seven *MERCURY* ASTRONAUTS

The United States' first space heroes, these men began training at the Langley Research Center of the National Aeronautics and Space Administration in 1961. The Mercury *flights proved that people could be sent into space and returned safely to Earth. The Mercury Project was then followed by the* Gemini *flights and the* Apollo *lunar landings.*

1. M. Scott Carpenter, Lieutenant
2. L. Gordon Cooper, Captain
3. John H. Glenn, Jr., Colonel
4. Virgil I. "Gus" Grissom, Captain
5. Walter M. Schirra, Jr., Lieutenant Commander
6. Alan B. Shepard, Jr., Lieutenant Commander
7. Donald K. "Deke" Slayton, Captain

Seven Corporal Works of MERCY

From the traditional doctrines of the Roman Catholic church.

1. Bury the dead
2. Clothe the naked
3. Feed the hungry
4. Give drink to the thirsty
5. House the homeless
6. Tend the sick
7. Visit the fatherless and afflicted

Seven METALLOIDS

From alchemy; these are the seven metal "spirits" once believed to have mystical properties.

1. Alum
2. Antimony
3. Salammoniac (ammonium chloride)
4. Salt
5. Saltpeter
6. Sulfur
7. Vitriol (sulfuric acid)

Seven METALS

From alchemy, a science of the Middle Ages. Also called the Seven Bodies, these seven metals were considered to have special mystical properties. They are listed in order from superior to inferior. Each is followed by its respective planet and day of the week.

1. Gold: Sun/Sunday
2. Silver: Moon/Monday
3. Mercury: Mercury/Wednesday
4. Copper: Venus/Friday
5. Iron: Mars/Tuesday
6. Tin: Jupiter/Thursday
7. Lead: Saturn/Saturday

Seven MODES (MUSIC)

The modes were the musical scales commonly used during the pre-Renaissance era. Each mode can be heard by playing only the white keys of a piano. Today only the Ionian and Aeolian modes are commonly used for popular and art music, but folk tunes in several of the modes are familiar. Sample melodies are listed for the five most common modes; the tunes given are not all "perfect fits" but do provide a good general guide to how the modes differ. Each mode is followed by its keynote, description of sound, and sample melody.

1. Ionian/C/major/"Home on the Range"
2. Dorian/D/minor, one altered note/"Scarborough Fair"
3. Phrygian/E/eerie/(rare)
4. Lydian/F/major, one altered note/"Star-Spangled Banner"
5. Mixolydian/G/major, slightly sad/"Norwegian Wood" (Lennon and McCartney)
6. Aeolian/A/pure minor/"House of the Rising Sun"
7. Locrian/B/strange, unfinished/(not normally used)

Seven MULES OF NOTRE DAME (FOOTBALL)

Seven linemen (and their respective positions) at Notre Dame in 1924 who became widely known due to their prowess on the football field. See also Four Horsemen of Notre Dame.

1. Ed Huntsinger (end)
2. Charles Collins (end)
3. Joe Bach (tackle)
4. Edgar "Rip" Miller (tackle)
5. Noble Kizer (guard)
6. John Weibel (guard)
7. Adam Walsh (center)

Seven NEW THINGS

From the New Testament, Revelation 21:1–22:21. See also Seven Sevens of the Book of Revelation.

1. New Heaven
2. New Earth
3. New Peoples
4. The Lamb's Wife: New Jerusalem
5. New Temple
6. New Light
7. New Paradise and Its River of the Water of Life

Seven NOTES OF THE MAJOR SCALE

The names of the notes of the scale, presented in six different versions. Version One gives the names as used in music theory, the study of composition, and musical analysis. The remaining versions give the names as used in different vocal training methods from the 1500s to the present day. The names of each system are derived from one or more of the syllables used. Version Six, with the first three notes named do-re-mi, is probably the most familiar version of the system. The syllables derive from a Latin poem: Ut queant laxis, Resonate fibris, Mira gestorum, Famuli tuorem, Solve polluti, Labii reatum, Sancte Johannes. These exact names are seen in Version Five. For Version Six, ut became do because it is easier to sing and it sounds better. The last note, si, from S.J., became ti to avoid confusion with sol, and because it sounds more final. See also Twelve Notes of the Chromatic Scale.

		Bocedization (1500s)	Bebization (1600s)	Damenization (1700s)	Solmization (1900s)	Modern Solfege
1.	Tonic	bo	la	da	ut	do
2.	Supertonic	ce	be	me	re	re
3.	Mediant	di	ce	ni	mi	mi
4.	Subdominant	ga	de	po	fa	fa
5.	Dominant	lo	me	tu	sol	sol
6.	Submediant	ma	fe	la	la	la
7.	Leading tone	ni	ge	be	si	ti

Seven Ps, Seven PECCATAS

See Seven Deadly Sins.

Seven PERSONAGES (NEW TESTAMENT)

From Revelation 12:1–14:20. Each personage appears during the time of the final days. See also Seven Sevens of the Book of Revelation.

1. The Woman: Israel
2. Satan: a Red Dragon with Seven Heads and Ten Horns
3. The Child: Christ
4. The Archangel

5. The Jewish Remnant
6. The Beast out of the Sea
7. The Beast out of the Earth

Seven PILLARS OF WISDOM
See Seven Liberal Arts.

Seven PLAGUES
See Seven Vials.

Seven PLANETS
In the age before telescopes, the seven planets visible to the unaided eye were the only ones known. At that time, "planets" were heavenly bodies that did not behave as stars; ancients grouped the sun and the moon with the planets because they traversed the sky differently from stars. As with many numbered lists, these were correlated to mystical lists of various philosophical systems. Each planet is followed by its respective Roman, Greek, and Babylonian names.

1. Sun/Sol/Helios or Apollo/Shamush
2. Moon/Luna or Diana/Artemis/Sin
3. Mars/Mars/Ares/Marduk
4. Mercury/Mercury/Hermes/Ishtar
5. Jupiter/Jupiter/Zeus/Nabu (Nebo)
6. Venus/Venus/Aphrodite/Nergal
7. Saturn/Saturn/Cronos/Ninib

Seven Types of PLASTIC
Developed by the plastics industry in the 1970s to aid in recycling. Nearly every plastic product manufactured in the United States is marked with one of these numbers and a corresponding set of initials identifying the material used. In general, recycling centers accept only products marked 1 or 2, but research efforts toward greater recycling are continuing. Each label is followed by its meaning and example products.

1. P.E.T./P.E.T.E. (polyethylene terephthalate): beverage containers, "boil-in-bag" pouches
2. H.D.P.E. (high density polyethylene): milk and detergent bottles
3. P.V.C. (polyvinyl chloride or "vinyl"): house siding, blister packs, plumbing pipe
4. L.D.P.E./L.L.D.P.E. (low-density polyethylene, linear low-density polyethylene): shrink wrap, garbage bags
5. P.P. (polypropylene)
6. P.S. (nonfoamed polystyrene): plastic knives and forks
   Foam P.S. (foamed polystyrene or "styrofoam"): coffee cups, packaging
7. A.B.S. (acrylonitrile butadiene styrene)
   Acetate (cellulose acetate)
   Acrylic (methyl acrylic)
   Eng. Therm (engineering thermoplastics)
   Mixed Therm (mixed thermoplastics)
   Nylon (polyamide)
   OTHER (all other plastics)

Seven PLEASURES

According to The Rape of the American Puritan Ethic *(1963), by humorist Allan Sherman, these are the seven basic pleasures humans share with other creatures.*

1. Eat
2. Drink
3. Sleep
4. Shit
5. Piss
6. Fuck
7. Play

PLEIADES

From Greek mythology; the seven daughters of Atlas and Pleione, who exist as a cluster of stars in the constellation Orion. Because only six stars are visible in the Pleiades,

Merope is said to be ashamed to show her face among her sisters, for they married gods, and she married a mortal.

1. Alcyone
2. Celaeno
3. Electra
4. Maia
5. Merope
6. Sterope
7. Taygete

Seven PRIMORDIAL RAYS (THEOSOPHY)

From Theosophy, a mystical religion founded in 1875 by Helena Petrovna Blavatsky. The Theosophical concept known as the Septenary Law states that these seven rays support and influence every action in the universe.

Ray	Plane	Kingdom	Chakra	Shape	Food
I.	adi-atomic	shambala	head	circle	protein
II.	logoic	hierarchy	heart	triangle	fats
III.	mental	deva	throat	square	carbohydrate
IV.	buddhic	humanity	base of spine	circle squared	unknown
V.	manasic	animal	brow	sphere, lens	vitamins
VI.	astral	plant	solar plexus	cube	water
VII.	physico-etheric	mineral	sacral	pyramid	mineral salts

Politics	Nation-soul	Nation's Personality	Gas
fascism	India and China	U.K. and Germany	nitrogen
democracy	U.K. and U.S.A.	Brazil	oxygen
socialism	unknown	China and France	hydrogen
city-state	Germany and Austria	India and Italy	carbon dioxide
oligarchy	France	Austria	ammonia
theocratic despotism	Italy and Spain	U.S.A. and Russia	incense-laden
communism	Russia	Spain	nitrous oxide

Color	Qualities	Musical Note	Planets
scarlet, white	will and power	do	Sun, Uranus
indigo	love, wisdom	sol	Jupiter, Neptune
green	active intelligence	fa	Earth, Saturn
yellow	art, harmony through conflict	mi	Mercury
orange	concrete knowledge, science	re	Venus
blue, rose	devotion and idealism	ti	Mars, Jupiter
violet	ceremonial order and ritual	la	Moon, Earth

Sense	Endocrine	Nervous Equipment
sight	pineal	cerebrum
intuition	thymus	midbrain
hearing	thyroid	medulla
taste	adrenals	cerebellum
concrete touch	pituitary	peripheral
pain	pancreas	sympathetic
smell	gonads	parasympathetic

Seven Cornices of PURGATORY

From the Divine Comedy, *by Italian poet Dante Alighieri (1265–1321), a philosophical poem in one hundred cantos recounting an imaginary journey through Hell, Purgatory, and Heaven, and considered a masterpiece of world literature. Dante divided Purgatory into three levels. He placed the first three cornices in the first level, Lower Purgatory, the region of Love Perverted. The fourth cornice exists by itself in Middle Purgatory, or Love Defective. Upper Purgatory, or Excessive Love of Secondary Love, houses the final three cornices. A region known as Ante-Purgatory is reserved for excommunicates, the indolent, the unshaven, and the "preoccupied."* See also Seven Deadly Sins, Nine Circles of Hell, Ten Heavens of Paradise. *Each entry is followed by the type of sinner found therein.*

1. Superbia: the Proud
2. Invidia: the Envious
3. Ira: the Wrathful

4. Acedia: the Slothful
5. Avaritia: the Covetous
6. Gula: the Gluttonous
7. Luxuria: the Lustful

Seven Root RACES OF MANKIND
A tenet of Theosophy (a mystical religion founded by Helena Petrovna Blavatsky in 1875) holds that each succeeding race will develop a higher sense or mental faculty than the last. The following list of senses begins with the most primitive and progresses toward the most advanced. According to this belief, humans are currently at Level Five.

1. Hearing
2. Touch
3. Speech
4. Sight
5. Mentality
6. Intuition and clairvoyance
7. Direct perception and clairaudience

Seven ROOTS OF SINFULNESS
See Seven Deadly Sins.

Seven SACRAMENTS
From the Roman Catholic tradition. Only a bishop can administer all seven.

1. Baptism: cleansing of the soul
2. Confirmation: coming of age
3. Holy Eucharist: communion with the blood and body of Christ
4. Penance: confession and redemption
5. Extreme Unction: anointing of the sick at time of death (last rites)
6. Holy Orders: being ordained a priest
7. Matrimony: marriage

Seven SACRED BOOKS

During the Enlightenment, these seven holy books of the world religions were recognized by European scholars. Also known as the Seven Bibles.

1. The Bible of the Christians
2. The Eddas of the Scandinavians
3. The Five King of the Chinese (see *Five Classics*)
4. The Qur'an
5. The Tripitaka of the Buddhists (see *Three Baskets of the Law*)
6. The Four Vedas of the Hindus (see *Four Vedas*)
7. Zendavesta of the Zoroastrians (see *Five Books of the Zendavesta*)

Seven SAGES

See Seven Wise Men of Greece.

The SEVEN SAMURAI

Directed by Japanese filmmaker Akira Kurosawa, The Seven Samurai *(1956) is considered to be among the finest films ever made. The story, later adapted by Hollywood as* The Magnificent Seven, *revolves around a group of warriors in the seventeenth century who are drawn together to defend a village against ruthless marauders. Each character is described, followed by the actor who played the part.*

1. Kambei Shimada/leader/Takashi Shimura
2. Kikuchiyo/would-be samurai (name means "thirteen")/Toshiro Mifune
3. Katsushiro/young samurai/Ko Kimura
4. Gorobei Katayama/wise warrior/Yoshio Inaba
5. Heihachi Hayashida/good-natured/Minoru Chiaki
6. Shichiroji/friend of Kambei/Daisuke
7. Kyuzo/swordsman/Seiji Miyaguchi

Seven SEALS

From the New Testament, Revelation 4:1–8:1. Each seal corresponds to a prophetic sign or vision; the first four are horses. See also Seven Sevens of the Book of Revelation.

1. Unnamed: white horse, the rider with a bow and crown
2. Peace Taken from Earth: red horse
3. Famine: black horse, the rider with a balance in each hand
4. Death: pale horse, the rider is death
5. The Martyred Remnant
6. Anarchy
7. Out of Which Came Seven Trumpets

Seven SEAS

The phrase "Seven Seas" occurs often in mythology and folklore as a poetical reference to the waters of the earth. There are no specific bodies of water corresponding to this title, but a collection of numbered lists would be incomplete without at least one example. Here are two.

GRECO-ROMAN

The following selection may be considered as authentic as any. If these seem unimpressive, substitute the Dead Sea, Aral Sea, Tyrrhenian Sea, or any of the lesser bodies of water in the Mediterranean area.

1. Adriatic Sea
2. Aegean Sea
3. Black Sea
4. Caspian Sea
5. Ionian Sea
6. Mediterranean Sea
7. Red Sea

ACCORDING TO OCEANOGRAPHERS

Oceans and ocean regions may be used as the Seven Seas.

1. Antarctic
2. Arctic
3. Indian
4. North Atlantic
5. North Pacific

6. South Atlantic
7. South Pacific

Seven SENSES
See Five Senses.

Seven SEVENS OF THE BOOK OF REVELATION
As the final book of the New Testament, the Book of Revelation contains many mystical passages and includes exactly seven lists of seven. Each of these lists appears in this chapter under its own heading.

1. Seven Churches in Asia
2. Seven Seals
3. Seven Trumpets
4. Seven Personages
5. Seven Vials
6. Seven Dooms
7. Seven New Things

Seven SISTERS (COLLEGES)
Once known as the Seven Sisters, these were at one time considered the equivalent of the Ivy League for women.

1. Barnard; New York, N.Y.
2. Bryn Mawr; Bryn Mawr, Pa.
3. Mount Holyoke; South Hadley, Mass.
4. Radcliffe; Cambridge, Mass.
5. Smith; Northampton, Mass.
6. Vassar; Poughkeepsie, N.Y.
7. Wellesley; Wellesley, Mass.

Seven SISTERS (PETROLEUM)

At one time these were the seven biggest oil companies doing business in the United States; this nickname has fallen into disuse since the breakup of Gulf Oil.

1. British Petroleum
2. Gulf Oil
3. Mobil Oil
4. Royal Dutch/Shell Oil
5. Standard Oil of California
6. Standard Oil of New Jersey
7. Texaco

Seven SISTERS (WOMEN'S MAGAZINES)

Top women's magazines in the United States.

1. *Better Homes and Gardens*
2. *Family Circle*
3. *Good Housekeeping*
4. *Ladies' Home Journal*
5. *McCall's*
6. *Redbook*
7. *Woman's Day*

Seven SLEEPERS

A mystical tale appearing in the Qur'an and other ancient texts tells of seven prophetic youths of Ephesus who fled to a cavern in Mount Celion in Rome during the persecution of Decius. There they slept for hundreds of years. It was believed that prophesies were made based on the motions of the Seven as they turned in their sleep.

1. Constantine
2. Dionysius
3. John
4. Maximian
5. Malchus

6. Martinian
7. Serapion

SOPHIA'S SEVEN DAUGHTERS
See Seven Liberal Arts.

Seven SORROWS OF MARY
From the traditional doctrines of the Roman Catholic church. See also Seven Joys of Mary.

1. Prophesy of Simeon
2. Flight into Egypt
3. Three Day's Disappearance of the Child Jesus
4. Betrayal of Christ
5. Crucifixion
6. Descent from the Cross
7. Entombment

Seven STATIONS OF THE JOURNEY TOWARD GOD (SUFISM)
From Sufism, a mystical sect of Islam.

1. Repentance
2. Abstinence
3. Renunciation
4. Poverty
5. Patience
6. Trust in God
7. Acquiescence to the Will of God

Seven SUMMITS
Includes the highest peak on each continent. The goal of some mountain climbers is to climb these. Each entry is followed by its number of feet above sea level.

1. Mount Everest (Asia): 29,028
2. Mount Aconcagua (South America): 22,834
3. Mount McKinley (North America): 20,320
4. Mount Kilimanjaro (Africa): 19,340
5. Mount Elbrus (Europe): 18,510
6. Mount Vinson Massif (Antarctica): 16,864
7. Mount Kosciusko (Australia): 7,310

Seven against THEBES

Greek mythology tells of seven Argive heroes who fought against Thebes.

1. Adrastus: king of Argos
2. Amphiaraus: seer
3. Capaneus
4. Hippomedon
5. Parthenopaeus
6. Polynices: deposed king of Thebes
7. Tydeus: son-in-law of Adrastus

Seven Basic THEMES

A saying among the writing community holds that there are only seven different themes.

1. Love
2. Hate
3. Loneliness
4. Happiness
5. Sadness
6. Jealousy
7. Revenge

Seven TINCTURES OF HERALDRY

Sometimes called the Seven Smalts, these seven hues are the most standard colors found on hereditary coats of arms. However, in precise heraldic terms, there are only five stan-

dard colors. Gold (yellow) and silver (white or gray) are called not colors but metals. One also encounters, rarely, tenné (orange), brown, and other tinctures. The term "proper" is used to describe an object illustrated with its natural coloring. The abbreviation and English name for each follows.

1. or/O./gold (shown as yellow)
2. argent/A. (Ar.)/silver (shown as white or gray)
3. azure/B. (Az.)/blue
4. gules/G./red
5. sable/S./black
6. vert/V./green
7. purpure/P./purple

Seven TITANS

From Greek mythology; these are the children of Uranus (heaven) and Gaia (earth). While the Seven Titans figure in most versions, the Greek poet Hesiod (fl. 800 B.C.E.) listed Twelve Titans: six male (Cocus, Cronos, Crius, Hyperion, Iapetus, and Oceanus) and six female (Mnemosyne, Phoebe, Rhea, Tethys, Thea, and Themis).

1. Briareus
2. Coeus
3. Hyperion
4. Iapetus (Japetus)
5. Oceanus
6. Saturn (Cronos)
7. Titan

Seven TRUMPETS

From the New Testament, Revelation 8:2–11:19. A sign occurs at the sounding of each trumpet. See also Seven Sevens of the Book of Revelation.

1. Hail and Fire
2. Sea Becomes Blood
3. Star Falls out of Heaven

4. Darkening the Day
5. Locusts with Scorpion Stings
6. Death of the Third Part of Men
7. Elders Fall and Worship God

Seven Principles of UNITARIAN UNIVERSALISM

Unitarian Universalism is a small but rich noncreedal religious tradition formed out of Protestant Unitarianism in Europe and Universalism in the United States. An organization known as the Seventh Principle Project works toward environmental goals. The statement of principles says that Unitarian Universalists covenant together to affirm and promote the following.

1. The inherent worth and dignity of every person
2. Justice, equity, and compassion in human relations
3. Acceptance of one another and encouragement to spiritual growth in our congregations
4. A free and responsible search for truth and meaning
5. The right to conscience and the use of the democratic process within our congregations and in society at large
6. The goal of world community with peace, liberty, and justice for all
7. Respect for the interdependent web of all existence, of which we are a part.

Seven VIALS

From the New Testament, Revelation 15:1–16:21. Each vial or bowl contains a plague, making Seven Plagues. See also Seven Sevens of the Book of Revelation.

1. Upon the Earth: noisome sores upon men which had the mark of the beast
2. Upon the Sea: The sea became blood, every living soul died in the sea
3. Upon Rivers and Fountains: They became blood
4. Upon the Sun: Blasphemers were scorched
5. Upon the Empire of the Antichrist: His kingdom was full of darkness
6. Upon the River Euphrates: The river dried up
7. Into the Air: destruction of the political and economic Babylon

Seven VICES
See Seven Deadly Sins.

Seven VIRTUES
The Seven Virtues occur in many forms. Here are two versions. The Roman Catholic list combines the Three Graces *and the* Four Virtues, *while the second list derives from a combination of different biblical sources.*

Roman Catholic

1. Faith
2. Hope
3. Charity (Love)
4. Justice
5. Temperance
6. Prudence
7. Fortitude

General Christian

1. Humility
2. Prudence
3. Temperance
4. Fortitude
5. Justice
6. Awe
7. Mercy

Seven VOWELS
The Greek alphabet, containing seven vowels, was often used in ancient times as a model of the perfection of the number seven. Each is followed by the corresponding Greek character and planet.

1. Alpha/Aα/Moon

2. Epsilon/Eϵ/Mercury
3. Eta/Hη/Venus
4. Iota/Iι/Sun
5. Omicron/Oo/Mars
6. Upsilon/Υυ/Jupiter
7. Omega/Ωω/Saturn

WATERGATE SEVEN
These seven men were arrested for breaking into the Democratic campaign headquarters in the Watergate Building in Washington, D.C., in 1972. Their illegal activities were overseen by members of the Republican party and their discovery led to the resignation of President Richard Nixon in 1974.

1. Bernard L. Baker
2. Virgilio R. Gonzales
3. E. Howard Hunt, Jr.
4. G. Gordon Liddy
5. James W. McCord
6. Eugenio R. Martinez
7. Frank A. Sturgis

Seven WISE MEN OF GREECE
Also known as the Seven Sages. Sometimes Anacharsis of Scythia is included in place of Chilo of Sparta. Each is followed by his respective motto.

1. Solon of Athens: Know thyself.
2. Pittacus of Mitylene: Seize Time by the forelock.
3. Thales of Miletus: Who hateth suretyship is sure.
4. Chilo of Sparta: Consider the end.
5. Bias of Priene: Most men are bad.
6. Cleobulus of Lindus: The golden mean; or, Avoid extremes.
7. Periander of Corinth: Nothing is impossible to industry.

Seven WONDERS OF THE WORLD

The greatest tourist attractions of the last two thousand years. The earliest reference to the Seven Wonders of the World occurred in the fifth century B.C.E. in the writings of the historian Herodotus. Callimachus of Cyrene (305–240 B.C.E.), chief librarian of Alexandria, wrote A Collection of Wonders around the World, *but the work was destroyed along with the library, and the contents of the collection are unknown. The present list was created in the Middle Ages, long after many of the Seven Wonders had ceased to exist. Nevertheless, these Seven Wonders represent some of the greatest achievements in the history of architecture and sculpture the world has ever seen. (The Walls of Babylon is sometimes included in place of the Pharos of Alexandria.)*

ANCIENT

1. The Great Pyramid of Khufu (Cheops) at Giza, greater Cairo, Egypt. Usually the entire group of Egyptian pyramids is listed, but the Great Pyramid is what places the pyramids among the Seven Ancient Wonders of the World. Built as his own tomb by Egyptian pharaoh Khufu around 2560 B.C.E., the Great Pyramid is the only one of the Seven Wonders still standing. Constructed of over two million limestone blocks, each weighing several tons, the pyramid stands 482 feet high and covers 13 acres. Each side, aligned to one of the *Four Directions*, is 756 feet long. An entrance in the north wall leads to the burial chamber. Construction of the Great Pyramid took about twenty years.

2. The Hanging Gardens of Babylon, built by king Nebuchadnezzar II (reigned 605–562 B.C.E.) on the banks of the Euphrates River south of Baghdad, Iraq. It is believed that Nebuchadnezzar built the gardens as a gift to his wife Amytis to emulate the mountainous surroundings of Media, whence she came. Construction has also been credited to legendary queen Semiramis of Assyria. The gardens were composed of massive stepped terraces supported on stone columns and connected by stairways. Mounds of earth were piled on the terraces and thickly planted with trees, flowers, and plants. Irrigation was provided by streams of water drawn upward by pumping machines.

3. The Statue of Zeus at Olympia, on the western coast of Greece about 93 miles from Athens, built by renowned Greek sculptor Phidias

around 440 B.C.E. An enormous statue representing the patron of the Olympic games, it was built as an addition to the Temple of Zeus at that site. The statue showed Zeus seated in a throne, his head almost touching the ceiling. The throne was decorated with sphinxes and winged figures of Victory. Zeus's head sported a wreath of olive leaves, and in his right hand he held a figure of Victory made from ivory and gold. His left hand held a scepter on which perched an eagle. Zeus's robe and sandals were gold, and the entire statue was encrusted with precious stones, ebony, and ivory.

4. The Temple of Artemis at Ephesus, near Selcuk, about 30 miles south of Izmir in Turkey. Believed by some to be the most beautiful structure on earth, the temple was built about 550 B.C.E. in honor of the Greek goddess of the hunt. Sponsored by Croesus, the king of Lydia, and designed by the Greek architect Chersiphron, it was destroyed in 401 by Saint John Chrysostom. With a rectangular foundation, the marble building had a decorated facade overlooking a large courtyard. More than 100 columns 60 feet high supported a terrace measuring 260 by 430 feet. Within the temple, fine paintings and bronze sculptures decorated the walls.

5. The Mausoleum at Halicarnassus, now Bodrum, on the Aegean Sea in southwest Turkey, a gigantic tomb and monument to Mausolus of Caria. Mausolus was a Persian satrap (territorial governor) whose rule lasted from 377 to 353 B.C.E. Conceived and built by his wife and sister Artemisia, the tomb was completed around 350 B.C.E. It was destroyed in 1494 by the Knights of Saint John of Malta, who dismantled it and used the blocks to fortify a crusader castle. The Mausoleum was 140 feet high and had a rectangular foundation measuring 100 by 120 feet. A stepped podium 60 feet high, with sides decorated with statues, led to the burial chamber. The sarcophagus, surrounded by Ionic columns, was made of white alabaster decorated in gold. Above it, a colonnade supported a pyramid roof decorated with statues. At the top of the tomb was a giant statue of a chariot pulled by four horses. The entire structure was made of polished stone and marble.

6. The Colossus of Rhodes, a giant bronze statue of the Greek sun god Helios erected by the citizens of Rhodes near the harbor of Mandraki. Completed in 282 B.C.E., the statue took twelve years to construct.

Around 226 B.C.E., an earthquake nearly destroyed it, making it the shortest lived of the Seven wonders; it broke at the knees and toppled. Reconstruction was not undertaken, in accord with the advice of an oracle. The Colossus remained where it had fallen until 654, when it was dismantled by Arab invaders and sold. Usually pictured as straddling Mandraki Harbor, the statue most probably stood on one side or the other. It was a 110-foot sculpture of Helios standing upright, set on a white marble base. Cast in bronze, it was made of many pieces and assembled and fortified with an iron and stone framework. Constructed in part to celebrate the unity of three peaceful city-states on the Isle of Rhodes, the statue symbolized peace and freedom and inspired French sculptor Auguste Bartholdi in his design of the Statue of Liberty.

7. The Pharos of Alexandria, a lighthouse on the ancient island of Pharos, now a promontory within the city of Alexandria. Named for Alexander the Great, Alexandria was once the capital of Egypt. The city's harbor was treacherous, and a lighthouse was necessary to ensure the safety of ships entering and leaving the port. Begun by Ptolemy I (Soter) (c. 367–283 B.C.E.) and completed by his son Ptolemy II (Philadelphus) (309–264 B.C.E.), construction of the lighthouse continued over the course of many years. Earthquakes in 956, 1303, and 1323 so damaged the structure that in 1480 Egyptian sultan Qaitbay took stone and marble from the lighthouse to build a fort for Alexandria's defense. For centuries, the Pharos was the tallest building on earth. Standing about 40 stories high and built of white marble, it was composed of three sections. The lowest section, 240 feet high, was square with a cylindrical core. The octagonal middle section rose an additional 110 feet. The circular top section, 24 feet high, housed a giant mirror that could reflect light over 42 miles away. During the day the mirror reflected sunlight, and at night the light from a fire was used. Legend has it that light from the mirror was also used to detect and burn enemy ships.

MEDIEVAL

During the Middle Ages many temples and monuments were substituted for the Ancient Wonders that no longer existed. Along with the wonders described here, many other magnificent constructions have appeared on the list, including the Colosseum of Rome

(Italy), Stonehenge (England), the Temple of Tenochtitlan (Mexico), the Catacombs of Alexandria (Egypt), the Porcelain Tower of Nanking (China), the Mosque of Saint Sophia (Turkey), the Sistine Chapel (the Vatican), and Machu Picchu (Peru).

1. The Temple of Abu Simbel, south of Aswan, Egypt. Built in honor of the three deities Ra-Harakhte, Ptah, and Amun-Ra, the temple was constructed by order of the pharaoh Ramses II (1292–1225 B.C.E.) using forced labor. The temple still stands, although it is partially damaged. The facade, 108 feet high and 125 feet wide, is guarded by four colossal statues of the seated pharaoh, each 65 feet in height. The inner sanctum houses statues of the three deities and the pharaoh. In the 1960s, the Temple of Abu Simbel was transported to higher ground to save it from rising water levels behind Aswan High Dam.

2. The Temple of Angkor Wat, in Angkor Thom, northwestern Kampuchea (Cambodia). Dedicated to the Hindu god Vishnu by the Khmer king Suryavarman II (reigned 1131–50), the temple is one of the most famous monuments in Asia. It covers an area of about two hundred acres; its five towers are believed to represent the five peaks of Mount Meru, center of the Hindu (and Buddhist) universe, and it features the longest continuous bas-relief in the world. Angkor Wat is presently a Buddhist temple; its image appears on the national flag of Kampuchea.

3. The Giant Monoliths of Rapa Nui, also known as Easter Island, about two thousand miles from the coast of Chile. Rapa Nui was first populated by Polynesians about 400 C.E., but the precise history of the sculptures is not certain. Over six hundred giant stone statues dot the shoreline and interior of the island, the largest weighing 70 tons and rising over 40 feet. These monoliths, correctly called Moai, were carved from volcanic rock in the interior of the island, and many were transported to the coasts. Over the centuries, all the Moai standing along the coast were torn down by the islanders themselves, but recent efforts have raised many of the statues.

4. The Gate of All Nations and the Throne Hall of Persepolis, 37 miles northeast of Shiraz, Iran. The present Persian name of the city is Takht-e-Jamshid, but the ancient name of the city was Parsa, known in Greek as Persepolis. The city once boasted many large constructions, but the

most glorious were the Gate of All Nations and the Throne Hall commissioned by Xerxes I, king of Persia, around 470 B.C.E. Persepolis and the greater part of its monuments were destroyed by Alexander in 330 B.C.E., but over the last century archaeological investigations have uncovered much of what remains. The Gate of All Nations was built at the end of two monumental staircases with symbols of Ahura Mazda and carvings representing the peoples of the world. The gate leads to the Throne Hall, known as the Hundred-column Hall for its precise columnar architecture.

5. The Taj Mahal, in the city of Agra, about 125 miles south of New Delhi, India. The most beautiful taj (mausoleum) on earth, built from 1630 to 1656. Emperor Shah Jehan, of the Mogul dynasty, ordered it built in honor of his wife, Mumtaz Mahal, who died giving birth to her fourteenth child. The complex consists of a main gateway, a garden, a mosque, a resthouse, and the actual mausoleum or tomb. Four domed minarets, rising 132 feet, stand at the corners of the structure surrounding a large central dome. The tomb is encased in white marble and red sandstone, adorned with impressive sculpture, and inlaid with precious gems and metals.

6. The Leaning Tower of Pisa, Italy. Famous for its slow, continuing tilt, this bell tower in the city of Pisa was constructed over the period 1174–1350. Currently about fifteen inches out of line, the tower leans about one-twentieth of an inch every year. Rising 180 feet above the street, the tower's walls are thirteen feet thick at its base. Each floor has 30 columns, and there are three hundred steps to the top of the tower. Efforts to restore it and prevent it from eventually collapsing have been undertaken, but no solution has yet been found.

7. The Great Wall of China started as a series of individual earthworks erected by the rulers of different independent states to prevent Mongols from invading from the north. The sections were not connected until the Ch'in (Qin) Dynasty, about 220 B.C.E. Ch'in Shih-huang-ti (Qin Shihuangdi), the first emperor of the dynasty, used forced labor to build the wall, and construction continued for centuries, each dynasty adding more height, depth, and breadth. During the Ming dynasty (1368–1644), watchtowers and cannons were added. The wall is over fifteen hundred miles long and roughly follows the southern border of the Mongolian

plain. Its average height is 25 feet and its average width is 12 feet. It is the only artificial construction on earth that can be seen from space.

MODERN

In the 1950s, at the height of the Cold War, these technological marvels were called the "new" Seven Wonders of the World. Since that time, many innovations have surpassed even these wonders.

1. Empire State Building (New York City): tallest building, 102 floors
2. Golden Gate Bridge (San Francisco): longest suspension bridge, 4,200 feet
3. Hoover Dam (Nevada/Arizona): largest dam, 726 feet high, 1,244 feet wide
4. Jodrell Bank Telescope (England): biggest telescope, 250 feet
5. *Nautilus* (United States): first atomic submarine
6. Panama Canal (Panama): longest canal, 50 miles
7. *Sputnik I* (Soviet Union): first artificial satellite

NATURAL

Apart from temples, monuments, and technological marvels, there are the Seven Wonders of the Natural World.

1. Grand Canyon (Arizona): 1 mile deep, 18 miles wide, 217 miles long
2. Amazon River (Brazil): highest-volume river, 3,900 miles long, 100 miles wide at its mouth
3. Himalayas (India/Asia): highest mountain range, average elevation 20,000 feet
4. Niagara Falls (United States/Canada): highest-volume waterfall, 212,000 cubit feet/second
5. Ayres Rock (Australia): giant desert rock, 6 miles long, 1,000 feet high
6. Sahara Desert (North Africa): largest desert, 3.5 million square miles
7. Great Barrier Reef (Australian coast): largest coral reef, 1,250 miles long

Seven WORKS OF MERCY
See Seven Corporal Works of Mercy.

Seven Levels of the ZIGGURAT
In Assyrian, ziquratu means "summit." Ziggurats were stepped pyramids with four corners oriented to the Four Directions. *The structures typically had seven terraces dedicated to seven deities, although some ziggurats had only three terraces. These mystical structures represented the union of heaven and earth, with each level representing one step closer to heaven. Levels are listed here from least important (bottom) to most important. Each deity is followed by its respective color.*

1. Saturn (black)
2. Jupiter (orange)
3. Mars (red)
4. Sun (gold)
5. Venus (yellow)
6. Mercury (blue)
7. Moon (silver)

EIGHTS

The ancient Greeks associated Eight with Rhea, mother of the universe, and saw Eight as a symbol of wisdom. To many ancient mystics, Eight represented the wheel of the year, symbolized by the *Four Seasons* and the *Four Solar Festivals*. Buddhists followed the *Eightfold Path* leading to enlightenment. Carl Jung labeled Eight the double quaternity, representing completeness, the unity of the spiritual and corporeal.

Significant biblical Eights included the number of people saved from the flood, the position of David as the eighth child among his brothers, and the number of days after birth before circumcision. In Christian belief, the seven days of creation were followed by the Eighth Day (or Octave), a symbol of eternity. Christian baptismal fonts were thus constructed with an octagonal shape representing the eternal bliss of heaven.

The EIGHT (ART)

Unable to get their work recognized by conservative art galleries, eight artists led by Robert Henri formed The Eight in 1907 and organized their own exhibition in New York City in 1908. Breaking away from the academic establishment, they created the Ashcan School (also known as the New York Realists), focusing on realistic art depicting scenes of everyday urban life—partly in reaction to the impressionistic art of the group known as Ten American Painters.

1. Arthur B. Davies (1862–1928)
2. William J. Glackens (1870–1938)
3. Robert Henri (1865–1929)
4. Ernest Lawson (1873–1939)
5. George Luks (1866–1933)
6. Maurice Pendergast (1859–1924)
7. Everett Shinn (1876–1953)
8. John Sloan (1871–1951)

Big Eight (ACCOUNTING)
See Big Six (Accounting).

Eight BEATITUDES
From Matthew 5:3–12, part of the Sermon on the Mount, these words are believed to have been spoken by Jesus of Nazareth and are some of the most powerful and often quoted words in the Bible. Some reckon the number of beatitudes as nine, for at the end of the sermon Jesus says, "Blessed are ye, when men shall revile you, and persecute you, and shall say all manner of evil against you falsely, for my sake . . . for great is your reward in heaven." (Symbols follow.)

1. Blessed are the poor in spirit, for theirs is the kingdom of heaven. (dove)
2. Blessed are they that mourn, for they shall be comforted. (inverted torch)
3. Blessed are the meek, for they shall inherit the earth. (lamb)
4. Blessed are they which do hunger and thirst after righteousness, for they shall be filled. (scales)
5. Blessed are the merciful, for they shall obtain mercy. (broken sword)
6. Blessed are the pure in heart, for they shall see God. (lily)
7. Blessed are the peacemakers, for they shall be called the children of God. (olive branch)
8. Blessed are they which are persecuted for righteousness' sake, for theirs is the kingdom of heaven. (starred crown)

BIG EIGHT IN FOOTBALL

In college football, these eight universities are known as the Big Eight conference. (Team names follow.)

1. Colorado: Buffaloes
2. Iowa State: Cyclones
3. Kansas: Jayhawks
4. Kansas State: Wildcats
5. Missouri: Tigers
6. Nebraska: Cornhuskers
7. Oklahoma: Sooners
8. Oklahoma State: Cowboys

Eight Shots in BILLIARDS

Pool players strive to master each of these.

1. Break: hitting a full rack of balls
2. Straight shot: hitting the object ball with the cue ball
3. Rail shot: cue ball is touching the rail
4. Off the rail shot: hitting the rail with the cue ball, then hitting the object ball
5. Bank shot: hitting the object ball, which then hits the rail
6. Massé shot: hitting the cue ball high so that it curves
7. Jump shot: hitting the cue ball low so that it jumps
8. Combination shot: hitting with the cue ball another ball and then the object ball (also called Billiard shot)

Eight CANONICAL HOURS

At one time Christian calendars divided the year not only into holy days and holy weeks but also into precise segments of time, each with its own prayers and rituals. The early Christian church had only seven canonical hours; Tertia (Terce) was a later addition. Prime, Terce, Sext, and Nones were the Four Hours of the Day, while Vespers, Complin, Matins, and Lauds were the Four Watches of the Night.

1. Matins (midnight)
2. Lauds (early morning: dawn or "cockcrow")
3. Prima or Prime (6 A.M.)
4. Tertia or Terce (9 A.M.)
5. Sexts or Sext (noon)
6. Nona or Nones (3 P.M.)
7. Vespers (evening: between 3 and 6 P.M.)
8. Compline or Complin (after sunset: 7 P.M. or at retiring)

Eight Degrees of CHARITY

Described by Rabbi Moses Ben Maimonides in 1135, this progression of eight forms or levels of charity still serves as a guide to enlightened giving.

1. Give with reluctance and regret.
2. Give cheerfully but not proportionally to the distress of the sufferer.
3. Give cheerfully and proportionately but not until asked.
4. Give cheerfully, proportionally, and unasked, but put it directly into the sufferer's hand.
5. Give so that the sufferer knows you but you don't know them.
6. Give so that you know the sufferer but they don't know you.
7. Give so that both you and they are unknown to each other.
8. Prevent poverty by teaching them a trade or getting them a job.

CHICAGO EIGHT

See Chicago Seven.

Eight CHURCH MODES

Thirteenth-century Western music used these eight modes or scales to construct music. They were known as church modes because at that time, essentially, all music was religious music. In the twentieth century, this system was more or less abandoned and replaced by the Seven Modes. *See also* Six Rhythmic Modes.

	Tonic	Dominant	Range
1. Dorian	D	A	D–D
2. Hypodorian	D	F	A–A
3. Phrygian	E	C	E–E
4. Hypophrygian	E	A	B–B
5. Lydian	F	C	F–F
6. Hypolydian	F	A	C–C
7. Mixolydian	G	D	G–G
8. Hypomixolydian	G	C	D–D

In 1547, four more were added to the system.

	Tonic	Dominant	Range
9. Aeolian	A	E	A–A
10. Hypoaeolian	A	C	C–C
11. Ionian	C	G	C–C
12. Hypoionian	C	E	G–G

Again, in the 1900s, more were added.

	Tonic	Dominant	Range
13. Locrian	B	F	B–B
14. Hypolocrian	B	D	F–F

Eight Gods of the DIRECTIONS
From Hindu mythology. (Their kingdoms follow in parentheses.)

1. Indra: east (heaven)
2. Varuna: west (waters)
3. Kubera: north (wealth)
4. Yama: south (death)
5. Soma: northeast (moon)
6. Vayu: northwest (air)
7. Agni: southeast (fire)
8. Surya: southwest (sun)

Eight DOCTORS

The popular television show Doctor Who *was made in England from 1963 to 1990. The gimmick was that since the Doctor is an alien, he can regenerate. Seven different actors played him during the course of the series, and in 1996 an eighth actor appeared in a special television movie that continued where the series left off.*

1. William Hartnell, 1963–66
2. Patrick Troughton, 1966–69
3. Jon Pertwee, 1969–74
4. Tom Baker, 1974–80
5. Peter Davison, 1981–84
6. Colin Baker, 1984–87
7. Sylvester McCoy, 1987–90
8. Paul McGann, 1996

GANG OF EIGHT

See Moscow Eight.

Eight HOLY DAYS OF PAGANS

The Four Sabbaths of Pagans *and the* Four Solar Festivals *constitute the Eight Holy Days of Pagans. Neo-Paganism, called Wicca, Wise-craft, or Witchcraft by some participants, has been reconstituted from pre-Christian religions of Europe, the British Isles, and other places around the world. Neo-Pagans generally celebrate these days, but the names, dates, and forms of the events vary widely among celebrants.*

	Name	*Approximate Date(s)*	*Occasion*	*Celebration of*
1.	Samhain	October 31	Halloween	death
2.	Yule	December 20–23	Winter Solstice	hibernation
3.	Imbolc	February 2	Candlemas	purification
4.	Ostara	March 20–23	Spring Equinox	rejuvenation
5.	Beltane	April 30	May Eve	fertility
6.	Litha	June 20–23	Summer Solstice	passion and joy
7.	Lughnassad	August 1	August Eve	increase
8.	Mabon	September 20–23	Autumnal Equinox	abundance

216

Eight Trigrams of the I CHING

From the philosophy of ancient China. For a brief discussion of the origin and use of these, see Four Symbols of the I Ching.

		Trigram	Character	Element	Description	Interpretation
1.	Ch'ien	☰	father	heaven	creative	strong
2.	K'un	☷	mother	earth	receptive	devoted, yielding
3.	Chên	☳	first son	thunder	arousing	inciting movement
4.	K'an	☵	second son	water	abysmal	dangerous
5.	Kên	☶	third son	mountain	keeping still	repose
6.	Sun	☴	first daughter	wind, wood	gentle	penetrating
7.	Li	☲	second daughter	fire	clinging	light giving
8.	Tui	☱	third daughter	lake	joyous	joyful

Eight IMMORTALS

These eight mystical figures were legendary Chinese sages who attained the goal of immortality. They are often represented in Chinese art by their symbols.

	Name	Symbol	Kingdom or Patronage
1.	Lü Tung-Pin	sword	supernatural powers
2.	Chung-Li Ch'üan	fan	resurrection
3.	Lan Ts'ai-Ho	flower basket	flowers
4.	Ho Hsien-Ku	lotus	the house
5.	Han Hsiang-Tzu	flute	the power of growing
6.	Li T'ieh-Kuai	gourd	beggars
7.	Ts'ao Kuo-Chiu	castanets	theatrical art
8.	Chang Kuo-Lao	tube drum	magic power

Eight IS ENOUGH
This television series aired on ABC during 1977–81. It starred Dick Van Patten, as Tom Bradford, and his eight children. (Actors follow in parentheses.)

1. David (Grant Goodeve)
2. Mary (Lani O'Grady)
3. Joannie (Lauri Walters)
4. Susan (Susan Richardson)
5. Nancy (Dianne Kay)
6. Tommy (Willie Aames)
7. Elizabeth (Connie Newton)
8. Nicholas (Adam Rich)

IVY LEAGUE EIGHT
The top U.S. universities in terms of academic standards.

1. Brown University (Providence, R.I.)
2. Columbia University (New York, N.Y.)
3. Cornell University (Ithaca, N.Y.)
4. Dartmouth College (Hanover, N.H.)
5. Harvard University (Cambridge, Mass.)
6. Princeton University (Princeton, N.J.)
7. University of Pennsylvania (Philadelphia, Pa.)
8. Yale University (New Haven, Conn.)

LEAGUE OF EIGHT
Established in Switzerland in the 1300s, the League of Eight served as a model of peaceful coexistence for the kingdoms of Europe. The original Swiss cantons, originally city-states, have now become more or less equivalent to counties.

Three Forest Cantons

1. Uri
2. Schwyz
3. Unterwalden (Nidwalden and Obwalden)

4. Lucerne
5. Zürich
6. Glarus
7. Zug
8. Berne

Eight MARKS OF CADENCY (HERALDRY)

In European heraldry, the science of hereditary coats of arms, a father's coat of arms is generally borne by his sons, with each son adding one small figure or charge to differentiate his coat of arms from his father's. These added figures are known as marks of cadency. There are no standard charges beyond the eighth son; some heralds give the ninth son a double quatrefoil; others give him an anchor and reserve the double quatrefoil for the tenth son. These charges appear frequently on coats of arms, so the appearance of one of these charges does not automatically indicate that those arms are borne by a son of that rank.

1. Label
2. Crescent
3. Mullet
4. Martlet
5. Annulet
6. Fleur-de-Lys
7. Rose
8. Cross Moline

Eight MOONS OF NEPTUNE

Until 1989, Triton and Nereid were the only known moons of Neptune. The six moons discovered during the flight of Voyager 2 *in 1986 are all irregularly shaped. See also* Four Rings of Neptune. *Research into the moons of our solar system is ongoing, so more moons may be discovered in the future. (Diameters in miles follow in parentheses.)*

Inner Moons

1. Naiad (37)
2. Thalassa (50)
3. Despina (90)
4. Galatea (120)

Outer Moons

5. Larissa (110)
6. Proteus (415)
7. Triton (1680)
8. Nereid (211)

MOSCOW EIGHT

Also known as the Gang of Eight, these top-level Kremlin men officially called themselves the State Committee for the State of Emergency. On August 19, 1991, in a failed coup attempt, they placed Soviet premier Mikhail Gorbachev under arrest, announced he was ill and took control of the government. Anatoly Lukyanov, speaker of the parliament, was called "the ninth member" of the junta. Several other high-ranking officials supported the group, including foreign minister Alexander Bessmertnykh, chief of staff Valeri Boldin, and military chief of staff Mikhail Moiseyev. Within two days they had all been arrested or fired. Pugo committed suicide and the rest were finally pardoned.

1. Gennadi Yanayev, vice-president
2. Vladimir Kryuchkov, head of the KGB (secret service)
3. Dmitri Yazov, minister of defense
4. Boris Pugo, minister of the interior
5. Valentin Pavlov, prime minister
6. Oleg Baklanov, first deputy chairman, Soviet Defense Council
7. Vasily Starodubtsev, member of parliament, chairman of the Peasants Union
8. Alexander Tizyakov, president, Association of State Enterprises and Industrial Construction, Transport, and Communications Facilities

Eight OFFICES OF CANONICAL HOURS
See Eight Canonical Hours.

OGDOAD OF HERMOPOLIS

In ancient Egyptian mythology, the Ogdoad, or group of eight deities, ruled before the creation of the world, personifying the primeval forces of chaos. The deities were grouped in pairs, with one male and one female deity in each pair, representing one aspect of the universe before creation. (The female deities' names follow the males'; their kingdoms follow in parentheses.)

1, 2.   Nun, Naunet (primeval waters)
3, 4.   Heh, Hehet (the infinity of space and eternity)
5, 6.   Kek, Keket (the darkness)
7, 8.   Amun, Amaunet (invisibility)

Eight Sizes of OLIVES

These terms were standardized for the olive industry by the California Olive Growers. (Number of olives per pound follows in parentheses.)

1.   Small (128–40)
2.   Medium (106–121)
3.   Large (95–105)
4.   Extra Large (65–88)
5.   Jumbo (51–60)
6.   Colossal (41–50)
7.   Super Colossal (26–40)
8.   Leviathan (1)

Eight PARTS OF SPEECH

The eight major categories of words. Many subcategories also exist, such as transitive verb, pronoun, and expletive. (Examples follow descriptions.)

1. Noun: a thing or object (*tree, cat, justice*)
2. Verb: action word (*drive, fall, put*)
3. Adjective: modifies nouns (*red, tall, warm*)
4. Adverb: modifies verbs (*carefully, cleverly, witlessly*)
5. Article (determiner): points to a noun (*a, the, these, that*)
6. Preposition: describes relationship between things (*beside, near, under*)
7. Conjunction: connects phrases (*and, but, or*)
8. Interjection: exclamation (*Oh! Pshaw!, For pete's sake!*)

Eightfold PATH

The Buddhist way of enlightenment, these eight paths are symbolized by an eight-spoked wheel. The Eightfold Path is Buddhism's basic list of correct moral and spiritual behavior.

1. Right Understanding (or right view)
2. Right Thought (or right aspiration)
3. Right Speech
4. Right Action (or right conduct)
5. Right Livelihood
6. Right Effort
7. Right Mindfulness (or right awareness)
8. Right Concentration (or right rapture, right faith)

Eight PHASES OF THE MOON

The moon goes through this complete cycle every four weeks. The moon's cycle is also frequently expressed in four phases: new moon, first quarter, full moon, and last quarter.

1. New Moon
2. Waxing Crescent
3. First Quarter (Half Moon)
4. Gibbous
5. Full Moon
6. Gibbous
7. Last Quarter (Half Moon)
8. Waning Crescent

Eight POSITIONS (HERALDRY)

In British heraldry, concise terminology is used to describe each object on a given coat of arms. Lions and other four-legged, nonhooved animals appear in these eight basic positions. In addition, the term "reguardant" (head turned to face the viewer) is frequently added to one of these descriptives.

1. Rampant: erect, one hind foot on the ground (ubiquitous)
2. Salient: leaping, two hind feet on the ground (uncommon)
3. Passant: walking, one foreleg raised (very common)
4. Statant: standing, four feet on the ground (occasional)
5. Sejant Erect: seated, both forelegs raised (extremely rare)
6. Sejant: seated, cat-style (very rare)
7. Couchant: crouching (uncommon)
8. Dormant: lying down (uncommon)

Eight PROPHETS OF MONOTHEISM (ISLAM)

One of the basic tenets of Islamic philosophy holds that there is one God. Prophets throughout history who have proclaimed the one true God are seen as part of the Islamic tradition. Besides Mohammed, Muslims recognize these eight.

1. Adam
2. Isa (Jesus)
3. Yahya (John the Baptist)
4. Yusuf (Joseph)
5. Idris (Enoch)
6. Haroon (Aaron)
7. Musa (Moses)
8. Ibrahim (Abraham)

Eight Levels of PSYCHOLOGICAL EXISTENCE

Established by psychologist Clare W. Graves, these eight levels represent eight progressively complex states of psychological existence. His theories were based on his own research and the work of several other psychologists including Abraham Maslow (see Five Levels of Needs). *He first published these in an article in* The Futurist

(1974). Understanding of the eight levels is intended to help people better understand their fellow human beings.

1. Reactive: has no values, is concerned with survival
2. Tribalistic: relies on chiefs and clan support, is superstitious
3. Egocentric: is aggressive, self-centered, angry, flamboyant, and abrasive
4. Absolutistic: is rigid, structured, promotes clearly defined roles, imposes own system upon others
5. Achievist: is a wheeler-dealer, competitive, manipulative, motivated by success
6. Personalistic: is concerned with human dignity and worth and social responsibility
7. Existential: values individual freedom, is inner-directed, tolerant, reasoning
8. Experientialistic: accepts existential dichotomies

Eight Divisions of the RADIO WAVE SPECTRUM

These terms for the eight divisions of the radio wave spectrum were established in 1947 in Atlantic City, New Jersey, at a convention of the International Telecommunications union. VHF and UHF are the two divisions commonly used for television broadcast and reception. (Wave types in parentheses.)

1. VLF: Very Low Frequency (myriametric)
2. LF: Low Frequency (kilometric)
3. MF: Medium Frequency (hectometric)
4. HF: High Frequency (decametric)
5. VHF: Very High Frequency (metric)
6. UHF: Ultra High Frequency (decimetric)
7. SHF: Super High Frequency (centimetric)
8. EHF: Extremely High Frequency (millimetric)

Eight REINDEER

The beloved poem "A Visit from St. Nicholas" by American educator Clement Clarke Moore (1779–1863), popularly known as "The Night before Christmas," is respon-

sible for providing the names of the eight reindeer that pull Santa Claus's magical sleigh. The German names Donner and Blitzen mean "thunder" and "lightning." More recently, a red-nosed reindeer named Rudolf entered popular culture (1944).

1. Dasher
2. Dancer
3. Prancer
4. Vixen
5. Comet
6. Cupid
7. Donner
8. Blitzen

Eight VOICES
See Four Voices.

Eight WINDS
See Four Winds.

Eight Steps to Attainment in YOGA
The eastern philosophy involved in the practice of yoga divides into two forms. Hatha yoga consists of the Fourfold Path, here shown as the first four steps. The complete group of steps represents the eight steps of raja yoga.

1. Yama: control of self
2. Niyama: purity of thought
3. Asana: control of the body
4. Pranayama: absorption of vital forces
5. Pratyahara: introspection
6. Dharana: concentration
7. Dhyana: meditation
8. Samadhi: ecstasy

Eight Superior Powers of an Adept in YOGA

1. Anima: to shrink to the size of an atom
2. Mahima: to increase in size
3. Garima: to become very heavy
4. Laghima: to become very light
5. Prapti: to bring anything within reach
6. Prakamya: to realize desire
7. Isitva: to create matter by the power of thought
8. Vasitva: to dominate all objects

Eight Signs of the ZODIAC (ANCIENT INDIA)

These eight signs were the standard zodiacal signs in India, 5,000 years ago.

1. Edu (ram)
2. Yal (harp)
3. Nand (crab)
4. Amma (mother)
5. Tuk (scales)
6. Kani (dart)
7. Kuda (pitcher)
8. Min (fish)

NINES

Nine, consisting of three Threes or a trinity of trinities, was assigned only the most sacred, mystical, and important concepts in ancient cultures of the world. Nine was commonly seen as the product of Three and Three, not as Ten minus One, and thus represented wholeness, completeness, and perfection.

The ancient Greeks saw Nine as combining order (Four) with crisis (Five), thus representing opportunity. Nine was also associated with Hera, goddess of matrimony. According to Pythagoras, Humanity was a full chord (eight notes) and the ninth note was Deity. Those who followed the Pythagorean system called Nine the unsurpassable limit, the point at which the digits begin to repeat.

The belief that cats had nine lives was based on the ancient concept of Nine as a symbol of the infinite. The phrases "dressed to the nines" (to perfection) and "on Cloud Nine" (bliss) derived from the concept of the perfection of Nine.

In astrology, a novile (two planets at a 40-degree angle, equaling one-ninth of a circle) was believed to signify a charismatic or transcendental force leading to an increase in positive spiritual energy, often called karma. Noviles also related to coming of age, marriage, and other important ceremonies.

In mathematics, Nine was christened the magic number due to the unusual patterns formed in calculations involving nines. A brief survey of the Nine column of a multiplication table will reveal just one of these aspects. The nine numbers (one of each digit except zero) may also be arranged in a square with three across and three down in which every row, column, and diagonal adds up to fifteen; the whole figure was considered by some a magic square with the power of a talisman.

Nine AGANIPPIDES
See Nine Muses.

Nine ALIGNMENTS (DUNGEONS AND DRAGONS)
From the popular suite of role-playing adventure games known as Dungeons and Dragons. Each player creates a character to portray during the game. The character's alignment, which governs that character's behavior throughout the game, is decided before the game begins. The alignment is described according to two designations, Law (lawful, neutral, or chaotic) and Principle (good, neutral, or evil). There are nine possible combinations of these factors.

1. Lawful Good (LG)
2. Neutral Good (NG)
3. Chaotic Good (CG)
4. Lawful Neutral (LN)
5. True Neutral (N)
6. Chaotic Neutral (CN)
7. Lawful Evil (LE)
8. Neutral Evil (NE)
9. Chaotic Evil (CE)

Nine AONIDES
See Nine Muses.

Nine ARTS
The nine basic areas of the creative arts. Note that these do not match the nine arts overseen by the Nine Muses.

Triad of Spatial Arts

1. Architecture
2. Sculpture
3. Painting

Triad of Temporal Arts

4. Musicry (music composition)
5. Story
6. Poetry

Triad of Dynamic Arts

7. Music (music performance)
8. Theatre
9. Dance

Nine Festivals of BAHA'I

The Baha'i Faith celebrates nine Holy Days commemorating events in the lives of its founder, Baha'u'llah, and his predecessor, the Bab. Work ceases on these Holy Days.

1. Feast of Naw-Ruz: Baha'i New Year ("new day") (March 21)
2. First Day of Ridvan: beginning, Feast of Ridvan (April 21)
3. Ninth Day of Ridvan: commemorating when Baha'u'llah first declared his mission, 1863 (April 29)
4. Twelfth Day of Ridvan: (May 2)
5. Declaration of the Bab: the Bab declared his mission, 1844 (May 23)
6. Ascension of Baha'u'llah: Baha'u'llah died, 1892 (May 29)
7. Martyrdom of the Bab: the Bab executed, 1850 (July 9)
8. Birth of the Bab: the Bab born in Iran, 1819 (October 20)
9. Birth of Baha'u'llah: Baha'u'llah born in Iran, 1817 (November 12)

Nine BEATITUDES
See Eight Beatitudes.

Nine CASTALIDES
See Nine Muses.

Nine CHOIRS OF ANGELS
Dionysius the Pseudo-Areopagite (fl. 500 C.E.) authored The Celestial Hierarchy, *a mystical work in which the nine orders of angels were first described. Pope Gregory the Great (Gregory I, 590–604) also described nine distinct levels of angels, but his version differed somewhat from that of Dionysius. Italian poet Dante Alighieri (1265–1321) also wrote works that touched on the hierarchy of angels and produced yet another version of this list.*

According to Dionysius the Pseudo-Areopagite	According to Gregory I	According to Dante
First Hierarchy		
1. Seraphim	Seraphim	Seraphim
2. Cherubim	Cherubim	Cherubim
3. Thrones	Thrones	Powers
Second Hierarchy		
4. Dominations (Dominions)	Dominions	Principalities
5. Virtues	Principalities	Virtues
6. Powers	Powers	Dominions
Third Hierarchy		
7. Principalities	Virtues	Thrones
8. Archangels	Archangels	Archangels
9. Angels	Angels	Angels

Nine CIRCLES OF HELL
From the Divine Comedy, *by Italian poet Dante Alighieri (1265–1321). He divided Hell into four levels. Upper Hell, for those who have committed the Sins of the Leopard, houses the first five circles. The First Nether Hell, for the Sins of the Lion,*

houses the sixth and seventh circles. The Second Nether Hell, for the Sins of the Wolf, houses the eighth circle, wherein are contained panderers and seducers, flatterers, sorcerers, thieves, and other such sinners. The ninth circle is contained in the Third Nether Hell, especially reserved for various kinds of traitors. See also Seven Cornices of Purgatory, Ten Heavens of Paradise.

1. The Unbaptized and Virtuous Pagans (Limbo)
2. The Lustful
3. Gluttons
4. Hoarders and Spendthrifts
5. The Wrathful
6. Heretics
7. The Violent
8. Fraud Simple (Malbowges)
9. Fraud Complex (Cocytus)

Nine CITHERIDES
See Nine Muses.

Nine CRUSADES
In general, the crusades were military expeditions launched by various Western Christians in an attempt to convert or massacre unbelievers in the East. Each crusade had specific aims, and not all were directed against Eastern peoples. The Children's Crusade, or Slaughter of the Innocents, in which nearly 50,000 children perished, is called the Fifth Crusade by some but is not included by others; the numbering of the subsequent crusades varies accordingly. Some consider the first three or four crusades to be the only true crusades.

1. First Crusade (1096–99) "The People's Crusade"
2. Second Crusade (1147–49) "The Monks' Crusade"
3. Third Crusade (1189–92) "The Kings' Crusade"
4. Fourth Crusade (1202–04) "The Knights' Crusade"
5. Children's Crusade (1212) "The Children's Crusade"
6. Fifth Crusade (1217–19)

7. Sixth Crusade (1228–29) "The Pope's Crusade"
8. Seventh Crusade (1248–49)
9. Eighth Crusade (1270)

ENNEAD OF THE ETRUSCANS
Nine gods worshiped in ancient times by the inhabitants of Etruria (now Tuscany, Italy).

Three Chief Deities

1. Juno
2. Minerva
3. Tinia

Six Lesser Deities

4. Vulcan
5. Mars
6. Saturn
7. Hercules
8. Sumamus
9. Vedius

ENNEAD OF HELIOPOLIS
These nine deities, or Pesedjet, were the nine chief gods and goddesses of the ancient Egyptian pantheon.

1. Atum or Ra-Atum-Khepra
2, 3. Shu, Tefnut; children of Atum
4, 5. Geb, Nut; children of Shu and Tefnut
6, 7. Osiris, Isis; brother and sister
8. Set or Seth, Sutekh; brother and husband of Nephthys
9. Nephthys; daughter of Geb and Nut

ENNEAD OF THE SABINES

A group of nine deities worshiped by the Sabines, an ancient pre-Roman sect.

1. Hercules
2. Romulus
3. Esculapius
4. Bacchus
5. Aeneas
6. Vesta
7. Santa
8. Fortuna
9. Fides

ENNEAGRAM

The Enneagram is believed to derive from a 2,500-year-old system of Eastern mysticism. It has lately become popular in many areas of self-therapy and self-investigation. Basically, the Enneagram shows nine different human personality types and the correlations between each type. Knowledge of the Enneagram is said to help improve one's interpersonal relationships. The ideal type of each follows the description.

1. The Perfectionist: critical of self and others, astute, feels ethically superior, uses "should" a lot (ruler)
2. The Giver: demands approval, seeks to be loved and appreciated, is caring and supportive, can be manipulative (goddess)
3. The Performer: seeks to be loved for performance and achievement, obsessed with status, competitive, can be effective leader or competent promoter (magician)
4. The Romantic: attracted to ideals, able to help other people through their pain, artistic and sensitive, creative and passionate (artist)
5. The Observer: intellectual, maintains emotional distance from others, protects privacy, feels drained by other people's needs, can be excellent decisionmaker (mystic, philosopher)
6. The Trooper: identifies with the underdog, antiauthoritarian, self-sacrificing, can be afraid to take action because exposure leads to attack, can be a loyal soldier or a great team player (hero)

7. The Epicure: the eternal youth, superficial and adventurous, has trouble with commitment, wants to stay emotionally high, can be a good synthesizer or theoretician (magical child)

8. The Boss: protective, combative, loves a fight, respects opponents who stand and fight, can be an excellent leader and a powerful supporter (warrior)

9. The Mediator: ambivalent, sees all points of view, knows other people's needs better than their own, can be an excellent peacemaker, counselor, or negotiator (saint)

Additional Attributes

		Passion	Fixation	Avoidance	Virtue
1.	The Perfectionist	anger	resentment	anger	serenity
2.	The Giver	pride	flattery	needs	humility
3.	The Performer	deceit	vanity	failure	honesty
4.	The Romantic	envy	melancholy	feeling lost	balance
5.	The Observer	greed	stinginess	emptiness	detachment
6.	The Trooper	fear	cowardice	deviance	courage
7.	The Epicure	gluttony	planning	pain	sobriety
8.	The Boss	excess	vengeance	weakness	innocence
9.	The Mediator	laziness	indolence	conflict	action

Sacred Idea	Idealization	Talking Style	Domain
perfection	I am righteous	sermon	sentimental
freedom	I am helpful	advice	security
hope	I am successful	propaganda	fantasy
originality	I am elite	lament	intellectual
omniscience	I know	treatise	social
faith	I am loyal	setting limits	work and rest
work	I am okay	story	hierarchical
truth	I am competent	guilt trip	moral
love, charity	I am comfortable	saga	spiritual

GANG OF NINE

These nine major manufacturers of IBM-clone computers joined together in 1988 in order to more effectively compete against IBM. The gang remained cohesive for less than one year, but it did contribute positively to the burgeoning home computer industry. The largest company, Compaq, was the leader.

1. AST Research
2. Compaq Computer Corporation
3. Epson America
4. Hewlett-Packard
5. NEC Information Technology
6. Olivetti and Company
7. Tandy Corporation
8. Wyse Technology
9. Zenith Data Systems

Nine Great LIVES

This work by Greek historian Plutarch (c. 46–c. 120), more commonly known as Plutarch's Lives, *examines the biographies of five remarkable Greeks and four notable Romans. This work differed from most biographies of Plutarch's day in that he included critical chapters drawing parallels between Alcibiades and Coriolanus and between Demosthenes and Cicero. William Shakespeare used some of Plutarch's material for his plays* Julius Caesar *and* Antony and Cleopatra.

1. Themistocles (c. 527–c. 460 B.C.E.), Athenian statesman and general
2. Pericles (d. 429 B.C.E.), Athenian statesman, made Athens a center of culture
3. Aristides (c. 530–c. 468 B.C.E.), Athenian statesman and commander
4. Alcibiades (c. 450–c. 404 B.C.E.), Athenian politician and general
5. Gaius Marcius Coriolanus (fl. 400 B.C.E.), Roman hero at siege of Corioli
6. Demosthenes (c. 385–322 B.C.E.), Athenian statesman, greatest Greek orator
7. Marcus Tullius Cicero (106–43 B.C.E.), Roman orator
8. Gaius Julius Caesar (100–44 B.C.E.), Roman general, statesman
9. Marc Antony (c. 83–30 B.C.E.), Roman soldier, statesman

Nine HIPPOCRENIDES
See Nine Muses.

Nine INTELLIGENCE QUOTIENT LEVELS
This hierarchy of levels of intelligence was formulated by psychologist Lewis M. Ter-
man (1877–1956) of Stanford University. While the labels on Terman's list and
even the concept of the IQ have declined from general use, the list is still a useful guide
to the definitions of these terms as they were used by psychologists in the mid-twentieth
century. (IQ test scores in parentheses.)

1. Genius (140+)
2. Very Superior (120–140)
3. Superior (110–120)
4. Average (90–110)
5. Dull (80–90)
6. Borderline (70–80)
7. Moron (50–70)
8. Imbecile (25–50)
9. Idiot (0–25)

Nine Festivals of JUDAISM
These are the nine greatest holidays of the Hebrew calendar. (Hebrew month and day
and corresponding month follow.)

1. Rosh Hashanah: Day of Remembrance (new year) (Tishri 1) (October)
2. Yom Kippur: Day of Atonement (Tishri 10) (October)
3. Sukkot: Feast of Tabernacles (commemorating wandering in the desert) (Tishri 15) (October)
4. Simhat Torah: Rejoicing of the Law (ninth day of Sukkot) (Tishri 23) (October)
5. Hanukkah: Festival of Lights (Kislev 25) (December)
6. Purim: Victory over Oppression (commemorating events in the Book of Esther) (Adar 14) (March)
7. Pesach: Passover (Nisan 15) (April)

8. Yom Ha'Shoah: Holocaust Remembrance Day (Nisan 27) (May)
9. Shavuot: Torah given to Israelites (Sivan 6–7) (June)

Nine MUSES

In Greek mythology, the Muses were nine beautiful goddesses who represented the nine arts. They were the daughters at Mnemosyne, goddess of memory. (The Nine Arts of today differ somewhat from the nine represented by these Muses.) Many women poets have been referred to as the Tenth Muse, including the Greek poet Sappho (fl. 600 B.C.E.) and Mexican poet Juana Inés de la Cruz (1651–95). See also Three Muses, Five Muses. (Symbols follow in parentheses.)

1. Calliope, Muse of epic poetry (tablet and stylus, scroll)
2. Clio, Muse of history (scroll, open chest of books)
3. Erato, Muse of lyric poetry, love poetry (lyre)
4. Euterpe, Muse of music (flute)
5. Melpomene, Muse of tragedy (mask of tragedy, club, sword)
6. Polyhymnia, Muse of sacred song (posture of meditation)
7. Terpsichore, Muse of dancing, choral song (lyre)
8. Thalia, Muse of comedy (mask of comedy, shepherd's crook)
9. Urania, Muse of astronomy (staff and globe)

NOVENSILES

See Ennead of the Sabines.

Nine OLD MEN

The nickname of the inner circle of top animators at Walt Disney Studios during the golden era of animation (1930s–1960s). The Nine Old Men also worked on designs for Disneyland and Disney World attractions. In addition to the Nine, Disney's circle of animators included Woolie Reitherman, director of The Jungle Book, *and Ub Iwerks, the chief creator of Mickey Mouse. (Famous characters the nine designed and animated follow their names.)*

1. Les Clark
2. Marc Davis: Tinker Bell (in *Peter Pan*)
3. Norm "Fergie" Ferguson: Witch (in *Snow White and the Seven Dwarfs*)
4. Ollie Johnston: *Pinocchio*
5. Milt Kahl: Mowgli (in *The Jungle Book*)
6. Ward Kimball: Jiminy Cricket (in *Pinocchio*)
7. Eric Larson
8. John Lounsbery: elephants (in *The Jungle Book*)
9. Frank Thomas: Bambi

Nine PLANETS

Astronomers currently recognize nine planets circling our sun. In addition, the asteroid belt, lying between Mars and Jupiter, contains over two thousand asteroids, of which the largest is Ceres (diameter 470 miles).

		Distance from Sun (miles)	Equatorial Diameter (miles)	Number of Moons	Number of Major Rings
1.	Mercury	36 million	3,031	0	
2.	Venus	67 million	7,519	0	
3.	Earth	93 million	7,900	1	
4.	Mars	141 million	4,223	2	
5.	Jupiter	483 million	88,700	16	very thin rings
6.	Saturn	886 million	74,980	18	3
7.	Uranus	1.78 billion	32,490	15	9
8.	Neptune	2.79 billion	30,700	8	4
9.	Pluto	3.67 billion	1,400	1	

Nine POINTS OF THE LAW

Success in a lawsuit is based on these nine points. The term Nine Points of Law, which derives from an old English saying, survives in our modern expression "Possession is nine-tenths of the law."

1. A Good deal of money
2. A Good deal of patience

3. A Good cause
4. A Good lawyer
5. A Good counsel
6. Good witnesses
7. A Good jury
8. A Good judge
9. Good luck

Symbology of the Nine PRIMARY NUMBERS

One of the most ancient forms of divination is numerology, or divination by numbers. Generally, a subject's number is determined by adding up the numerical values of the letters of his or her name or date of birth. The digits of the sum are added to each other, and re-added if necessary, until a single digit results. There are endless variations upon the interpretations and meanings assigned to the nine digits; only a few are given here.

Digit	Meaning	Planet	Power	Symbol(s)	Ideal Type
1.	aggression	Sun	creativity	crown, circle	pioneer
2.	balance	Moon	harmony	yin and yang, scales	helpmate
3.	expression	Mars	idealism	palate, scroll	artist
4.	steadiness	Mercury	ritual	pyramid, swastika	mason
5.	adventure	Jupiter	knowledge	keystone, ship	scribe
6.	dependability	Venus	love	lighthouse, rainbow	teacher
7.	mystery	Saturn	spirituality	book	mystic
8.	success	Uranus	fate	the city	gleaner
9.	power	Neptune	humankind	castle, fasces	metaphysician

Nine RINGS OF URANUS

Listed from the outermost to the innermost. See also Three Rings of Saturn, Four Rings of Neptune.

1. Epsilon
2. Delta
3. Gamma
4. Eta
5. Beta
6. Alpha
7. Four
8. Five
9. Six

Nine SPHERES

According to the system of astronomy devised by Egyptian mathematician Ptolemy (fl. 200 C.E.), the celestial bodies rest on these nine nesting spheres, within which Earth occupies the central point. Beyond the ninth sphere came the Primum Mobile and the Empyrean, or Abode of the Deity. See Ten Heavens of Paradise.

1. Sphere of the Moon
2. Sphere of Mercury
3. Sphere of Venus
4. Sphere of the Sun
5. Sphere of Mars
6. Sphere of Jupiter
7. Sphere of Saturn
8. Sphere of the Firmament
9. Sphere of the Crystalline

Nine VALKYRIES

In Norse and Teutonic mythology, the Valkyries were fierce warrior women who fought beside Odin, the chief god. The name Valkyrie means "chooser of the slain." Brünnhilde is perhaps the best-known Valkyrie, as she appears as a prominent character in Richard Wagner's famous opera cycle, the Ring Des Niebelungen, *as well as in numerous parodies of it. See* Three Rhinemaidens, Four Operas of the Ring Cycle.

1. Gerhilde
2. Helmwige
3. Waltraute
4. Schwertleite
5. Ortlinde
6. Grimgerde
7. Rossweisse
8. Siegrune
9. Brünnhilde

Nine WORLD RELIGIONS

The Baha'i Faith was founded by Persian prophet Mirza Husein Ali (1817–92), also called Baha'u'llah, in the latter half of the nineteenth century. It teaches that there are nine great religions in the world, each one having developed out of or been influenced by the previous religions. The Baha'i symbol is a nine-pointed star or nine-petaled lotus representing the nine great religions of the world.

1. Taoism
2. Hinduism
3. Buddhism
4. Zoroastrianism
5. Judaism
6. Christianity
7. Islam
8. Bábi (the precursor of Baha'i)
9. Baha'i

Nine WORTHIES OF THE KING

Nickname given to the nine privy councilors of William III (William of Orange) of England (reigned 1689–1702).

Four Whigs

1. William Cavendish, duke of Devonshire (1640–1707)
2. Charles Sackville, earl of Dorset (1638–1706)

3. James Scott, duke of Monmouth (1649–85)
4. Edward Russell, earl of Orford (1653–1727)

Five Tories

5. Thomas Osborne, marquis of Carmarthen (1631–1712)
6. Henry Herbert, earl of Pembroke (1654–1709)
7. Daniel Finch, earl of Nottingham (1647–1730)
8. John Churchill, duke of Marlborough (1650–1722)
9. Sir John Lowther, viscount Lonsdale (1655–1700)

Nine WORTHIES OF LONDON

The chronicle of these worthies is told by English poet Richard Johnson, well-known creator of the Seven Champions of Christendom.

1. Sir William Walworth, fishmonger, twice Lord Mayor (1374, 1381); defended London Bridge against Kentish peasants (1381).
2. Sir Henry Pritchard; feasted Edward III with five thousand followers (1356)
3. Sir William Sevenoke; built twenty almshouses and a free school (1418)
4. Sir Thomas White, merchant tailor; as Lord Mayor kept citizens loyal to Queen Mary during rebellion of Sir Thomas Wyatt (1554); founded St. John's College, Oxford (1560)
5. Sir John Bonham; commander of the army raised against Turkish ruler Suleiman (1565)
6. Christopher Croker; hero at the siege of Bordeaux
7. Sir John Hawkwood, one of the Black Prince's knights; commander of the detachment that defeated Milan (1392)
8. Sir Hugh Caverley; rid Poland of a monstrous bear
9. Sir Henry Maleverer, called Henry of Cornhill, crusader (early 1400s)

Nine WORTHIES OF THE WORLD

These nine men were identified by English printer William Caxton (c. 1422–91) in his original preface to Le Morte D'Arthur *as the nine greatest men ever to have lived.*

The list, which did not originate with Caxton, was commonly circulated in the Middle Ages.

Three Pagans

1. Hector, legendary prince of Troy
2. Alexander the Great (356–323 B.C.E.), conqueror of the known world
3. Julius Caesar (100–44 B.C.E.), Roman emperor

Three Jews

4. Joshua, legendary conqueror of Canaan
5. David, legendary king of Jerusalem
6. Judas Maccabaeus (d. 160 B.C.E.), defended the Temple against Antiochus

Three Christians

7. Arthur, legendary king of the Britons
8. Charlemagne (768–814), king of the Franks, emperor of the West
9. Godfrey of Bouillon (c. 1061–1100), leader of the First Crusade

TENS

To ancient mystics, Ten, like Nine, represented perfection and completion. Ten was found to be made up of the sum of One, Two, Three, and Four, and thus formed a perfect triangle; as seen, for example, in the standard arrangement of ten bowling pins.

In ancient Mesopotamian belief, Ten represented Adad, god of storm, while for the Sumerians, Ten symbolized Ishkur, god of thunder, lightning, and flood. Astrologers interpreted a decile (two planets at a 36-degree angle, equaling one-tenth of a circle) as a foreteller of special gifts, exceptional mental ability, great technical insight, or success in one's career.

The human body, having ten fingers and ten toes, gave rise to the use of Ten as the base of our counting system. In cabala, a mystical Jewish philosophy of the Middle Ages, the Ten Sephiroth (also called the numbers or the counting) are said to be emanations of God, representing the whole of creation. The presence of the Ten Commandments in the Old Testament provided a much-followed example for lists of ten basic dos and don'ts for many modern businesses and organizations.

Ten AMENDMENTS OF THE CONSTITUTION
(BILL OF RIGHTS)
See Twenty-seven Amendments.

Ten AMERICAN PAINTERS

Group of artists formed in 1898 to spread impressionism across the United States. Their impact on the world of American art was followed in 1907 by the Ashcan School (See The Eight).

1. John Fabian Carlson (1875–1945)
2. Edwin Evans (1860–1946)
3. Frederick Carl Frieseke (1874–1939)
4. Childe Hassam (1859–1935)
5. James Taylor Harwood (1860–1940)
6. Robert Reid (1863–1929)
7. Richard Emile Miller (1875–1943)
8. John Henry Twachtman (1853–1902)
9. Elihu Vedder (1836–1923)
10. J. Alden Weir (1852–1919)

Ten AVATARS OF VISHNU

See Twenty-two Incarnations of Vishnu.

Ten BASEBALL PLAYER POSITIONS

The first nine player positions may be seen in any amateur game; the tenth was added officially for professional teams in order for them to be able to substitute a hitter for the pitcher. (Abbreviations follow.)

1. Pitcher (P)
2. Catcher (C)
3. First base (FB or 1B)
4. Second base (SB or 2B)
5. Third base (TB or 3B)
6. Right field (RF)
7. Center field (CF)
8. Left field (LF)
9. Shortstop (SS)
10. Designated hitter (DH)

BIG TEN (FOOTBALL)

These Midwestern universities compete in football as the Big Ten conference.

1. Illinois: Fighting Illini
2. Indiana: Fighting Hoosiers
3. Iowa: Hawkeyes
4. Michigan: Wolverines
5. Michigan State: Spartans
6. Minnesota: Gophers
7. Northwestern: Wildcats
8. Ohio State: Buckeyes
9. Purdue: Boilermakers
10. Wisconsin: Badgers

Ten Systems of the Human BODY

All the organs and processes of the human body belong in one of these anatomical categories.

1. Circulatory
2. Digestive
3. Endocrine
4. Excretory
5. Integumenary (skin)
6. Muscular
7. Nervous
8. Reproductive
9. Respiratory
10. Skeletal

Ten Provinces of CANADA

Canada has ten provinces, listed below, as well as two territories: Northwest Territories (NT) and the Yukon (YT). (Postal codes follow.)

1. Alberta (AL)
2. British Columbia (BC)
3. Manitoba (MB)
4. New Brunswick (NB)
5. Newfoundland and Labrador (NF)
6. Nova Scotia (NS)
7. Ontario (ON)
8. Prince Edward Island (PE)
9. Quebec (PQ)
10. Saskatchewan (SK)

Ten COMMANDMENTS

Also called the Ten Words or the Decalogue, these commandments appear in Exodus 20:3–17. A passage from John 13:34, "Love one another," is sometimes called the Eleventh Commandment. Presented here is the Protestant version of the list; the Jewish and Roman Catholic versions contain minor variations.

1. Thou shalt have no other gods before me.
2. Thou shalt not make any graven image.
3. Thou shalt not take the name of the Lord thy God in vain.
4. Remember the sabbath day to keep it holy.
5. Honor thy father and thy mother.
6. Thou shalt not kill.
7. Thou shalt not commit adultery.
8. Thou shalt not steal.
9. Thou shalt not bear false witness against thy neighbor.
10. Thou shalt not covet thy neighbor's house, thou shalt not covet thy neighbor's wife, nor his manservant, nor his maidservant, nor his ox, nor his ass, nor anything that is thy neighbor's.

DECALOGUE
See Ten Commandments.

DECAPOLIS LEAGUE

A group of ten cities in the Mediterranean area that united for mutual benefit around 60 B.C.E.

1. Damascus
2. Dion
3. Gadara
4. Gerasa
5. Hippos
6. Kanatha
7. Della
8. Philadelphia
9. Raphana
10. Scythopolis (Beth-Shan, now called Beisan)

DECATHLON

This ten-in-one Olympic event consists of ten different track and field sports. The athlete who gains the highest total score in these ten individual events is declared the decathlon winner. See also Pentathlon *(among the Fives) and* Heptathlon *(in the Sevens).*

1. 100-meter dash
2. 400-meter dash
3. 1,500-meter run
4. 110-meter high hurdles
5. Javelin
6. Discus
7. Shot put
8. Pole vault
9. High jump
10. Long jump

Ten GURUS (SIKHISM)

From the religion of Sikhism, the name of which derives from the Punjabi word sishya, *or disciple. The term* guru, *as it is usually understood by Westerners who have a pass-*

248

ing knowledge of Hinduism, means a devoted spiritual leader. However, in Sikhism, a guru, or bride of God, is held in much higher esteem and is roughly equivalent to an apostle of Christianity. Sikhism was preached by the Gurus until 1708, when the Tenth Guru declared that Sri Guru Granth Sahib, a scripture containing the hymns of the Sikh gurus and various saints, was to be recognized as the Guru of the Sikhs.

1. Sri Guru Nanak Dev Ji (1469–1539), founder of Sikhism
2. Sri Guru Angad Dev Ji (1504–52)
3. Sri Guru Amar Das Ji (1467–1574)
4. Sri Guru Ram Das Ji (1534–81)
5. Sri Guru Arjan Dev Ji (1563–1606), son of Sri Guru Ram Das Ji
6. Sri Guru Har Gobind Ji (1595–1644)
7. Sri Guru Har Rai Sahib Ji (1630–61)
8. Sri Guru Har Krishan Sahib Ji (1656–64), son of Sri Guru Har Rai Sahib Ji
9. Sri Guru Teg Bahadur Ji (1621–75)
10. Sri Guru Gobind Singh Ji (1666–1708), son of Sri Guru Teg Bahadur Ji

Ten Levels of HARDNESS (MINERALS)

German mineralogist Friedrich Mohs (1773–1839) created a scale, also known as Mohs' Scale, that lists minerals from softest to hardest. Hardness is defined not as how tough the material is, but rather by how well it resists heat. Mohs' system of ten levels was revised and expanded in the early twentieth century, and a system of fifteen levels resulted: talc, gypsum, calcite, fluorite, apatite, orthoclase, vitius pure silica, quartz, topaz, garnet, fused zirconia, fused alumina, silicon carbide, boron carbide, and diamond.

1. Talc
2. Gypsum
3. Calcite
4. Fluorite
5. Apatite
6. Orthoclase
7. Quartz

8. Topaz
9. Corundum
10. Diamond

Ten HEAVENS OF PARADISE

From the Divine Comedy, *by Italian poet Dante Alighieri (1265–1321). See also* Seven Cornices of Purgatory, Nine Circles of Hell, *and* Nine Spheres. *(Each circle's virtue and inhabitants are also listed here.)*

1. Heaven of the Moon: fortitude (the inconstant in vows)
2. Heaven of Mercury: justice (the ambitious of the active life)
3. Heaven of Venus: temperance (lovers)
4. Heaven of the Sun: prudence (theologians, teachers, historians)
5. Heaven of Mars: fortitude (warriors)
6. Heaven of Jupiter: justice (the just)
7. Heaven of Saturn: temperance (contemplatives)
8. Starry Heaven ("Zodiac"): faith, hope, charity (Christ, Mary, and other divine persons)
9. Crystalline Heaven: "Primum Mobile"
10. Empyrean

HOLLYWOOD TEN

Ten influential people in Hollywood who refused to testify before the House Committee on Un-American Activities in 1947 and were convicted of contempt. After their appeals were denied, all served prison terms in 1950 of six months to one year. They were also fined, fired from their jobs, and blacklisted for many years. Each person is listed here along with one or two of his major credits. The six shown with an asterisk (*) also appeared in the 1976 film Hollywood on Trial.

1. Alvah Bessie,* received Academy Award nomination for original story for *Objective, Burma!* (1945)
2. Herbert Biberman, directed *Salt of the Earth* (1954)
3. Lester Cole,* wrote screenplay for *Objective, Burma!* (1945)
4. Edward Dymtryk,* directed *The Caine Mutiny* (1954)

5. Ring Lardner, Jr.,* cowrote *Woman of the Year* (1942), for which he shared an Academy Award for original screenplay; also wrote *M*A*S*H* (1970), for which he won an Academy Award for screenplay adaptation

6. John Howard Lawson, wrote *Smash Up: The Story of a Woman* (1947)

7. Albert Maltz,* received Academy Award nomination for screenplay adaptation for *Pride of the Marines* (1945)

8. Samuel Ornitz, cowrote *Hell's Highway* (1932)

9. Adrian Scott, cowrote *Mr. Lucky* (1943); produced *The Boy with Green Hair* (1948)

10. Dalton Trumbo,* director, shared an Academy Award as cowriter of *Papillon* (1973)

Ten MUSES
See Nine Muses.

Ten ORDINARIES (HERALDRY)

The ordinaries are the basic geometric shapes that commonly appear on hereditary coats of arms. Heralds disagree as to which ten abstract charges should be called ordinaries, and even disagree on whether there are ten. However, this list may be considered as authentic as any other. (Diminutives follow.)

1. Bend (bendlet)
2. Pale (pallet, endorse)
3. Fess (bar, barrulet)
4. Chevron (chevronel)
5. Cross
6. Saltire
7. Chief (fillet)
8. Pile (passion nail)
9. Bend Sinister (bendlet sinister, baton)
10. Pall

PAC TEN (FOOTBALL)

The Pacific Eight conference consists of these universities minus Arizona and Arizona State.

1. Arizona: Wildcats
2. Arizona State: Sun Devils
3. California: Golden Bears
4. Oregon: Ducks
5. Oregon State: Beavers
6. Southern California: Trojans
7. Stanford: Cardinals
8. University of California, Los Angeles (UCLA): Bruins
9. Washington: Huskies
10. Washington State: Cougars

Ten PERSECUTORS OF CHRISTIANITY

These were ten emperors of Rome who instituted harsh laws against Christian churches and practitioners.

1. Nero (37–68)
2. Domitian (51–96)
3. Trajan (52 or 53–117)
4. Marcus Aurelius (121–80)
5. Lucius Septimius Severus (146–211)
6. Decius (201–251)
7. Valerian (d. c. 269)
8. Maximian (286–305)
9. Aurelian (c. 212–75)
10. Diocletian (245–313)

Ten PHILOSOPHICAL MISTAKES

From the landmark book of the same name by American philosopher Mortimer J. Adler (1985), in which he discusses the errors that plague modern philosophy. See also Six Great Ideas.

1. Human Existence (the fallacy of reductionism)
2. Human Society (failure to understand how the basic forms of human association are both natural and conventional)
3. Human Nature (the denial of human nature)
4. Freedom of Choice (the misunderstanding of freedom of choice as opposed to determinism)
5. Happiness and Contentment (the mistake in the identification of happiness)
6. Moral Values (the mistake that makes good and evil subjective)
7. Knowledge and Opinion (the mistake of not acknowledging the contributions of philosophy are as important as those of the sciences)
8. Words and Meanings (the failure to recognize that ideas are meanings)
9. The Intellect and the Senses (the mistake about the human mind)
10. Consciousness and Its Objects (the mistake about consciousness)

Ten PLAGUES OF EGYPT

Listed in Exodus 7–11. (Hebrew terms are given here.)

1. Dam: blood (water turned to blood)
2. Tzfardeyah: frogs
3. Kinim: lice
4. Arov: beasts (epidemic among Egypt's beasts)
5. Dever: blight (flies)
6. Sh'hin: boils
7. Barad: hail (or fiery hail)
8. Arbeh: locusts
9. Hosheh: darkness
10. Makat B'horot: slaying of the firstborn

Ten REQUISITES OF GOOD BEHAVIOR (BUDDHISM)

These are the ten basic rules of conduct for Buddhist laity. Each phrase belongs in the middle of the following sentence: "The training in aversion and abstinence from . . . I undertake."

1. Destroying life
2. Taking what is not given to me
3. Sexually immoral conduct
4. False speech
5. Slander
6. Harsh or impolite talk
7. Frivolous or senseless talk
8. Covetousness
9. Malevolence
10. Heretical views

Ten SEPHIROTH

In cabala, a mystical Jewish philosophy of the Middle Ages, the Sephiroth or Sefirah are said to be emanations of God. Daath, the abyss or forbidden knowledge, is said to be the Eleventh Sephir.

Hebrew Term	English Term	Representing
1. Kether or Keter Elyon	supreme crown	heavenly plane, transcendence
2. Hokhma or Chokmah	wisdom	great father
3. Bina or Binah	intelligence, understanding	great mother
4. Hesed or Chesed	mercy	ruler of the universe
5. Geburah or Gevurah	power, justice	cleansing force
6. Rahamin or Tiferet, Tiphareth	compassion, beauty, harmony	rebirth
7. Nezah or Netzach	firmness, endurance	spiritual passion
8. Hod	majesty, splendor	rational thought
9. Yesod	victory, foundation	fertility
10. Malkut or Malkuth, Shekkinah	the kingdom, Earth, or Shekina, God's spouse	earthly plane

Corresponding Deities, Religious Concepts	Corresponding Angel
satori (Zen Buddhism), nirvana	Metatron
Saturn, Cronos, Thoth, Atum, Ptah	Ratziel
Virgin Mary, Rhea, Isis, Demeter	Tzaphqiel
Zeus, Jupiter	Tzadqiel
Mars, The Charioteer (tarot card)	Khameal
Ra, Apollo, Mithra, Osiris, Jesus Christ	Raphael
Aphrodite, Venus, Hathor	Haniel
Mercury, Judgment (tarot card)	Michael
Artemis, Luna, Diana, Sin	Gabriel
Persephone, Geb, The World (tarot card)	Sandalphon

Ten TALENTS (QUAKERISM)

The ten fundamental beliefs of the Society of Friends, known as Quakers.

1. God's spiritual light, lightening every soul
2. The indwelling of the Spirit with the disciple
3. The headship of Christ in the church
4. The priesthood of all true believers
5. The freedom of the Gospel ministry
6. The spiritual equality of the sexes
7. Spiritual baptism and communion only—no sacraments
8. The unlawfulness of war
9. The unlawfulness of oaths
10. The duty of brotherly love and simplicity of life

Ten VIRTUES OF JAINISM

This ancient branch of Hinduism is believed to have been founded by legendary sage Rishabha.

1. Forgiveness
2. Humility
3. Honesty
4. Purity

5. Truthfulness
6. Self-restraint
7. Asceticism
8. Study
9. Detachment
10. Celibacy

Ten VIRTUES OF TAOISM

Taoism is a Chinese philosophy based on the doctrines of Lao Tzu (sixth century B.C.E.).

1. Filial piety
2. Loyalty to emperors and teachers
3. Kindness to all creatures
4. Patience and reproof of wrongdoing
5. Self-sacrifice to help the poor
6. Liberating slaves and planting trees
7. Digging wells and making roads
8. Teaching the ignorant and promoting welfare
9. Studying the Scriptures
10. Making proper offerings to the Gods

Ten VIRTUES OF THE VIRGIN

From the doctrines of the Roman Catholic church.

1. Chastity
2. Prudence
3. Humility
4. Faith
5. Piety
6. Obedience
7. Poverty
8. Patience
9. Charity
10. Compassion

Ten WARS OF THE UNITED STATES
(Dates and final agreements follow.)

1. American Revolution, 1775–81; Peace of Paris, 1783
2. War of 1812, 1812–15; Treaty of Ghent
3. Mexican War, 1846–48; Treaty of Guadalupe Hidalgo
4. American Civil War, 1861–65; Lee surrendered at Appomattox
5. Spanish-American War, 1898–99; Treaty of Paris
6. World War I, 1914–18 (U.S. entered 1917); Treaty of Versailles
7. World War II, 1939–45 (U.S. entered 1941); Germany and Japan surrendered separately
8. Korean War, 1950–53; armistice signed at Panmunjom
9. Vietnam War, 1950–75 (U.S. entered 1961); ceasefire 1973, U.S. withdrew 1975
10. Persian Gulf War, 1990–91; U.S. withdrew

Ten WORDS
See Ten Commandments.

ELEVENS

Being one beyond Ten, Eleven has represented transgression and incompleteness. The Anglo-Saxon word for Eleven was aend-lefene (one left), meaning One more after Ten. The Book of Matthew contained the phrase "at the eleventh hour," meaning "just in time," indicating the belief that Ten was the logical stopping point and that Eleven was One beyond that point.

Eleven is held sacred by followers of Agama Tirtha, the primary religion of Bali. Agama Tirtha is a complex synthesis of Buddhism, animism, Sivaism, and Hinduism and encompasses many ancient rituals from these diverse sources. The Eka Dasa Rudra, "Festival of the Eleven Powers," a ritual believed to restore the balance between good and evil in the universe, is the most spectacular sacred ceremony of the Balinese people.

In cabala, the *Ten Sephiroth* surrounded the hidden Eleventh Sephir, representing forbidden knowledge—again, One step beyond Ten. In astrology, an undecile (two planets at a 33-degree angle, equaling one-eleventh of a circle) was believed to forebode psychic gifts. The legend of the Eleven Thousand Virgins of Saint Ursula, massacred at Cologne by a party of Huns, had its rise in the name of Ursula's handmaid, Undecimella, which means "eleven thousand."

Eleven BELIEFS (BAHA'I)
The eleven basic tenets of the Baha'i Faith. Founded by Persian prophet Baha'u'llah in 1844, Baha'i is a relatively recent world religion that incorporates Hindu, Muslim, and Zoroastrian aspects. See also Nine World Religions.

Three Pillars

1. The Oneness of God
2. The Oneness of Mankind
3. The Oneness of All Religions

Eight Precepts

4. Independent Investigation of Truth
5. The Essential Harmony of Science and Religion
6. Equality of Men and Women
7. Elimination of Prejudice of All Kinds
8. Universal Compulsory Education
9. A Spiritual Solution of the Economic Problem
10. A Universal Auxiliary Language
11. Universal Peace Upheld by a World Government

Eleven CONFEDERATE STATES OF AMERICA
The Confederate States of America was the political entity of the South that existed during the American Civil War. South Carolina seceded in 1860. The remaining ten states seceded in 1861. Kentucky, lying between the North and South, remained officially neutral during the conflict.

1. South Carolina
2. Mississippi
3. Florida
4. Alabama
5. Georgia
6. Louisiana
7. Texas
8. Tennessee
9. North Carolina
10. Arkansas
11. Virginia

Eleven CRICKET PLAYER POSITIONS

Cricket, a team sport, is the national pastime of England.

1. Bowler
2. Wicketkeeper
3. First slip
4. Second slip
5. Gully
6. Third man
7. Cover-point
8. Mid-off
9. Mid-on
10. Square leg
11. Deep fine leg

Eleven DYNASTIES OF CHINA

China has been ruled by these eleven major dynasties, with intervening periods of disruption. Prior to the first dynasty, the era of the semilegendary Emperor Yu is known as the Hsia Dynasty (c. 1994–c. 1523 B.C.E.). In 1912, the Republic of China was declared by Chinese revolutionary Sun Yat-Sen (1866–1925).

1. Shang or Yin (c. 1523–1027 B.C.E.); bronze-age, agricultural, writing developed
2. Chou (1027–256 B.C.E.); age of Confucius, Lao Tzu, and Mencius

Warring States Period (403–221 B.C.E.); division into many minor political entities

3. Kin or Ch'in (221–207 B.C.E.); unification under Emperor Shih Huang-ti, abolition of feudalism, completion of Great Wall
4. Han (206 B.C.E.–220 C.E.); further unification under Liu Pang, Confucianism and Buddhism flourish

Three Kingdoms Period (220–65); division into three states

5. Tsin or Chin (265–420); expansion to the southeast
6. Sui (581–618); reunification
7. T'ang (618–906); expansion, era of great poets Li Po, Po Chu-i, and Tu Fu

Five Dynasties and Ten Kingdoms Period (907–60); warfare and corruption

8. Sung (960–1279); new central government, Neo-Confucianism
9. Yuan or Mongol (1260–1368); Mongols under Kublai Khan
10. Ming (1368–1644); established by Emperor Chu Yuanchang, development of fine porcelain, architecture, drama, and the novel
11. Chi'ing or Manchu (1644–1912); Manchu supremacy, decline of central authority, opium wars, end of monarchy

Eleven FOOTBALL PLAYER POSITIONS
In the National Football League of the United States, eleven players are used on each team. See Twelve Football Player Positions *for the Canadian assortment.*

Offense

1. Quarterback
2. Fullback
3. Tailback or runningback
4. Wide receiver or split end
5. Tight end
6. Slotback or flanker
7. Left tackle
8. Right tackle
9. Left guard
10. Right guard
11. Center

1. Strong safety
2. Free safety
3. Left cornerback
4. Right cornerback
5. Left outside linebacker
6. Right outside linebacker
7. Left inside linebacker
8. Right inside linebacker
9. End
10. End
11. Noseguard

OCEAN'S ELEVEN

This "rat pack" caper movie of 1960 starred the following eleven Hollywood actors as veterans of the Eighty-second Airborne Division who plan to rob five Las Vegas casinos just after midnight on New Year's Eve. Cesar Romero also starred as former gangster Duke Santos, and Angie Dickinson as Beatrice Ocean, Danny's wife.

1. Frank Sinatra: Danny Ocean, leader of the gang
2. Dean Martin: Sam Harmon, entertainer
3. Sammy Davis, Jr.: Josh, demolitions expert and garbage collector
4. Peter Lawford: Jimmy Foster, Danny's best friend
5. Richard Conte: Tony Bergdorf, electrician and ex-con
6. Joey Bishop: "Misty" O'Connors, retired boxer
7. Norman Fell: Peter Reimer, demolitions expert
8. Henry Silva: Roger Cornell
9. Clem Harvey: Louie Jackson, cowboy
10. Richard Benedict: "Curly" Steffans
11. Buddy Lester: Vince Massler

Eleven POWERS (YOGA)

Eleven qualities that are developed through the use of kundalini yoga, and the abilities they make possible. With proper meditation, these powers provide a constant source of inspiration for oneself and others.

1. Tolerance (to tolerate difficulties)
2. Courage (to face obstacles with courage)
3. Cooperation (to see others as your brothers and sisters)
4. Accommodation (to be above any clash of personality)
5. Discernment (to give correct value to your thoughts, words, and actions and to those of others)
6. Judgment (to make clear, quick, accurate, and unbiased decisions)
7. Withdrawal (to withdraw your thoughts while you perform any given activity)
8. Elimination (to eliminate wasted thoughts and actions)
9. Inner development (to develop inner trust and unconditional love)
10. Understanding (to gain knowledge)
11. Ascension (to rise above)

Eleven PRINCIPLES OF THE CODE OF SELF-REGULATION (MOVIES)

The Motion Picture Association of America adopted these rules voluntarily in order to assure audiences that they would not be exposed to "objectionable" content in films. The first ten principles were initially adopted; the eleventh was added later. The code became more or less obsolete with the introduction of the movie rating system. (See Five Movie Ratings.*)*

1. The basic dignity and value of human life shall be respected and upheld. Restraint shall be exercised in portraying the taking of life.
2. Evil, sin, crime, and wrong-doing shall not be justified.
3. Special restraint shall be exercised in portraying criminal or antisocial activities in which minors participate or are involved.
4. Detailed and protracted acts of brutality, cruelty, physical violence, torture, and abuse shall not be presented.
5. Indecent or undue exposure of the human body shall not be presented.

6. Illicit sex relationships shall not be justified. Intimate sex scenes violating common standards of decency shall not be portrayed.

7. Restraint and care shall be exercised in presentations dealing with sex aberrations.

8. Obscene speech, gestures, or movements shall not be presented. Undue profanity shall not be permitted.

9. Religion shall not be demeaned.

10. Words or symbols contemptuous of racial, religious, or national groups shall not be used so as to incite bigotry or hatred.

11. Excessive cruelty to animals shall not be portrayed and animals shall not be treated inhumanely.

Eleven RODGERS AND HAMMERSTEIN MUSICALS

The duo of composer Richard Rodgers and lyricist Oscar Hammerstein II created a new style of theater known as the American musical with their debut show Oklahoma! *in 1943. In addition to this groundbreaking musical, their most important works for the stage were* Carousel, South Pacific, The King and I, *and* The Sound of Music. Cinderella *was the only Rodgers and Hammerstein musical done directly for television.*

	Year Opened	Year Filmed
1. *Oklahoma!*	1943	1955
2. *Carousel*	1945	1956
3. *State Fair*		1945
4. *Allegro*	1947	
5. *South Pacific*	1949	1958
6. *The King and I*	1951	1956
7. *Me and Juliet*	1953	
8. *Pipe Dream*	1955	
9. *Cinderella*	First broadcast 1957	
10. *Flower Drum Song*	1958	1961
11. *The Sound of Music*	1959	1965

Eleven SOCCER PLAYER POSITIONS

Presented in three different versions.

2-3-5 Formation

1. Goalkeeper
2. Center forward
3. Left forward
4. Right forward
7. Left defender
8. Right defender
9. Center midfielder
10. Left midfielder
11. Right midfielder

W-M Formation

1. Goalkeeper
2. Center striker
3. Left wing
4. Right wing
5. Left fullback
6. Right fullback
7. Left inside forward
8. Right inside forward
9. Center midfielder
10. Left midfielder
11. Right midfielder

1-3-3-3 with Sweeper Formation

1. Goalkeeper
2. Sweeper
3. Striker
4. Left winger
5. Right winger
6. Left defensive back
7. Center defensive back
8. Right defensive back

9. Center midfielder
10. Left midfielder
11. Right midfielder

Eleven SIBYLS

In classical Rome, a sibyl was the priestess of an oracle. Roman scholar Marcus Terentius Varro (116–27 B.C.E.) preserved this list of the locations of the eleven greatest sibyls of the age. (Their symbols follow.)

1. Sibylla Persia, lantern and serpent
2. Sibylla Libyea, flaming torch
3. Sibylla Erythreia, white rose and sword
4. Sibylla Cimmeria, cross
5. Sibylla Cumana, ancient stone manger
6. Sibylla Delphica, crown of thorns
7. Sibylla Cania, reed and candle
8. Sibylla Phrygia, banner representing resurrection
9. Sibylla Tiburtine, bundle of rods
10. Sibylla Hellespontia, flowering branch
11. Sibylla Europa, sword

TWELVES

Twelve was once called the great cosmic number, divisible by one, two, three and four, thus containing all the mystical significance of those numbers. The Anglo-Saxon word for Twelve was twa-lef (two left), meaning Two beyond Ten. Like its partner Ten, Twelve was seen as a logical stopping point in numerical progression. After Twelve, numbers advanced by adding whole numbers to, or multiplying by, Ten.

A dodecad (grouping of twelve gods or holy persons) figured prominently in the belief systems of many ancient cultures and religions. The *Twelve Tribes of Israel, Twelve Apostles of Christianity, Twelve Gods of the Norse Aesir,* and *Twelve Olympians* of the Greek and Roman pantheons are just a few familiar examples. Medieval Christians held that Twelve represented faith (the trinity) diffused to the four corners of the earth. The zodiac, with twelve signs and twelve houses, was based on belief in the mystical power of Twelve.

Twelve was used as a basis for counting systems in many ancient lands, and some remnants of these duodecimal systems still remain. We have twelve hours in a day, twelve months in a year, and 360 (three times ten times twelve) degrees in a circle because of the prominence of Twelve. The number 360 itself, because it contained the product of these three highly mystical numbers, was also used by the Romans for the number of days in a year. However, their devotion to 360 created a calendar that shortened the year to such an extent that several adjustments were needed, including the skipping of eleven days in 1753, in order to rectify the discrepancy.

Twelve ANGRY MEN

This original television play by Reginald Rose debuted in 1955. Two years later, Henry Fonda starred in the film version. The story focuses on the deliberations of twelve jurors in a murder trial. Initially, eleven of the men are sure the accused is guilty, but Juror Number Eight refuses to make such an important decision so quickly.

1. Martin Balsam (jury foreman)
2. John Fiedler (meek bank teller)
3. Lee J. Cobb (angry bully)
4. E. G. Marshall (snobby stockbroker)
5. Jack Klugman (grew up in slum)
6. Edward Binns (working man)
7. Jack Warden (self-centered sports fan)
8. Henry Fonda (architect)
9. Joseph Sweeney (observant old man)
10. Ed Begley (illogical bigot)
11. George Voskovec (quiet immigrant)
12. Robert Webber (shallow advertising executive)

Twelve APOSTLES

Also known as the Twelve Disciples, these men were the first followers of Jesus of Nazareth (Matthew 10:2–4, Mark 3:16–19). After Jesus' death, Judas was replaced by Matthias, who was known as the Thirteenth Apostle. Four later followers of Jesus are sometimes called apostles; they were Paul, Barnabas, Silas, and James.

1. Andrew
2. Bartholomew
3. James the Greater
4. James the Less
5. John
6. Jude, or Thaddeus, son of James
7. Judas Iscariot
8. Matthew
9. Peter or Simon Peter
10. Philip

11. Simon Zelotes (Zealot)
12. Thomas

Twelve APOSTLES (MORMON)

In the Church of Jesus Christ of Latter-day Saints, Jesus is believed to have appeared in North America; these were his twelve apostles during his travels here. Also known as the Twelve Elders, Twelve Disciples, or Nephite Twelve, they appear in the Book of Mormon, 3 Nephi 19:4. Three of the Nephite Disciples elected to remain on earth and preach. According to 3 Nephi 28:25, their names are forbidden to be written.

1. Nephi
2. Timothy, brother of Nephi
3. Jonas, his son
4. Mathoni
5. Mathoninah, brother of Mathoni
6. Kumen
7. Kumenonhi
8. Jeremiah
9. Shemnon
10. Jonas
11. Zedekiah
12. Isaiah

Twelve Levels of the BEAUFORT SCALE (WINDS)

The Beaufort Scale was devised by English admiral Sir Francis Beaufort (1774–1857) in 1805 for indicating wind velocities. There are actually thirteen levels on the scale; the first is zero, representing calm winds of less than one mile per hour. (Wind speeds, in miles per hour, follow.)

1. Light Air: 3 or less
2. Slight Breeze: 7 or less
3. Gentle Breeze: 12 or less
4. Moderate Breeze: 18 or less
5. Fresh Breeze: 24 or less

6. Strong Breeze: 31 or less
7. Moderate Gale: 38 or less
8. Fresh Gale: 46 or less
9. Strong Gale: 54 or less
10. Whole Gale: 63 or less
11. Storm: 72 or less
12. Hurricane: 82 or less

Twelve BOXING CATEGORIES

The super heavyweight category was created in 1980. (Weight limits, in pounds, follow.)

1. Light flyweight (106)
2. Flyweight (112)
3. Bantamweight (119)
4. Featherweight (126)
5. Lightweight (132)
6. Light welterweight (140)
7. Welterweight (147)
8. Light middleweight (157)
9. Middleweight (165)
10. Light heavyweight (179)
11. Heavyweight (201)
12. Super heavyweight (unlimited)

Twelve CAESARS

The first twelve emperors of Rome.

	Full Name	Birth and Death	Emperor
1. Julius Caesar	Gaius Julius Caesar	100–44 B.C.E.	49–44 B.C.E.
2. Augustus	Gaius Octavius	63 B.C.E.–14 C.E.	27 B.C.E.–14 C.E.
3. Tiberius	Tiberius Claudius Nero Caesar	42 B.C.E.–37 C.E.	14–37
4. Caligula	Gaius Caesar	12–41	37–41
5. Claudius	Tiberius Claudius Drusus Nero Germanicus	10 B.C.E.–54 C.E.	41–54
6. Nero	Nero Claudius Caesar Drusus Germanicus	37–68	54–68
7. Galba	Servius Sulpicius Galba	c. 5 B.C.E.–69 C.E.	68–69
8. Otho	Marcus Salvius Otho	32–69	69
9. Vitellius	Aulus Vitellius	15–69	69
10. Vespasian	Titus Flavius Sabinus Vespasianus	9–79	69–79
11. Titus	Titus Flavius Sabinus Vespasianus	c. 40–81	79–81
12. Domitian	Titus Flavius Domitianus Augustus	51–96	81–96

Twelve DAYS OF CHRISTMAS

In the original festival of the birth of Jesus Christ, celebrations continued for twelve days. Here are the calendar dates of the Twelve Days of Christmas in both Western and Orthodox Christian divisions, and one popular version of the twelve gifts that are given in the familiar song. A common variation of this song has ten drummers drumming and twelve lords a-leaping.

1. December 25 (January 6), a partridge in a pear tree
2. December 26 (January 7), two turtledoves
3. December 27 (January 8), three French hens
4. December 28 (January 9), four calling birds
5. December 29 (January 10), five gold rings
6. December 30 (January 11), six geese a-laying
7. December 31 (January 12), seven swans a-swimming

8. January 1 (January 13), eight maids a-milking
9. January 2 (January 14), nine ladies dancing
10. January 3 (January 15), ten lords a-leaping
11. January 4 (January 16), eleven pipers piping
12. January 5 (January 17), twelve drummers drumming

THE DIRTY DOZEN

This 1967 Robert Aldrich film told the story of twelve military men, all convicted of serious crimes, who go on a suicide mission behind German lines during World War II. The film also starred Lee Marvin as Major Reisman, Richard Jaeckel as Sergeant Barron, and Ernest Borgnine and George Kennedy as high-ranking officers.

1. Charles Bronson: Joseph Wladislaw (speaks German)
2. Jim Brown: Robert Jefferson
3. Tom Busby: Milo Vladek
4. Ben Carruthers: Glenn Gilpin
5. John Cassavetes: Victor Franko (antisocial, uncooperative)
6. Stuart Cooper: Roscoe Lever
7. Trini Lopez: Pedro Jimenez
8. Colin Maitland: Seth Sawyer
9. Al Mancini: Tassos Bravos
10. Telly Savalas: Archer Maggott (religious zealot, racist)
11. Donald Sutherland: Vernon Pinkley (low intelligence)
12. Clint Walter: Samson Posey (Native American, strong)

Twelve DISCIPLES

See Twelve Apostles.

DODECANESE

Twelve Greek islands in the Aegean Sea; the name means The Twelve. Increased to fifteen by the addition of the islands of Kos and Rhodes in 1912 and Kastellorizon in 1923, the islands are still known as the Dodecanese.

1. Astypalaia
2. Ikaria
3. Kalimnos
4. Karpathos
5. Kasos
6. Khalki
7. Leros
8. Lipsos
9. Nisiros
10. Patmos
11. Syme
12. Tilos

Twelve ELDERS
See Twelve Apostles (Mormon).

Twelve FACE CARDS
In the standard deck of playing cards, there are four suits with thirteen ranks in each suit. Three of these thirteen ranks are "face cards" that portray human characters. Though there were probably no specific characters intended to be represented by the original face cards, the following twelve mythological or highly romanticized characters correspond to the twelve face cards in some symbolical systems.

1. Jack of Spades: Ogier
2. Queen of Spades: Palas
3. King of Spades: David, king of the Jews
4. Jack of Hearts: La Hire
5. Queen of Hearts: Judith
6. King of Hearts: Charlemagne
7. Jack of Diamonds: Hector
8. Queen of Diamonds: Rachel
9. King of Diamonds: Caesar
10. Jack of Clubs: Lancelot
11. Queen of Clubs: Argine
12. King of Clubs: Alexander the Great

Twelve FEDERAL RESERVE BANKS

The letter of one of these twelve banks is printed boldly on every piece of United States paper currency. The same letter is always used as the first character of the serial number on that bill.

A. Boston, Mass.

B. New York, N.Y.

C. Philadelphia, Pa.

D. Cleveland, Oh.

E. Richmond, Va.

F. Atlanta, Ga.

G. Chicago, Il.

H. Saint Louis, Mo.

I. Minneapolis, Minn.

J. Kansas City, Kan.

K. Dallas, Tex.

L. San Francisco, Calif.

Twelve FOOTBALL PLAYER POSITIONS (CANADIAN)

In the Canadian Football League, twelve players are used on each team. See also Eleven Football Player Positions *for the U.S. assortment.*

Offense

1. Quarterback
2. Fullback
3. Tailback or runningback
4. Split end
5. Wide receiver
6. Tight end
7. Slotback or flanker
8. Left tackle
9. Right tackle
10. Left guard
11. Right guard
12. Center

1. Strong Safety
2. Free Safety
3. Left cornerback
4. Right cornerback
5. Defensive back
6. Left outside linebacker
7. Right outside linebacker
8. Left inside linebacker
9. Right inside linebacker
10. End
11. End
12. Noseguard

Twelve GATES OF THE CITY OF JERUSALEM
See Twelve Tribes of Israel.

Twelve GODS OF THE NORSE AESIR
There are many gods and goddesses in the Norse pantheon, but these twelve are the primary deities of the Aesir. (See Three Gods: Norse.) *The well-known trickster god Loki is also among the Aesir but is not one of the twelve chief deities.*

1. Odin or Wodin, Woṭan, "The Mad One"; father of the gods, god of wisdom
2. Frigga or Frigg, Frija, Fricka; mother of the gods, goddess of the home, family, and children
3. Thor or Thunar, Donner, "Thunder"; god of thunder, provider of rain
4. Balder or Baldur; god of light
5. Tyr or Tywaz; god of war, sacrifice, and valor
6. Bragi; god of poetry and learning
7. Heimdal or Heimdall; god of perception, guardian of the rainbow bridge, teacher
8. Hod or Hodur, Hödr; brother of Balder, slain by Vali

9. Vidar or Vitharr, "Silent God" or "Wide-ruling One"
10. Uller or Ull, Wuldor, "Glory"; bow god, god of the hunt and of winter
11. Skadi; goddess of the hunt
12. Forseti or Foseti, Forsete; patron god of the Frisians

Twelve HISTORICAL BOOKS OF THE OLD TESTAMENT
The books of the Old Testament have been divided by scholars into five distinct groups including this one, made up of the sixth through seventeenth books. See Five Books of Moses.

1. Joshua
2. Judges
3. Ruth
4. 1 Samuel
5. 2 Samuel
6. 1 Kings
7. 2 Kings
8. 1 Chronicles (also called 1 Paralipomenon)
9. 2 Chronicles (also called 2 Paralipomenon)
10. Ezra
11. Nehemiah
12. Esther

Twelve HOUSES (ASTROLOGY)
Astrologers who use divination by the stars divide the heavenly chart into twelve Houses, each representing the state of matters in a different area of the subject's life.

1. House of Life
2. House of Fortune (Riches)
3. House of Brethren
4. House of Parents and Relatives
5. House of Children
6. House of Health
7. House of Marriage

8. House of Death
9. House of Religion
10. House of Dignities
11. House of Friends and Benefactors
12. House of Enemies

Twelve IMAMS (SHI'ITE)

Twelve prophets recognized by Shi'ite Muslims. Among Shi'ites are two sects known as Seveners and Twelvers because they venerate the seventh Imam and twelfth Imam, respectively. A school of theology among Twelvers includes Muhammad and Fatima among the Twelve Imams, making a group of fourteen.

1. Ali ibn Abi Talib
2. al-Hasan ibn Ali
3. al-Husayn ibn Ali
4. Ali ibn al-Husayn, Zayn al-Abidin
5. Muhammad al-Baqir
6. Ja'far al-Sadiq
7. Musa al-Kazim
8. Ali al-Rida
9. Muhammad Jawad al-Taqi
10. Ali al-Naqi
11. al-Hasan al-Askari
12. Muhammad al-Mahdi, al-Qa'im al-Hujjah

Twelve LABORS OF HERCULES

In Greek mythology, the gods gave Heracles (Hercules) twelve tasks, deemed impossible, in order that he might prove himself. Each labor is detailed in a separate tale, and each feat required great strength as well as cunning and ingenuity. Eurystheus, mentioned in the third labor, was Heracles' master. See Four Hesperides.

1. Slay the Nemean Lion
2. Destroy the Lernaean Hydra
3. Bring the Arcadian Stag to Eurystheus

4. Capture the Boar of Erymanthus
5. Clean the Stables of King Augeas
6. Kill the Carnivorous Birds near Lake Stymphalis
7. Capture the Bull ravaging Crete
8. Capture the Mares of Diomedes of Thrace
9. Steal Hippolyta's Girdle
10. Capture the Carnivorous Oxen of Geryon
11. Steal some Golden Apples from Hesperides' Garden
12. Capture Cerberus, the Guardian of Hades

Twelve Levels of the MODIFIED MERCALLI INTENSITY SCALE
(EARTHQUAKES)
In 1931, Harry Wood and Frank Neumann devised this scale for rating the intensity of earthquakes. Unlike the Richter Scale, which is an often-misunderstood mathematical measure based on a logarithmic pattern, the Mercalli Scale is based on the observable effects of an earthquake and is more easily understood by the general public.

1. Not felt.
2. Felt by persons at rest.
3. Felt noticeably by person indoors, vibration similar to the passing of a truck.
4. Felt outdoors by a few, walls make a cracking sound, some sleepers are awakened, standing cars rock noticeably.
5. Felt by nearly everyone, some dishes and windows break, unstable objects overturn.
6. Heavy furniture moves, buildings receive slight damage.
7. Well-built buildings are slightly damaged, badly designed buildings receive considerable damage, some chimneys break.
8. Structures designed especially for earthquakes receive slight damage, some buildings partially collapse, factory stacks fall, heavy furniture overturns.
9. Specially designed structures are heavily damaged, buildings thrown out of plumb, shifted off foundations.
10. Some sturdy wood and most sturdy masonry and frame structures destroyed, rails bent.

11. Few masonry structures remain standing, bridges destroyed, rails greatly bent.
12. Damage total, lines of sight distorted, objects thrown into the air.

Twelve MINOR PROPHETS OF THE OLD TESTAMENT
The last twelve books of the Old Testament are known as the Minor Prophets. See Five Books of Moses.

1. Hosea (Osee)
2. Joel
3. Amos
4. Obadiah (Abdias)
5. Jonah
6. Micah
7. Nahum
8. Habakkuk
9. Zephaniah (Sophoniah)
10. Haggai (Aggeus)
11. Zecharaiah
12. Malachi

Twelve MONTHS OF THE GREGORIAN CALENDAR
The Gregorian calendar is used by the United States and most of the Western Hemisphere. The final four months were originally numbered seven through ten because before the months of July and August were added to the calendar, there were only ten months. (Namesakes, birthstones, and flowers follow.)

1. January (Janus); garnet, carnation or snowdrop
2. February (Februarius, Roman fertility festival); amethyst, violet or primrose
3. March (Mars); aquamarine or bloodstone, jonquil or daffodil
4. April (Aphrodite); diamond, sweet pea or daisy
5. May (Maia, Roman goddess of fertility); emerald, lily of the valley
6. June (Juno); pearl or agate, rose

7. July (Julius, Roman emperor Julius Caesar); ruby, alexandrite, or moonstone, larkspur or water lily
8. August (Augustus, Roman emperor Augustus Caesar); peridot or sardonyx, gladiolus
9. September (septem, seven); sapphire, aster
10. October (octo, eight); opal, tourmaline, or rose sapphire, calendula, cosmos, or dahlia
11. November (novem, nine); topaz, chrysanthemum
12. December (decem, ten); turquoise or blue zircon, poinsettia, narcissus, or holly

Twelve MONTHS OF THE HEBREW CALENDAR
Tishri, the first month, falls in October.

1. Tishri
2. Cheshvan (Heshvan)
3. Kislev
4. Teveth (Tebet)
5. Shevat (Shebat)
6. Adar
7. Nisan (Abib)
8. Iyar
9. Sivan
10. Tamuz
11. Av (Ab)
12. Elul

Twelve MONTHS OF THE HINDU CALENDAR
Baisakh is sometimes used as the first month. Chait begins in March.

1. Chait
2. Baisakh
3. Jeth
4. Asarh

5. Sawan
6. Bhadon
7. Asin
8. Kartik
9. Aghan
10. Pus
11. Magh
12. Phagun

Twelve MONTHS OF THE MUSLIM CALENDAR

1. Muharram
2. Safar
3. Rabi I
4. Rabi II
5. Jumada I
6. Jumada II
7. Rajab
8. Sha'ban
9. Ramadan
10. Shawwal
11. Dhu'l-Qa'dah
12. Dhu'l-Hijja

NEPHITE TWELVE
See Twelve Apostles (Mormon).

Twelve NOTES OF THE CHROMATIC SCALE
The chromatic scale includes every note within the octave and is composed entirely of half steps. The scale thus has twelve notes (thirteen including the octave) instead of the more familiar seven of the major scale. See Seven Notes of the Major Scale.

1. C
2. C sharp (D flat)
3. D
4. D sharp (E flat)
5. E
6. F
7. F sharp (G flat)
8. G
9. G sharp (A flat)
10. A
11. A sharp (B flat)
12. B

Twelve OLYMPIANS

In Greek and Roman mythology, these twelve deities were the chief gods and goddesses who dwelled on Mount Olympus.

Greek Name	Roman Name	Kingdom	Symbol(s)
1. Zeus	Jupiter	the sky	thunderbolt, eagle
2. Hera	Juno	marriage	cow eyes, peacock
3. Apollo	Apollo	music, wisdom	lyre, laurel
4. Hades	Pluto	the underworld	helmet of invisibility
5. Hestia	Vesta	the hearth, the home	fireplace
6. Hephaestus	Vulcan	the forge	anvil
7. Artemis	Diana	the hunt	spear, stag
8. Athena	Minerva	wisdom, justice	aegis, owl
9. Ares	Mars	war	helmet of war, vulture
10. Hermes	Mercury	the messenger	caduceus, wings
11. Poseidon	Neptune	the sea	trident, horse
12. Aphrodite	Venus	beauty, love	dove, swan

Twelve PATRIARCHS

See Twelve Tribes of Israel.

Twelve SOFTBALL PLAYER POSITIONS
Softball differs slightly from baseball in the equipment used, and in organized softball leagues there is one extra player in the outfield and one extra hitter. (Abbreviations follow.)

Field Players

1. Pitcher (P)
2. Catcher (C)
3. First base (1B)
4. Second base (2B)
5. Third base (3B)
6. Right field (RF)
7. Right center (RC)
8. Left field (LF)
9. Left center (LC)
10. Shortstop (SS)

Substitutes

11. Designated hitter (DH)
12. Extra hitter (EH)

Twelve SONS OF JACOB
See Twelve Tribes of Israel.

Twelve STEPS
This step-by-step system of self-improvement and self-maintenance was devised by the founders of Alcoholics Anonymous, an organization that helps its members control their addiction to drinking. The Twelve Steps have also been adopted by many other organizations that are directed toward helping people control their addictive behavior.

1. We admitted we were powerless over alcohol—that our lives had become unmanageable.

2. We came to believe that a Power greater than ourselves could restore us to sanity.
3. We made a decision to turn our will and our lives over to the care of God, *as we understood Him.*
4. We made a searching and fearless moral inventory of ourselves.
5. We admitted to God, to ourselves, and to another human being the exact nature of our wrongs.
6. We were entirely ready to have God remove all these defects of character.
7. We humbly asked Him to remove our shortcomings.
8. We made a list of all persons we had harmed, and became willing to make amends to them all.
9. We made direct amends to such people wherever possible, except when to do so would injure them or others.
10. We continued to take personal inventory and when we were wrong promptly admitted it.
11. We sought through prayer and meditation to improve our conscious contact with God, *as we understood Him,* praying only for the knowledge of His will for us and the power to carry that out.
12. Having had a spiritual awakening as a result of these steps, we tried to carry this message to alcoholics and to practice these principles in all our affairs.

Twelve TASKS OF HERCULES
See Twelve Labors of Hercules.

Twelve TITANS
See Seven Titans.

Twelve TRIALS OF HERCULES
See Twelve Labors of Hercules.

Twelve TRIBES OF ISRAEL

The Twelve Tribes of the Israelites descended from the Twelve Sons of Jacob, also known as the Twelve Patriarchs. Each tribe was represented by a gemstone on the breastplate of the high priest (Exodus 39:10–13), but variations occur among different translations of these gemstones. In Ezekiel 48:31–34, the city of Jerusalem is described as having twelve gates, three on each side, named for the Twelve Tribes. In Numbers 1–2, the Tribe of Levi is not counted among the twelve, and Manassah and Ephraim, both sons of Joseph, take the place of the tribes of Levi and Joseph. (Locations of gates follow.)

1. Judah (sardius, sardonyx, or ruby); north
2. Reuben (topaz); north
3. Gad (carbuncle, garnet, or yellow quartz); west
4. Asher (emerald or turquoise); west
5. Naphtali (sapphire); west
6. Dan (diamond or emerald); east
7. Simeon (ligure or jacinth); south
8. Levi (agate); north
9. Issachar (amethyst); south
10. Zebulon (beryl, chrysolite, or peridot); south
11. Joseph (onyx); east
12. Benjamin (jasper); east

Twelve TROJAN PLANETS

The Trojan Planets, as they are called, are actually asteroids that circle the Sun in Jupiter's orbit; there are seven ahead of Jupiter and five behind. Both groups are distanced from Jupiter by 60 degrees. The asteroids are named for participants in the Trojan War; the first group for the Greeks and the second group for the Trojans.

Ahead of Jupiter

1. Achilles
2. Hector
3. Nestor
4. Agamemnon

5. Odysseus
6. Ajax
7. Diomedes

Behind Jupiter

8. Patroclus
9. Priamus
10. Aeneas
11. Anchises
12. Troilus

Twelve Signs of the ZODIAC

One of the most familiar tools of divination, the ancient signs of the zodiac are still used by astrologers to forecast people's fate.

EUROPEAN

	Animal or Object	Dates	Symbol	Corresponding Mythical Meaning(s)
1. Aries	ram	March 21– April 19	♈	ram with the golden fleece
2. Taurus	bull	April 20– May 19	♉	bull that bore Europa across the seas
3. Gemini	twins	May 20– June 20	♊	Castor and Pollux, Hercules and Apollo, Triptolemus and Iasion
4. Cancer	crab	June 21– July 22	♋	northern limit of the sun
5. Leo	lion	July 23– August 21	♌	Nemean Lion slain by Hercules

6. Virgo	virgin	August 22– September 22	♍	Justitia; Erigone; Parthene, virgin daughter of Jupiter and Themis; Virgin Mary
7. Libra	scales	September 23– October 22	♎	equality of day and night
8. Scorpio	scorpion	October 23– November 21	♏	scorpion killed by Orion
9. Sagittarius	archer	November 22– December 21	♐	the centaur Chiron
10. Capricorn	goat	December 22– January 20	♑	southern limit of the sun
11. Aquarius	waterbearer	January 21– February 19	♒	the cupbearer, the rainy season
12. Pisces	fishes	February 20– March 20	♓	Aphrodite and Eros disguised

CORRESPONDENCES

Occupation	_Domain of Mastery_	_Mode of Experience_
soldier	military	fighting, war
farmer	agriculture	producing
journalist	media	writing and talking
cook	common sense	childhood
politician	government	love affairs
doctor	medicine	health
artist	art	beauty, diplomacy
business person	business	sex, death
teacher	academia	teaching, traveling
scientist	science	science, ambition
technician	technology	friendship
cleric	religion	martyrdom

Mode of Emotion	_Way of Problem Solving_
anger	state the problem clearly
contentment	study all resources
humor	list all ideas
sensitivity	examine assumptions
love	decide what is heart of the problem
analysis	break down into components
apology, affection	picture the problem
passion	incubate and gestate
wisdom	receive insight
seriousness	judge and verify
friendliness	synthesize with established methods
compassion	make a decision

Personality and Attitude	_Color_	_Art Form_
militant	red	straight lines
bullheaded	brown	rounded
mercurial	yellow	fine, short and sharp
maternal	silver	childlike
leonine	gold	ornate
critical	green	V-shaped angles
harmonious	light blue	curves
intense	red and black	heavy
philosophical	purple	large
saturnine	black	small
humanitarian	white	original
mystical	aqua	vague

Parts of Human Body Governed	Abstract Activity
head and face	cutting
neck	substantiating
arms and lungs	connecting
breasts and stomach	receiving
upper back and heart	centering
digestive tract	focusing
lower back and kidneys	balancing
sex and elimination organs	vortexional
thighs	expansional
knees and skin	structuring
ankles and circulation	synthesizing
feet and lymph system	evaporating

Element	Position in Hierarchy	Planet
fire	twelve (top)	Sun
earth	one	Moon
air	seven	Mercury
water	six	Jupiter
fire	eleven	Neptune
earth	two	Earth
air	eight	Saturn
water	five	Asteroids
fire	ten	Pluto
earth	three	Mars
air	nine	Uranus
water	four	Venus

Development of Western Philosophy	Historical Example
the astrological zodiac	Present era
common sense	Prehistory
rationalism	St. Thomas Aquinas
inspiration	Early Christians
altered states of consciousness	John Lilly and Carlos Castaneda
beginning of recorded history	Ancient Mesopotamia
science	Galileo
craftsmanship	Classical Romans
analytical philosophy	Wittgenstein
clarity and distinctiveness	Ancient Ionians
synthesis	Herbert Spencer and Karl Marx
harmony, beauty, balance, and form	Classical Greeks

Breakthrough in Western Philosophy	Metal	Gemstone(s)
zodiacal order of thought	iron	amethyst, diamond
sensory awareness	copper	emerald, moss agate
reason and logic	quicksilver	beryl, amethyst
conscious spirituality	silver	emerald, moss agate
ESP and clairvoyance	gold	ruby, diamond
invention of writing	quicksilver	hyacinth, pink jasper
science and mathematics	copper	diamond, opal
engineering and law	steel	topaz, malachite
linguistic analysis	tin	turquoise, carbuncle
philosophy	lead	white onyx, moonstone
synthetic philosophy	uranium	sapphire, opal
architecture and sculpture	tin	chrysolite, moonstone

CHINA

The Chinese zodiac groups birthdates by year, not month. Since the Chinese year does not begin when the Western year begins, the years shown here are approximate.

1. Rat (1996)
2. Ox (1997)
3. Tiger (1998)
4. Hare (1999)

5. Dragon (2000)
6. Snake (2001)
7. Horse (2002)
8. Sheep (2003)
9. Monkey (2004)
10. Rooster (2005)
11. Dog (2006)
12. Boar (2007)

JAPAN
The Japanese zodiac was derived from the Chinese system and is nearly identical to it.

1. Tatsu (dragon)
2. Tora (tiger)
3. Net (rat)
4. Mi (serpent)
5. U (hare)
6. Ushi (ox)
7. Inu (dog)
8. Saru (monkey)
9. Uma (horse)
10. I (boar)
11. Tori (rooster)
12. Hitsuji (goat)

ANCIENT SOURCES
The zodiac as we know it derives from a very ancient system of divination that was known all over the Mediterranean in many variations. Here are four.

Ancient Greece

1. Hydrokhoos (water pot)
2. Krios (ram)
3. Karkinos (crab)
4. Aigokeros (great-horned one)
5. Dopatkar and Didumoi (twins)

6. Leon (lion)
7. Zugos (yoke)
8. Ikhthues (fish)
9. Toxotes (archer)
10. Skorpion (scorpion)
11. Tauros (bull)
12. Parthenos (maiden)

Ancient Persia

1. Dul (water pot)
2. Varak (lamb)
3. Kalakang (crab)
4. Vahik (sea goat)
5. Dopatkar and Didumoi (twins)
6. Ser (lion)
7. Tarazuk (balance)
8. Mahik (fish)
9. Nimasp (centaur)
10. Gazdum (scorpion)
11. Tora (bull)
12. Khusak (virgin)

Ancient India

1. Khumba (pot)
2. Mesha (or Aja) (ram or goat)
3. Karkata (crab)
4. Mahara (sea monster)
5. Mithuna (lovers)
6. Simha (lion)
7. Tula (balance)
8. Mina (fish)
9. Dhanus (bow)
10. Vrischika (scorpion)
11. Vrishka (bull)

12. Kanya (virgin)

Ancient Babylon

 1. Gula (goddess)
 2. Zappu (or Hunga) (hair or worker)
 3. Al-Lul (crab)
 4. Suhurmas (goat-fish)
 5. Mastabagalgal (twins)
 6. Urgula (lioness)
 7. Zibanitu (scales)
 8. Simmah and Anunitum (two tails)
 9. Nimas (centaur)
10. Gir-Tab (scorpion)
11. Gudanna (bull)
12. Ab-Sin (furrow)

THIRTEEN AND UP

The ill luck associated with Thirteen originally derived from the unlucky thirteenth (intercalcary) month of the Babylonian calendar, and this superstition survives today. Thirteen was seen as the disruption of Twelve, the most perfect of all numbers. The thirteenth card in the tarot was Death, and the followers of rural European religions customarily met in groups of thirteen, giving rise to the belief among Christians that Thirteen was the number of evil and black magic.

However, Thirteen also had many precedents as a lucky number. There were thirteen Buddhas in India, thirteen Gods in Aztec belief, and thirteen layers on the rooftops of Japanese pagodas. In ancient Israel, Thirteen was the number of sacred items necessary for the tabernacle. Some early Christians interpreted Thirteen as representing Jesus and his twelve apostles, thus an omen of blessing and good fortune.

The thirteen original colonies are represented on the great seal of the United States, which shows an eagle with thirteen feathers in each wing, thirteen leaves in one talon, and thirteen arrows in the other, beneath a constellation of thirteen stars within a ring of thirteen clouds, along with several other Thirteens. The first U.S. flag had thirteen stripes, the first U.S. navy had thirteen ships, and George Washington and his twelve generals made Thirteen.

The mystical meanings assigned to numbers higher than Thirteen relied on combinations of interpretations already given to one or more of the lower numbers. For example, Fourteen, containing two Sevens, enclosed all the luck and power of that number multiplied by Two. In ancient Hindu belief, Four, and its double, Eight, were held sacred, and Sixty-four, composed of eight Eights, was seen as the most perfect and holy of numbers.

Thirteen CIRCUIT COURTS OF THE UNITED STATES

The U.S. circuit court system consists of thirteen courts, only eleven of which are actually numbered. The two additional circuit courts are listed here as numbers twelve and thirteen. (The states and territories included follow in parentheses.)

1. First Circuit: Boston, Mass. (Maine, Massachusetts, New Hampshire, Rhode Island, Puerto Rico)
2. Second Circuit: New York, N.Y. (Connecticut, New York, Vermont)
3. Third Circuit: Philadelphia, Pa. (Delaware, New Jersey, Pennsylvania, Virgin Islands)
4. Fourth Circuit: Richmond, Va. (Maryland, North Carolina, South Carolina, Virginia, West Virginia)
5. Fifth Circuit: New Orleans, La. (Louisiana, Mississippi, Texas)
6. Sixth Circuit: Cincinnati, Oh. (Kentucky, Michigan, Ohio, Tennessee)
7. Seventh Circuit: Chicago, Ill. (Illinois, Indiana, Wisconsin)
8. Eighth Circuit: St. Louis, Mo. (Arkansas, Iowa, Minnesota, Missouri, Nebraska, North Dakota, South Dakota)
9. Ninth Circuit: San Francisco, Calif. (Alaska, Arizona, California, Hawaii, Idaho, Montana, Nevada, Oregon, Washington, Guam, Northern Mariana Islands)
10. Tenth Circuit: Denver, Colo. (Colorado, Kansas, New Mexico, Oklahoma, Utah, Wyoming)
11. Eleventh Circuit: Atlanta, Ga. (Alabama, Florida, Georgia)
12. Federal Circuit: Washington, D.C.
13. District of Columbia: Washington, D.C.

Thirteen CLASSICS (CONFUCIANISM)

The sacred texts of Confucianism consist of these thirteen books, built on the original Five Classics. See also Six Classics.

1. Shih Ching or Mao Shih (Book of Odes)

2. Shu Ching or Shang Shu (Book of History or Book of Records)
3. I Ching or Chou I (Book of Changes)
4. Li Chi (Book of Rites)
5. Chou Li (Rites of Chou)
6, 7, 8, 9. I Li, Tso Chuan, Kung-yang Chuan, Ku-liang Chuan (commentaries on the Spring and Autumn Annals)
10. Lun Yü (Analects of Confucius)
11. Hsiao Ching (Classic of Filial Piety)
12. Ehr Ya (Dictionary of Terms)
13. Meng-tzu (Writings of Mencius)

Thirteen COLONIES

The United States of America was formed out of these thirteen British colonies in 1776.

1. Delaware
2. Pennsylvania
3. New Jersey
4. Georgia
5. Connecticut
6. Massachusetts
7. Maryland
8. South Carolina
9. New Hampshire
10. Virginia
11. New York
12. North Carolina
13. Rhode Island

Thirteen DWARFS

In The Hobbit *by J. R. R. Tolkien (1937), this band of dwarfs is known as Thorin and Company. The Lucky Fourteenth, Bilbo Baggins, is not a dwarf.*

1. Balin

2. Bifur

3. Bofur

4. Bombur

5. Dori

6. Dwalin

7. Fili Perish

8. Gloin

9. Kili Perish

10. Nori

11. Oin

12. Ori

13. Thorin Oakenshield

Thirteen GODS OF THE AZTECS

The Aztecs of central Mexico worshiped many gods and goddesses, but these thirteen constituted the primary Aztec pantheon.

1. Tezcatlipoca ("smoking mirror") (obsidian); supreme deity, sun god, god of night and sorcery
2. Huitzilopochtli; war god
3. Quetzalcoatl ("feathered serpent"); god of learning, civilization, regeneration, wind, and storms
4. Xiuhtecuhtli; fire god
5. Cioacoatl; water goddess
6. Tlaloc; rain god
7. Mictlantecuhtli; god of the dead
8. Tonantzin ("honored grandmother"); earth goddess
9. Ehecatl; wind god
10. Xipe Totec; fertility god
11. Centeotl; corn god
12. Ometecuhlti; god of creation
13. Omecihuatl; goddess of creation

Thirteen INTERVALS

Western music recognizes thirteen intervals, or distances between two notes, within an octave. (Alternate names follow in parentheses.)

1. Prime (unison, perfect unison)
2. Minor Second (half step)
3. Major Second (whole step)
4. Minor Third
5. Major Third
6. Fourth (perfect fourth)
7. Tritone (augmented fourth, diminished fifth, Diabolos in Musica)
8. Fifth (perfect fifth)
9. Minor Sixth
10. Major Sixth
11. Minor Seventh
12. Major Seventh
13. Octave (eighth, perfect octave)

Thirteen Principles of WICCAN BELIEF

Wicca or Witchcraft is an American revival of the old religions of the British Isles, earth-centered traditions of the Native Americans, and similar belief systems from around the world. The main tenet of Wicca is "An' (if) it harm none, do what thou wilt." These principles were composed by the Council of American Witches in 1974.

1. We practice rites to attune ourselves with the natural rhythm of life forces marked by the phases of the Moon and the seasonal Quarters and Cross Quarters.
2. We recognize that our intelligence gives us a unique responsibility toward our environment. We seek to live in harmony with Nature, in ecological balance offering fulfillment to life and consciousness within an evolutionary concept.
3. We acknowledge a depth of power far greater than that apparent to the average person. Because it is far greater than ordinary it is sometimes called "supernatural," but we see it as lying within that which is naturally potential to all.

4. We conceive of the Creative Power in the universe as manifesting through polarity—as masculine and feminine—and that this same Creative Power lies in all people, and functions through the interaction of the masculine and feminine. We value neither above the other, knowing each to be supportive to the other. We value sex as pleasure, as the symbol and embodiment of life, and as one of the sources of energies used in magickal practice and religious worship.

5. We recognize both outer worlds and inner, or psychological, worlds sometimes known as the Spiritual World, the Collective Unconscious, Inner Planes, etc.—and we see in the interaction of these two dimensions the basis for paranormal phenomena and magickal exercises. We neglect neither dimension for the other, seeing both as necessary for our fulfillment.

6. We do not recognize any authoritarian hierarchy, but do honor those who teach, respect those who share their greater knowledge and wisdom, and acknowledge those who have courageously given of themselves in leadership.

7. We see religion, magick and wisdom in living as being united in the way one views the world and lives within it—a worldview and philosophy of life which we identify as *Witchcraft—the Wiccan Way.*

8. Calling oneself "Witch" does not make a Witch—but neither does heredity itself, nor the collecting of titles, degrees and initiations. A Witch seeks to control the forces within her/himself that make life possible in order to live wisely and well without harm to others and in harmony with Nature.

9. We believe in the affirmation and fulfillment of life in a continuation of evolution and development of consciousness giving meaning to the Universe we know and our personal role within it.

10. Our only animosity towards Christianity, or towards any other religion or philosophy of life, is to the extent that its institutions have claimed to be "the only way" and have sought to deny freedom to others and to suppress other ways of religious practice and belief.

11. As American Witches, we are not threatened by debates on the history of Witchcraft, the origins of various terms, the legitimacy of various aspects of different traditions. We are concerned with our present and our future.

12. We do not accept the concept of absolute evil, nor do we worship any entity known as "Satan" or "the Devil," as defined by the Christian tradition. We do not seek power through the suffering of others, nor accept that personal benefit can be derived only by denial to another.
13. We believe that we should seek within nature that which is contributory to our health and well-being.

Thirteen VIRTUES

American statesman and philosopher Benjamin Franklin (1706–90) described his personal program of self-improvement in his autobiography. He listed these virtues (and descriptions) as ones he desired to acquire and improve on in his own behavior.

1. Temperance: Eat not to dullness; drink not to elevation.
2. Silence: Speak not but what may benefit others or yourself; avoid trifling conversation.
3. Order: Let all your things have their places; let each part of your business have its time.
4. Resolution: Resolve to perform what you ought; perform without fail what you resolve.
5. Frugality: Make no expense but to do good to others or yourself; i.e., waste nothing.
6. Industry: Lose no time; be always employed in something useful; cut off all unnecessary actions.
7. Sincerity: Use no hurtful deceit; think innocently and justly, and, if you speak, speak accordingly.
8. Justice: Wrong none by doing injuries, or omitting the benefits that are your duty.
9. Moderation: Avoid extremes; forbear resenting injuries so much as you think they deserve.
10. Cleanliness: Tolerate no uncleanliness in body, clothes, or habitation.
11. Tranquillity: Be not disturbed at trifles, or at accidents common or unavoidable.
12. Chastity: Rarely use venery but for health or offspring, never to dullness, weakness, or the injury of your own or another's reputation.
13. Humility: Imitate Jesus and Socrates.

Fourteen BOOKS OF THE APOCRYPHA

In addition to the Old Testament used by Jews and the New Testament used by Protes-
tants, there are fourteen biblical books known as the Apocrypha that are recognized by
the Roman Catholic church. The basis for the Hebrew celebration of Hanukkah is
found in the story of the Maccabees. A book known as The Rest of the Book of Esther
is found between Judith and The Wisdom of Solomon.

1. I Esdras
2. II Esdras
3. Tobit or Tobias
4. Judith
5. The Wisdom of Solomon
6. Ecclesiasticus or Sirach or The Wisdom of Jesus, Son of Sirach
7. Baruch
8. Jeremiah
9. Song of the Three
10. Daniel and Susanna
11. Daniel, Bel, and the Snake
12. Manasseh
13. I Maccabees
14. II Maccabees

Fourteen MANUS

According to Hindu belief, these are the rulers of the Earth.

1. Svayambhuva
2. Svarochisha
3. Uttama
4. Tamasa
5. Raivata
6. Chakshusha
7. Vaivasvata
8. Savarna
9. Daksha-Savarna
10. Brahma-Savarna

11. Dharma-Savarna
12. Rudya-Savarna
13. Rauchya
14. Bhautya

Fourteen STATIONS OF THE CROSS

In Roman Catholic tradition, these represent fourteen significant events in the final days of Jesus Christ's life on earth. Art depicting each event is displayed in churches as an aid to prayer.

1. Condemnation of Jesus
2. Receives the Cross
3. Falls for the First Time
4. Meets His Mother
5. Simon of Cyrene Bears His Cross
6. Veronica Wipes His Face
7. Falls a Second Time
8. Speaks to the Women of Jerusalem
9. Falls a Third Time
10. Stripped
11. Crucified
12. Dies
13. Body Is Taken Down
14. Laid in the Tomb

Fifteen Levels of HARDNESS

See Ten Levels of Hardness (Minerals).

Fifteen MOONS OF URANUS

Along with Nine Rings *Uranus has a total of fifteen moons of varying sizes, mostly named for women and faeries in the plays of Shakespeare. Eight of these moons were discovered during the journey of* Voyager 2 *in 1986. Research into the moons of our solar system is ongoing, so more moons may be discovered in the future. (Diameters in miles follow.)*

Small Inner Moons

1. Cordelia (16)
2. Ophelia (20)
3. Bianca (27)
4. Cressida (41)
5. Desdemona (36)
6. Juliet (52)
7. Portia (68)
8. Rosalind (34)
9. Belinda (42)
10. Puck (96)

Larger Outer Moons

11. Miranda (293)
12. Ariel (718)
13. Umbriel (725)
14. Titania (982)
15. Oberon (942)

Fifteen MYSTERIES OF THE ROSARY

In Roman Catholic tradition, the rosary is a special string of beads carried by the faithful and used as a tool in prayer. There are three sets of five large beads each, representing the Fifteen Mysteries, as well as additional smaller beads for other purposes.

Five Joyful Mysteries

1. Annunciation
2. Visitation of the Virgin by Saint Elizabeth
3. Birth of Christ
4. Christ's Presentation in the Temple
5. Jesus Talking with the Doctors

Five Sorrowful Mysteries

6. Agony of Christ in the Garden
7. Christ's Scourging
8. Crown of Thorns
9. Carrying the Cross to Calvary
10. Crucifixion

Five Glorious Mysteries

11. Resurrection
12. Ascension
13. Coming of the Holy Ghost
14. Assumption of Mary
15. Mary's Coronation in Heaven

Fifteen PARTICLES

These are the basic types of subatomic particles that constitute all that exists. Research into particle physics is ongoing, so more particles may be discovered in the future. (Symbols and abbreviations follow.)

1. deuteron (d)
2. electron (e)
3. neutron (n)
4. proton (p)
5. muon (μ)
6. lambda particle (λ)
7. sigma particle (Σ)
8. xi particle (Ξ)
9. alpha particle (α)
10. pion (π)
11. photon (γ)
12. neutrino (v)
13. radian (rad)
14. triton (t)
15. steradian (sr)

Fifteen TECTONIC PLATES

The Earth's surface is divided into tectonic plates that slowly but constantly shift position on the planet's surface. The shifting of the plates over millions of years causes the development of mountain ranges and fault lines, the creation of earthquakes and volcanoes, and numerous other geological events. Research into tectonic plates is ongoing, so more plates may be discovered in the future. (Locations and relative sizes follow.)

1. African: Africa (large)
2. Antarctic: Antarctica (large)
3. Arabian: Arabia (small)
4. Caribbean: Caribbea (small)
5. Caroline: north of New Guinea (small)
6. Cocos: Central America (small)
7. Eurasian: Eurasia (large)
8. Indian-Australian: India-Australia (large)
9. Juan de Fuca: Seattle area (small)
10. Nazca: Atlantic (large)
11. North American: North America (large)
12. Pacific: Pacific (large)
13. Philippine: Philippines (small)
14. Scotia: south of South America (small)
15. South American: South America (large)

Sixteen MOONS OF JUPITER

Jupiter, the largest planet of our solar system, has a large number of satellites. The four largest moons, called Jovian Moons or Galilean Satellites, were discovered by Italian scientist Galileo Galilei (1564–1642), the first person to use a telescope to view the planets. Here, the moons are listed in order from closest to furthest from Jupiter. The moons are named mainly for the mythical wives, lovers, and daughters of the Roman god Jupiter. Research into the moons of our solar system is ongoing, so more moons may be discovered in the future. (Diameters in miles in parentheses.)

Innermost Moons

1. Metis (25); lies within main ring
2. Adrastea (12); lies within main ring
3. Amalthea (150); reddest object in the solar system
4. Thebe (62)

Galilean Moons

5. Io (2262); most colorful moon in the solar system
6. Europa (1945); brightest moon in the solar system
7. Ganymede (3275); largest moon in the solar system
8. Callisto (3008); most geologically active moon in the solar system

Middle Moons

9. Leda (10); smallest moon of Jupiter
10. Himalia (115)
11. Lysithea (22)
12. Elara (47)

Outermost Moons

13. Ananke (19)
14. Carme (25)
15. Pasiphae (31)
16. Sinope (22)

Eighteen MOONS OF SATURN

Like Jupiter and Uranus, Saturn has a large and varied array of moons. This giant gas planet has eighteen known moons as well as several suspected moons that remain to be confirmed. The eight smallest moons are nonspherical. Observations from Voyager 1 *(1980) and* Voyager 2 *(1985) provided a great deal of information on the moons of Saturn, which are mainly named for Titans and demigoddesses and demigods in Roman mythology. See also* Three Rings of Saturn. *Research into the moons of our solar system is ongoing, so more moons may be discovered in the future. (Diameters in miles are in parentheses.)*

Small Inner Moons

1. Pan (12); within the Encke Gap in Saturn's A ring
2. Atlas (19); a shepherd satellite of the A ring
3. Prometheus (56); inner shepherd satellite of the F ring
4. Pandora (52); outer shepherd satellite of the F ring
5. Epimetheus (83); co-orbital with Janus
6. Janus (110); co-orbital with Epimetheus

Large Moons and Their Smaller Companion Moons

7. Mimas (244); has large crater named Herschel after its discoverer, astronomer William Herschel
8. Enceladus (310); highest albedo (reflectiveness) of any body in the solar system; may be the source of the material in Saturn's tenuous E ring
9. Tethys (650); has large crater named Odysseus and a huge valley named Ithaca Chasma; is accompanied in its orbit by Telesto and Calypso
10. Telesto (18); orbits 60 degrees ahead of Tethys
11. Calypso (16); orbits 60 degrees behind Tethys
12. Dione (696); densest of Saturn's moons after Titan; is accompanied in its orbit by Helene
13. Helene (20); orbits 60 degrees ahead of Dione

Outer Moons

14. Rhea (951)
15. Titan (3,200); densest of Saturn's moons, has an atmosphere
16. Hyperion (248); irregularly shaped
17. Iapetus (907)
18. Phoebe (124)

Nineteen MONTHS OF THE BAHA'I CALENDAR

The Baha'i Faith divides the calendar year into nineteen months of nineteen days each. Four intercalcary days, February 26–March 1, are added at the end of the eighteenth month (five days are added in leap year). Each month's Arabic name is an attribute of God. The first day of the year occurs on the vernal equinox; the first year of the Baha'i calendar was 1844. The first day of each month is listed here.

1. Baha, "splendor" (March 21)
2. Jalal, "glory" (April 9)
3. Jamal, "beauty" (April 28)
4. Azamat, "grandeur" (May 17)
5. Nur, "light" (June 5)
6. Rahmat, "mercy" (June 24)
7. Kalimat, "words" (July 31)
8. Kamal, "perfection" (August 1)
9. Asmá, "names" (August 20)
10. 'Izzat, "might" (September 8)
11. Mashiyyat, "will" (September 27)
12. 'Ilm, "knowledge" (October 16)
13. Qudrat, "power" (November 4)
14. Qawl, "speech" (November 23)
15. Masáil, "questions" (December 12)
16. Sharaf, "honor" (December 31)
17. Sultan, "sovereignty" (January 19)
18. Mulk, "dominion" (February 7)
19. Alá, "loftiness" (March 2)

Nineteen MONTHS OF THE MAYAN CALENDAR

In the ancient Mayan calendar, each month had twenty days, except the nineteenth month, which had only five. See also Twenty Days of the Month (Mayan).

1. Pop
2. Uo
3. Zip
4. Tzoz

5. Tzec
6. Xul
7. Yaxkin
8. Mol
9. Chen
10. Yax
11. Zac
12. Ceh
13. Mac
14. Kankin
15. Muan
16. Pax
17. Kayab
18. Cumhu
19. Uayeb

Twenty DAYS OF THE MONTH (AZTEC)

The ancient Aztec calendar named each day of the month after a common plant, animal, or quality.

1. Coatl ("snake")
2. Cuetzpalin ("lizard")
3. Calli ("house")
4. Ehecatl ("wind")
5. Cipactli ("crocodile")
6. Xochitl ("flower")
7. Quiahuitl ("rain")
8. Tecpatl ("flint")
9. Ollin ("rotation" or "movement")
10. Cozacuauhtli ("vulture")
11. Cuauhtle ("eagle")
12. Ocelotl ("jaguar" or "ocelot")
13. Acatl ("reed" or "cane")
14. Malinalli ("herb" or "dead grass")
15. Ozomahtli ("monkey")

16. Itzcuintli ("hairless dog")
17. Atl ("water")
18. Tochtli ("rabbit")
19. Mazatl ("deer")
20. Miquiztli ("death" or "skull")

Twenty DAYS OF THE MONTH (MAYAN)

The ancient Mayan calendar named each day of the month. See also Nineteen Months *of the Mayan Calendar.*

1. Imix
2. Ik
3. Akbal
4. Kan
5. Chicchan
6. Cimi
7. Manik
8. Lamat
9. Muluc
10. Oc
11. Chuen
12. Eb
13. Ben
14. Ix
15. Men
16. Cib
17. Caban
18. Etznab
19. Cauac
20. Ahau

Twenty-one EPISTLES OF THE NEW TESTAMENT

Biblical scholars have divided up the books of the New Testament into two major groups: the Four Gospels and the Twenty-one Epistles. The Acts of the Apostles and the Book of Revelation or Apocalypse are the two books that are not included in either group. The epistles, or letters, are messages written by Saint Paul and others to various churches and individuals. Each book is named for the person, church, or people to whom the letter was addressed, or for its author.

1. Romans
2. 1 Corinthians
3. 2 Corinthians
4. Galatians
5. Ephesians
6. Philippians
7. Colossians
8. 1 Thessalonians
9. 2 Thessalonians
10. 1 Timothy
11. 2 Timothy
12. Titus
13. Philemon
14. Hebrews
15. James
16. 1 Peter
17. 2 Peter
18. 1 John
19. 2 John
20. 3 John
21. Jude

Twenty-two ENIGMAS OF THE TAROT

The tarot is a deck of cards used in divination. It is similar to a standard deck of playing cards, except that there are fourteen ranks in each suit instead of thirteen, and there are 22 additional cards that carry no suit and represent specific characters, objects, and events. These 22 special cards are called the Enigmas, the Mysteries, or the Major Arcana. A full tarot deck consists of 78 cards: 22 Enigmas plus 56 Minor Arcana.

0. The Fool (le Fou)
I. The Magician (le Bateleur)
II. The Archpriestess (la Papesse)
III. The Empress (l'Imperatrice)
IV. The Emperor (l'Empereur)
V. The Archpriest (le Pape)
VI. The Lovers (l'Amoureux)
VII. The Chariot (le Chariot)
VIII. Justice (la Justice)
IX. The Hermit (l'Ermite)
X. The Wheel of Fortune (la Roue de la Fortune)
XI. Strength (la Force)
XII. The Hanged Man (le Pendu)
XIII. Death (la Mort)
XIV. Temperance (la Tempérance)
XV. The Devil (le Diable)
XVI. The Tower Struck by Lightning (le Feh du Ciel)
XVII. The Stars (les Etoiles)
XVIII. The Moon (la Lune)
XIX. The Sun (le Soleil)
XX. The Judgment (le Jugement)
XXI. The World (le Monde)

Twenty-two INCARNATIONS OF VISHNU
In the mythology of Hinduism, an avatar is an earthly incarnation of God (Vishnu). The Hindu believe that Vishnu appears on earth in many forms or incarnations. Among these 22, the first ten are known as the Ten Avatars of Vishnu. See also **Twenty-four Tirthankaras.**

1. Matsya (fish)
2. Kurma (tortoise)
3. Varaha (boar)
4. Narasimha (man-lion)
5. Vamana (dwarf)
6. Parasurama (Rama, a warrior with an axe)

7. Rama (the faithful husband)
8. Krishna (the adorable one)
9. Buddha (the founder of the faith)
10. Kalki (the bringer of righteousness—man on white horse yet to come)
11. Sanat Kumara (youth)
12. Sage Narada
13. Saints Nara and Narayana
14. Sage Kapila
15. Dattareya
16. Yajna
17. Rishabha (the founder of Jainism, a Hindu sect)
18. King Prithu
19. Dhanvarati
20. Balarama
21. Sage Veda Vyasa
22. Mohini

Twenty-two MYSTERIES
See Twenty-two Enigmas of the Tarot.

Twenty-four TIRTHANKARAS
Tirthankaras, literally "ford builders," are the major prophets of the Jain religion, an ancient branch of Hinduism founded by Rishabha. All the Tirthankaras are said to have lived many centuries B.C.E., but evidence of their existence is sketchy at best. Four in particular appear often in Jain literature and art and are usually represented by the symbols indicated here in parentheses. Each Tirthankara is believed to have experienced the Five Kalyanas.

1. Rishabha (bull)
2. Ajita
3. Sambhava
4. Abhinandana
5. Sumati
6. Padmaprabha

7. Suparsva
8. Candraprabha
9. Suvidhi or Puspadanta
10. Sitala
11. Sreyansa
12. Vasupujya
13. Vimala
14. Ananta
15. Dharma
16. Santi
17. Kunthu
18. Ara
19. Malli
20. Munisuvrata
21. Nami
22. Arishtanemi or Nemi (conch shell), c. 900 B.C.E.
23. Parsva (snake), c. 800 B.C.E.; "Beloved"
24. Vardhamana (lion), c. 599–492 B.C.E.; Mahavira, "Great Hero," Jina, "Conqueror"

Twenty-six LETTERS OF THE ALPHABET

The alphabet as we have it today is based on the Latin alphabet, which in turn derived from the Hebrew alphabet. Our present letter J evolved out of the letter I, and the letter U gave us V, W, and Y. Also presented are a few of the symbolic meanings that have been assigned to the letters.

1. A: mountain, pyramid, creation, birth
2. B: mother's breasts
3. C: the sea, the crescent moon
4. D: day, brilliance
5. E: the sun
6. F: fire
7. G: the creator
8. H: the twins, dualism, the threshold
9. I: the axis of the universe, the self, the number One

10. J: tree and root
11. K: connections
12. L: power
13. M: mountains
14. N: waves of the sea, the serpentine path
15. O: perfection, completion
16. P: the staff, the shepherd's crook
17. Q: the rising sun, the setting sun
18. R: support
19. S: serpent
20. T: hammer, ax, cross, conflict, sacrifice
21. U: chain
22. V: convergence, a receptacle
23. W: water waves
24. X: union, the cross of light
25. Y: crossroads, choices, decisions
26. Z: lightning, the destroyer

Twenty-six RUDIMENTS (DRUMMING)

Students of orchestral or band drumming must learn these fundamental snare-drum techniques.

1. Single-stroke roll
2. Double-stroke roll
3. Five-stroke roll
4. Seven-stroke roll
5. Nine-stroke roll
6. Ten-stroke roll
7. Eleven-stroke roll
8. Thirteen-stroke roll
9. Fifteen-stroke roll
10. Flam
11. Flam tap
12. Flamaque
13. Flam accent

14. Flam paradiddle
15. Ratamaque
16. Double ratamaque
17. Triple ratamaque
18. Drag
19. Double drag
20. Paradiddle
21. Double paradiddle
22. Paradiddle-diddle
23. Drag paradiddle
24. Drag paradiddle-diddle
25. Lesson 25
26. Ruff

Twenty-seven AMENDMENTS OF THE CONSTITUTION

The Constitution of the United States of America contains provision for the peaceable revision of itself in the form of amendments. The amendment process is so strict that in over two hundred years, only 27 amendments have been added to the constitution, although over a thousand have been officially proposed. The first ten amendments, added soon after the constitution was written, are collectively known as the Bill of Rights.

Bill of Rights

1. Freedom of religion, speech, and the press, and the rights of assembly and petition.
2. A well-regulated militia and the right to bear arms.
3. Soldiers forbidden to occupy households.
4. Unreasonable searches and seizures without a warrant forbidden.
5. The right to refuse to testify against oneself ("I take the fifth"), the rules of indictment and due process, provision against double jeopardy, and compensation for private property taken for public use.
6. The right to a lawyer and a speedy trial.
7. The right to a jury trial.
8. Cruel and unusual punishments forbidden.

9. Provides that one right does not eradicate another.
10. Powers not given to the national government are reserved for the states or the people.

Later Amendments

11. Limitation on judicial power.
12. President and vice-president elected by electoral college.
13. Abolition of slavery.
14. Citizenship rights to freed slaves.
15. The right to vote given to members of all races.
16. Income tax.
17. Election of senators given to the people.
18. Prohibits the manufacture, transport, sale, and consumption of alcohol ("Prohibition").
19. Right to vote given to women.
20. New government-elect begins in January following the November election.
21. Repeal of Amendment 18, the end of Prohibition.
22. Limitations on the president's stay in office.
23. Voting rights granted to citizens of Washington, D.C.
24. Abolition of poll (voting) tax.
25. Provision for replacing the vice-president.
26. Voting age set at eighteen.
27. Limitations on pay increases for members of Congress.

Twenty-eight POETIC FEET
A poetic foot is a group of two to four syllables. Metrical poetry is often classified by the arrangement of strong and weak syllables within the feet. Here, strongly accented syllables are shown by heavy dashes and unaccented syllables are shown by concave lines. Much of the poetry of William Shakespeare is in iambic pentameter: five feet per line, each foot an iamb, or one unaccented followed by one accented syllable. Most of the meters listed here are very rarely used in English.

Two Syllables

1. Pyrric   **U** **U**
2. Iamb   **U** —
3. Trochee   — **U**
4. Spondee   — —

Three Syllables

5. Tribrach   **U** **U** **U**
6. Anapest   **U** **U** —
7. Dactyl   — **U** **U**
8. Cretic   — **U** —
9. Amphibrach   **U** — **U**
10. Baccius   **U** — —
11. Palimbacchius — — **U**
12. Molossus   — — —

Four Syllables

13. Proceleusmatic   **U** **U** **U** **U**
14. First Paeon   — **U** **U** **U**
15. Second Paeon   **U** — **U** **U**
16. Third Paeon   **U** **U** — **U**
17. Fourth Paeon   **U** **U** **U** —
18. Major Ionic   — — **U** **U**
19. Minor Ionic   **U** **U** — —
20. Diiamb   **U** — **U** —
21. Ditroche   — **U** — **U**
22. Coriamb   — **U** **U** —
23. Antispastic   **U** — — **U**
24. First Epitritus **U** — — —
25. Second Epitritus — **U** — —
26. Third Epitritus — — **U** —
27. Fourth Epitritus — — — **U**
28. Dispondee   — — — —

318

Thirty-two DEGREES OF FREEMASONRY
Officially founded in 1717, Freemasonry is a secret organization with origins lost in antiquity. See also Three Degrees of Freemasonry.

Blue Lodge

1. Entered Apprentice
2. Fellowcraft
3. Master Mason

Lodge of Perfection

4. Secret Master
5. Perfect Master
6. Intimate Secretary
7. Provost and Judge
8. Intendent of the Building
9. Master Elect of Nine
10. Master Elect of Fifteen
11. Sublime Knight Elect
12. Grand Master Architect
13. Knight of the Ninth Arch
14. Grand Elect Prefect and Sublime Mason

Chapter of Rose Croix

15. Knights of the East or Sword
16. Prince of Jerusalem
17. Knight of the East and West
18. Knight of the Rose Croix

Chapter (or Council) of Kadosh

19. Pontiff or Grand Pontiff
20. Master of the Symbolic Lodge or Master ad Vitam
21. Noachite or Prussian Knight

22. Knight of the Royal Axe or Prince of Libanus
23. Chief of the Tabernacle
24. Prince of the Tabernacle
25. Knight of the Brazen Serpent
26. Prince of Mercy
27. Knight Commander of the Temple
28. Knight of the Sun or Prince Adept
29. Knight of Saint Andrew
30. Knight of Kadosh

Consistory

31. Grand Inspector Inquisitor Commander
32. Sublime Prince (Master) of the Royal Secret

Appendix: Correspondences among the Sevens

Seven is the most mystical and magical number in Western mythology. See the introduction to the chapter on Sevens for a detailed discussion of the causes of this development. Mystics used many methods in order to understand the workings of the universe. One method was to match information from two or more unrelated sources in order to find previously unrevealed wisdom. Because the number Seven was so important, many otherwise unrelated lists of seven were correlated to each other. The following list gives a sampling. See also *Seven Metals, Seven Planets.*

	Planets	Symbols of the Planets	Days of the Week	Archangles	Kingdoms of the Seven Archangels
1.	Sun	☉	Sunday	Michael	light
2.	Moon	☾	Monday	Gabriel	hope and dreams
3.	Mars	♂	Tuesday	Samael	destruction
4.	Mercury	☿	Wednesday	Raphael	civilizing angel
5.	Jupiter	♃	Thursday	Sachiel	administering angel
6.	Venus	♀	Friday	Anael	love
7.	Saturn	♄	Saturday	Cassiel	solicitude

	Deadly Sins	Liberal Arts	Directions	Metals	Parts of the Body	Virtues
1.	pride	grammar	zenith	gold	center	faith
2.	sloth	logic	nadir	silver	genitals	hope
3.	wrath	rhetoric	south	iron	head	charity
4.	envy	arithmetic	center	mercury	right leg	temperance
5.	gluttony	geometry	east	tin	left arm	justice
6.	lust	astronomy	west	copper	right arm	fortitude
7.	avarice	music	north	lead	left leg	prudence

	Gods (Greek)	Gods (Babylonian)	Levels of Classification	Tempers	Musical Modes
1.	Helios	Shamash	kingdom	enthusiastic	hypodorian
2.	Artemis	Sin	phylum	melancholy	mixolydian
3.	Ares	nergal	class	pathetic	dorian
4.	Hermes	Nabu (Nebo)	order	active	hypophrygian
5.	Zeus	Marduk	family	ecstatic	phrygian
6.	Aphrodite	Ishtar	genus	erotic	hypolydian
7.	Cronos	Ninib	species	sad	lydian

	Colors	Seas	Tinctures of Heraldry	Gemstones	Qualities
1.	gold	Mediterranean	or	topaz	constancy
2.	silver	Aegean	argent	pearl	innocence
3.	red	Red	gules	ruby	magnanimity
4.	blue	Ionian	purpure	amethyst	temperance
5.	orange	Caspian	azure	sapphire	loyalty
6.	yellow	Adriatic	vert	emerald	love
7.	black	Black	sable	diamond	prudence

	Vowels of the Greek Alphabet		Churches in Asia	Ancient Wonders of the World	Continents
1.	iota	I	Ephesus	Great Pyramid	Africa
2.	alpha	A	Smyrna	Hanging Gardens	Antarctica
3.	omicron	O	Pergamum	Statue of Zeus	Asia
4.	epsilon	E	Thyatira	Temple of Artemis	Australia
5.	upsilon	Y	Sartis	Mausoleum at Halicarnassus	Europe
6.	eta	H	Philadelphia	Colossus of Rhodes	North America
7.	omega	Ω	Loadicea	Pharos of Alexandria	South America

	Great Towns	Demons	Champions of Christendom	Hills of Rome
1.	Argos	Lucifer	Saint George	Aventine
2.	Athens	Beelzebub	Saint Andrew	Caelian
3.	Chios	Satan	Saint Patrick	Palatine
4.	Colophon	Astaroth	Saint David	Esquiline
5.	Rhodes	Leviathan	Saint Denis	Capitoline
6.	Salamis	Elimi	Saint James	Viminal
7.	Smyrna	Baalbarith	Saint Anthony	Quirinal

FOR FURTHER READING

The main books and scriptures consulted in compiling this volume (not an exhaustive list).

Alberigo, Guiseppe, *The Documents of Vatican II,* Maryknoll, New York: Orbis Books, 1967

Apel, Willi, *Harvard Dictionary of Music, Second Edition, Revised and Enlarged,* Cambridge, Massachusetts: Harvard University Press, 1969

The Apocrypha: Revised Standard Version, New York: Thomas Nelson and Sons, 1957

Boswell, John, and Dan Starer, *Five Rings, Six Crises, Seven Dwarfs, and 38 Ways to Win an Argument,* New York: Penguin Books, 1990

Bulfinch, Thomas, *Bulfinch's Mythology,* edited by Bennett Cerf et al., Random House Modern Library, no date (c. 1960)

Burton, Richard F., translator, *The Kama Sutra of Vatsyayana,* New York: Dutton, 1962.

Cirlot, J. E., *A Dictionary of Symbols, Second Edition,* translated from Spanish by Jack Sage, New York: Philosophical Library, 1971

Curtis, Natalie, *The Indians' Book,* New York: Bonanza Books, 1987

Dante Alighieri, *The Divine Comedy,* translated by Dorothy L. Sayers and Barbara Reynolds, Baltimore: Penguin Books, 1962

Dennys, Rodney, *Heraldry and the Heralds,* London: Jonathan Cape, 1982

Gibson, Walter R., and Litzka R. Gibson, *Complete Illustrated Book of the Psychic Sciences,* New York: Doubleday and Company, 1966

Halliwell, Leslie, *Halliwell's Film Guide, Eighth Edition,* edited by John Walker, New York: HarperCollins, 1991

Lehrner, Ernst, *Symbols, Signs, and Signets,* New York: Dover Publications, 1969; reprint of World Publishing Company, 1950

Lurker, Manfred, *The Gods and Symbols of Ancient Egypt,* London: Thames and Hudson, 1980

Mark, Lisbeth, *The Book of Hierarchies,* New York: William Morrow and Company, 1984

Neilson, William A., editor in chief, *Webster's Biographical Dictionary,* Springfield, Massachusetts: G. and C. Merriam Co., 1963

Plutarch, *The Parallel Lives,* Cambridge, Massachusetts: Harvard University Press, 1989

Powell, James N., *The Tao of Symbols,* New York: William Morrow and Company, 1982

Prabhupada, Swami, *Bhagavad Gita—As It Is,* Bhagavad Gita Book Trust, 1983

Scofield, C. I., *The Holy Bible: Authorized Version,* New York: Oxford University Press, 1937

Thomas, Bob, *Walt Disney: An American Original,* New York: Hyperion, 1994

Walker, Barbara G., *The Woman's Dictionary of Symbols and Sacred Objects,* San Francisco: Harper and Row, 1988

Wallechinsky, David, with Irving Wallace and Amy Wallace, *The Book of Lists,* New York: William Morrow and Company, 1977

Woodcock, P. G., *Short Dictionary of Mythology,* New York: Philosophical Library, 1953

INDEX

327

330

Nine Great LIVES, 235
NOBEL PRIZES, Six, 151
NOBLE GASES, Six, 151
NOBLE TRUTHS, Four, 88
NOISE LEVELS, Six Basic, 151–152
NONVIOLENT ACTION, Three Tactics of, 40
NONVIOLENT RESISTANCE, Three
    Principles of, 40
NORNS, Three, 41
NOTES OF THE CHROMATIC SCALE,
    Twelve, 281–282
NOTES OF THE MAJOR SCALE, Seven, 188
NOVENSILES. See ENNEAD OF THE
    SABINES.

OCEANIDES, Four, 88
OCEAN'S ELEVEN, 262
OCEANS, Five, 125
OFFICE OF THE LORD, Fourfold, 88
OFFICES OF CANONICAL HOURS, Eight.
    See OGDOAD OF HERMOPOLIS
OFFICES OF CHRIST, Three, 41
OGDOAD OF HERMOPOLIS, 221
OLD MEN, Nine, 237–238
OLIVES, Eight Sizes of, 221
OLODUS, Four, 88–89
OLYMPIANS, Twelve, 282
OLYMPIC RINGS, Five, 125
ORDERS, Four, 89
ORDINARIES, Ten (HERALDRY), 251

Ps, Four, 89
Ps, Seven. See DEADLY SINS, Seven.
Ps, Three. See Ps, Four.
PAC TEN (FOOTBALL), 252
PANCHA BOOTHAS, Five (PANCHA
    TATTWAS). See ELEMENTS, Five.
PARCAE, Three. See FATES, Three.
PARDONS OF GOD, Three, 41
PARTICLES, Fifteen, 304
PARTICLES, Three Basic, 42
PARTITIONS OF POLAND, Three, 42
PARTS OF SPEECH, Eight, 221–222
PATH, Eightfold, 222
PATRIARCHS OF CHRISTIANITY, Five, 126
PATRIARCHS, Three, 42
PATRIARCHS, Twelve. See TRIBES OF
    ISRAEL, Twelve.
PECCATAS, Seven. See DEADLY SINS, Seven.
PEERS, Five, 126
PENTATEUCH. See BOOKS OF MOSES,
    Five.
PENTATHLON, 126–127
PERSECUTORS OF CHRISTIANITY, Ten,
    252

PERSONAGES, Seven (NEW TESTAMENT),
    188–189
PHASES OF THE MOON, Eight, 222
PHASES OF THE MOON, Four. See PHASES
    OF THE MOON, Eight.
PHILOSOPHICAL MISTAKES, Ten,
    252–253
PILLARS OF ISLAM, Five. See ISLAM, Five
    Precepts of.
PILLARS OF WISDOM, Seven. See LIBERAL
    ARTS, Seven.
PLAGUES OF EGYPT, Ten, 253
PLAGUES, Seven. See VIALS, Seven.
PLANE CRASH, Four Causes of a, 90
PLANES OF EXISTENCE, Three. See MAN,
    Three Parts of.
PLANETS, Nine, 238
PLANETS, Seven, 189
PLANTS, Four Sacred, 90
PLASTIC, Seven Types of, 189–190
PLAY, Three Types of, 42–43
PLEASURES, Seven, 190
PLEIADES, 191
POETIC FEET, Twenty-eight, 317–318
POETICAL BOOKS OF THE OLD
    TESTAMENT, Five, 128
POINTS OF THE LAW, Nine, 238–239
POINTS OF VIEW, Three Literary, 43
POLITICAL LABELS, Five, 128
POLO, Four Positions in, 90
POSITIONS, Eight (HERALDRY), 223
POWERS, Eleven (YOGA), 263
PRIMARY COLORS OF LIGHT, Three, 43
PRIMARY COLORS OF PAINT, Three, 43
PRIMARY NUMBERS, Nine, Symbology of,
    239
PRIMORDIAL RAYS, Seven (THEOSOPHY),
    191–192
PRINCIPLES OF THE CODE OF SELF-
    REGULATION, Eleven (MOVIES),
    263–264
PROOFS, Five. See WAYS, Five.
PROPHETS OF MONOTHEISM, Eight
    (ISLAM), 223
PROPHETS OF THE OLD TESTAMENT,
    Four Major, 91
PROTOCOLS, Four, 91
PSYCHE, Three Parts of, 43–44
PSYCHOLOGICAL EXISTENCE, Eight
    Levels of, 223–224
PURGATORY, Seven Cornices of, 192–193
PYTHAGOREAN SOLIDS, Five, 128–129

QUADRILATERALS, Five, 129
QUADRUPLE ALLIANCE, 91–92